'Wow – Ray Poynter and the team have done it again! Without a doubt, mobile has changed the relationship between brands and customers and this is changing how market and social research will need to be conducted and delivered. *The Handbook of Mobile Market Research* is both timely and an invaluable resource for marketers and researchers of all ages and experiences. A practical guide that does not get bogged down in technology speak, but focuses more how to get things done and addresses the tough but important topics such as ethics, incentives, and the challenges of "in the moment". It will become an essential reference guide with practical tips and tricks for success (my favorite tip is "don't collect more data than can be analyzed with the resources available!").'

Peter Harris, EVP & Managing Director, Vision Critical Asia Pacific

'Poynter, Williams, and York have created an incomparable primer, truly the first of its kind, for the use of mobile technologies in the practice of market research. *The Handbook of Mobile Market Research* provides a deep-dive into mobile as an emerging marketing measurement and data collection platform, while also providing a holistic view of current and future opportunities for marketers as mobile and cross platform research methods continue to evolve.'

Kristin Luck, President and CMO, Decipher

'Ray Poynter does it again in *The Handbook of Mobile Market Research*, this time with the aid of co-authors Sue York and Navin Williams. Drawing upon decades of study in the methods of market research practice, Ray, Sue, and Navin clarify the manner in which mobile devices are changing market research today and will continue to shape it in the future. The book incorporates social media, big data, and other technology of our times to provide a detailed reference document of applications and implementation practices for mobile research. Most importantly, it provides what is the most comprehensive summary of research-on [mobile]-research available in the industry today. This book has something to offer researchers irrespective of their role – from methodologists to CEOs.'

Leslie Townsend, President, Kinesis Survey Technologies

'The whole point of Market Research is to understand consumer behaviour and decision making. In the early days of the industry there was very limited science or technology available to support researchers and their clients in this quest – but we made the best of what there was, and developed pragmatic approaches, based on the thinking of the time.

Now, with hugely improved science and technology available, how do responsible researchers and decision makers decide how and when to use new approaches like mobile? How do you separate the real from the hype, the wheat from the chaff? We all need to be able to make good decisions about our research methodologies, not be drawn into having to test every new fashion for ourselves.

The Handbook of Mobile Market Research cuts through this dilemma by presenting current thinking clearly, comprehensively, and completely objectively. Armed with this knowledge you will be able to adopt mobile research methodologies appropriately, and with confidence, knowing what you're gaining, and the potential downsides. If only keeping up with all new thinking was this easy!'

Phyllis Macfarlane, Training in Africa Programme Manager, GfK Verein, and former Chairman, GfK NOP

'In this book Ray, Sue, and Navin lift the lid on mobile marketing research to comprehensively reveal how the various components work and fit together. This is an essential read for any researcher contemplating or already undertaking mobile data collection.'

Guy Rolfe, Head Mobile Practice, Global Operations, Kantar

'The most complete guide for mobile market research I've ever seen! Informative, educative, and a must have for any researcher, either beginner or experienced mobile market research adopter.'

Adriana Rocha, co-founder and CEO of eCGlobal Solutions

'This book is a comprehensive and no-nonsense approach to the application of mobile survey technologies within market and social research. It introduces a range of topics related to the design, collection, and implementation within both qualitative and quantitative methodologies, outlining best practice and potential challenges within the mobile arena.

Organized into four sections, the book is superbly-written and tackles specific topics on technologies, applications, ethics, and future directions. An easy-to-digest and example-based approach, the book is a must for anyone wanting to either better understand or directly conduct mobile research.

Well done to the authors. This is a first-class reference that will both educate and guide those in our industry in the most practical and legitimate ways, to utilize the "new normal" of mobile data collection and utilization. Something for all of us to embrace.'

Suz Allen, R&D Director Sensory & Consumer Science, Asia Pacific, Campbell Arnott's

'Mobile market research promises to transform the industry far more than online surveys did, changing the face of both quantitative and qualitative research. Poynter, York, and Williams have written the definitive guide for mobile research. Even if a researcher tries to avoid mobile work, mobile will impact their own approaches, replacing certain methods and changing others. This is a must-read book for market researchers.'

Jeffrey Henning, president, Researchscape International

The Handbook of Mobile Market Research

Tools and Techniques for
Market Researchers

Ray Poynter, Navin Williams,
and Sue York

WILEY

Library of Congress Cataloging-in-Publication Data

Poynter, Ray.
   The handbook of mobile market research : tools and techniques for market researchers /
Ray Poynter, Navin Williams, Sue York.
      pages cm
   Includes bibliographical references and index.
   ISBN 978-1-118-93562-0 (hardback)
   1. Marketing research.   2. Mobile commerce.   3. Mobile communication systems.
I. Williams, Navin, 1972–   II. York, Sue, 1968–   III. Title.
   HF5415.2.P659 2014
   658.8′3–dc23

                                                                    2014022436

A catalogue record for this book is available from the British Library.

ISBN 978-1-118-93562-0 (hardback)
ISBN 978-1-118-93577-4 (ebk) ISBN 978-1-118-93576-7 (ebk)

Cover design by Wiley

Set in 11/13pt Gillsans by Aptara Inc., New Delhi, India

Printed in Great Britain by TJ International Ltd, Padstow, Cornwall, UK

Dedication

This book is dedicated to all those working to improve and advance the use and application of market research in today's dynamically changing world.

Contents

Foreword

There have been two critical events in recent years that have had a profound effect on the market research industry.

The first was the 'internet' – the advent of online as a research medium and information source. On the positive side, it brought greater cost-efficiency; provided the platform for a whole new range of collaborative and social networking services; facilitated the growth of panels and associated software (which has become a sub-industry now in its own right); became a source of freely volunteered information, and for many research projects, particularly those dealing with highly sensitive or personal topics, facilitated a much higher level of respondent honesty and detail.

On the downside, however, issues of sample duplication, respondent verification, professional respondents, and online response behaviour (such as straight-lining, etc.) raised a series of challenges and quality concerns that, in some cases, have not been fully resolved, even today.

The second critical event that is having (and will continue to have) a profound effect on our industry is the development of mobile – not just telephones, but also tablets, phablets, other portable devices, and the associated 'app' industry. These devices now allow us to capture 'immediacy' with technology greatly expanding our ability to measure 'real-time' behaviour, rather than reported behaviour.

This 'immediacy' also adds a whole new dimension to many of the benefits that the internet has brought – in many parts of the emerging world (e.g. the African continent), the mobile phone is currently the default access mechanism to the internet, rather than fixed line.

In this rapidly evolving communications ecosphere, the traditional question(s) of understanding what is the universe, who is the universe (phone buyer or phone user?), what can/will our sample represent, as well as the newer challenges of determining 'consent', 'awareness', and 'privacy' are all yet to be comprehensively answered and agreed. With this in mind, the provision of the most up-to-date best practices and guidance is indispensable for anyone who wishes to adopt this methodology for any research project.

As with all new methodological applications, the 'shifting sands' nature of the legislative arena(s) that govern their implementation make it imperative that best (current) practice guidelines are shared, developed, and improved constantly, so that suggested policy directives and legislative proposals remain consistent with business needs and applications.

The Handbook of Mobile Market Research is a companion book to Ray Poynter's *Handbook of Online and Social Media Research* and provides a real source of current best practice guidance for those wishing to better understand mobile and include it in their toolkit of research methodologies. The authors, Ray Poynter, Navin Williams, and Sue York, bring years of learning, global experience, and a passion for combining new approaches with rigour. For example Ray and Sue are the editors of ESOMAR's book *Answers to Contemporary Market Research Questions*, and Navin is one of the contributors.

The book helps advance the cause of high quality market research by answering your questions, providing you with guidance, removing your fears, but at the same time highlighting the many (evolving) challenges that continue to present themselves with the adoption of any such new medium. This *Handbook of Mobile Market Research* is THE essential and formative guide to better understanding, and optimizing, your adoption of mobile.

I hope you gain as much value and insight from this second volume in the Handbook series as we did; ESOMAR is proud and honoured to be associated with this important reference document, and we look forward to continuing to monitor the evolution of our industry and providing such pioneering guidance in partnership with Ray, Sue, and Navin.

FINN RABEN
ESOMAR Director General

Introduction

Mobile market research is one of the hottest topics in market research today. The interest in the subject has not been matched by information and advice on utilizing mobile market research.

Given the speed of change in the mobile ecosystem, for example the increase in the penetration of mobile devices and the growth and development of smartphones and tablets, and the number of different ways that market researchers are seeking to use mobile devices in research, there is a hunger for good information and advice. However, there is a shortage of published information on: how to conduct mobile market research, the opportunities, the best practices, and the potential challenges. The advice that does exist tends to be spread across conference presentations, blogs, white papers, and articles.

This book addresses the shortfall in material by pulling together the latest thinking, guidance from people conducting mobile market research, academic research, and practical advice. The book provides a single point of reference for anybody seeking to be involved in mobile market research, either as a user or provider of research.

WHO THE BOOK IS FOR

This book has been written for market researchers who are aiming to conduct mobile market research, for users of market research, and for people looking to research or understand mobile market research. A basic understanding of market research is assumed, including knowledge of core market research terms and processes. In some of the more specialist areas, such as international and business-to-business research, a brief note has been included to ensure that the reader is sharing the same assumptions as the authors.

Most of the book is based on an assumption that readers will be utilizing market research platforms, typically, in partnership with fieldwork suppliers and/or access panel companies. Whilst the book reviews some of the issues involved in creating customized research solutions, this is not its focus. The book is not specifically designed for people looking to write a research app, or design new mobile question types, or create a new mobile market research product – although it might provide some useful background for anybody looking to do one of these.

THE STRUCTURE OF THE BOOK

The book is divided into four parts, to help readers locate material relevant to their current needs.

PART I: MOBILE MARKET RESEARCH

The book starts with an overview of mobile market research, providing a holistic view of how mobile devices are being used in market research. Part I then goes on to look at mobile market research in action, looking at topics such as brand tracking, ad testing, and customer satisfaction research. This is followed by a chapter looking at the technology of mobile market research.

PART II: QUALITATIVE AND QUANTITATIVE RESEARCH

The second part of the book looks at how market researchers are using mobile devices in terms of qualitative and quantitative research. The qualitative section starts by providing an overview of qualitative mobile market research, before focusing on topics such as online focus groups, online discussions, mobile diaries, and mobile ethnography.

The quantitative section starts with an overview of quantitative mobile market research, followed by a chapter focusing on designing and conducting mobile surveys.

PART III: THE METHODS AND APPLICATIONS OF MOBILE MARKET RESEARCH

The third part of the book looks at several aspects of mobile market research, for example mobile CAPI, mobile CATI, mixed-mode research, using passive data, working with panels and online communities, and conducting research internationally.

PART IV: RESEARCHING THE MOBILE ECOSYSTEM, ETHICS, AND THE FUTURE

The final part of the book is a reference section, providing advice and information on a range of topics, including researching the mobile ecosystem, the ethics of mobile market research, and a summary of the research-on-research that has been conducted.

This section also contains a review of the evolving picture. The majority of the book focuses on mobile market research as it is being conducted at the moment, reserving the more speculative and forward looking elements for this chapter in the final part of the book.

REFERENCES TO BRANDS AND SERVICES

In some parts of the book certain brands and services are mentioned by name, for example mobile survey platforms or access panel companies. These references are there to clarify the sort of organization being referred to; these mentions are not recommendations, and the reference does not imply that these brands or services are better or worse than other providers.

ONLINE MATERIAL

In order to keep this book to a manageable length, some of the more detailed information has been made available online, at www.handbookofmobilemarketresearch.com. The online material includes an extended glossary, longer versions of the case studies referred to in the book, and more material on the research-on-research quoted in the book.

REPETITION

The book has been designed as a reference book and it is likely that many readers will search for specific topics and chapters, rather than read it cover to cover. Therefore, a balance has been struck between repeating definitions, caveats, and cases in multiple places and repeatedly asking the reader to refer to other sections and the glossary. This does mean some elements appear in more than one place.

A NOTE OF THANKS

In the final part of the book there is a list of the many people who have helped create this book – helped by supplying material, by reviewing ideas and copy, and by engaging in discussions about the book.

Special mention should be made to Reg Baker and the University of Georgia's Principles of Marketing Research course. This book has benefited from the material created for the mobile market research course supplied by the University of Georgia, created by Reg Baker, Ray Poynter, and Navin Williams.

PART I

Mobile Market Research

The first part of this book provides an introduction to mobile market research, illustrates how it is being used, and explores the technology that underpins mobile market research.

Chapter 1 is an overview of mobile market research and provides a context for the rest of the book. The next chapter focuses on how mobile market research is being used in different contexts, categories, and markets.

The third chapter explores and explains the key technologies being relevant to mobile market research.

Part I covers:

1.   Overview of Mobile Market Research
2.   Mobile Research in Action
3.   The Technology of Mobile Market Research

Overview of Mobile Market Research

INTRODUCTION

Mobile market research (sometimes abbreviated to MMR) is a topic that had been forecast as the next big thing in market research for more than ten years. By 2014, there was widespread agreement that it was finally coming of age and was already having a major impact on many aspects of market research, from quantitative to qualitative, and from local to global. In the future, most market researchers are likely to come into contact with mobile market research in their everyday work and therefore a good understanding of the opportunities, characteristics, limitations, and challenges of this mode is essential. Similarly, buyers and users of market research need to be aware of the implications of some or all of their research being collected via mobile devices.

WHAT DOES MOBILE MARKET RESEARCH MEAN?

Mobile market research refers to participants taking part in market research via mobile devices and market research about the use of mobile devices.

Until recently the term 'mobile market research' was largely synonymous with research conducted by or about mobile phones. However, since the arrival of additional mobile devices, such as tablets and phablets, the term 'mobile market research' has become broader.

More specifically, mobile market research typically refers to the following:

1. Quantitative research where the participants complete surveys on their mobile device.

2. Mixed-mode quantitative studies, where some participants complete surveys via a PC while others use a mobile device.

3. Quantitative research where participants allow applications on their mobile device to gather information about them or their environment, referred to as passive data collection.

4.   Qualitative research, where the mobile device either facilitates communication (e.g. taking part in an online focus group from a tablet), or facilitates data collection (e.g. collecting photos and recordings), or a combination of the two.

5.   Research communities where the mobile device is a key method of communication or participation.

6.   Face-to-face research where the interviewers are using mobile devices to collect data, sometimes referred to as mCAPI (CAPI utilizing a mobile device).

Using participants' mobile phones to take part in CATI interviews is not always classed as mobile market research, but that might change in the future and a chapter on mCATI (CATI with mobile phones) is included in this book.

STANDARDIZED SOLUTIONS FOR MOBILE MARKET RESEARCH

When mobile market research first appeared on the scene, market researchers planning to use it often had to be very tech savvy and prepared to help develop or test solutions. However, for most people those days are gone.

Most mobile research is conducted via the international survey platforms such as Confirmit, through the mobile services of access panels such as Research Now, or through a specialist provider such as Revelation, MobileMeasure, or Locately: note – there are large and growing numbers in each of these categories. For most researchers it is not necessary to develop their own software solutions. In the more developed research markets, researchers will tend to use a conventional sample source such as an access panel, customer list, or community.

WHY THE INTEREST IN MOBILE?

There are four key drivers of the widespread interest in mobile market research:

1.   The growing ubiquity of mobile devices.

2.   People having their phones with them all the time, facilitating 'in the moment' research.

3.   Growth in more powerful mobile devices, especially smartphones and tablets.

4.   Passive data collection, recording information about participants without their having to actively enter information.

1. THE UBIQUITY OF MOBILE PHONES

Data about the penetration of mobile phones, smartphones, and tablets changes all the time, but in order to emphasize the scale of the mobile phenomenon, consider the following data from the ITU's Measuring the Information Society (ITU 2013) report:

- *6.8 billion mobile phones estimated to be in use, compared with the global population of about 7.2 billion.*

- *By the end of 2012, over 50% of the world's population were living in areas with at least 3G coverage.*

- *By the end of 2013 there were almost 2 billion mobile broadband subscriptions – with Ericsson forecasting that by the end of 2018 this figure would be 6.5 billion.*

The world is quickly moving to a point where every economically active adult who wants a mobile phone will have one. The trend is very much towards devices with internet access, further widening the potential for mobile research. However, it should be noted that 6.8 billion devices does not mean that 6.8 billion people have a mobile device, as many people have more than one mobile device.

2. 'IN THE MOMENT'

There is a widespread belief in marketing and market research that interviews conducted 'in the moment', for example, when someone is making a purchase, finishing a meal, or staying at a hotel, will reveal more than a survey conducted at a later date. Traditional research has relied on participants recalling details of interactions with products, services, and advertising, days or even weeks after the event. 'In the moment' approaches capture the information while it is still fresh in people's minds.

Most users of mobile phones have them with them all the time, for example Pew estimated that in 2012, 44% of Americans slept next to their phones (Pew Research Center 2012). This 'always available' characteristic of mobile devices finally allows researchers to conduct studies much closer to the 'moment of truth', that is, closer to when a product or service is being experienced.

3. PUTTING THE 'SMART' IN MOBILE MARKET RESEARCH

Early forms of mobile market research relied on SMS, WAP, or downloaded software (such as apps written in languages such as Java) to conduct research. These options were technically limiting (especially in the case of SMS) and sometimes required a high degree of cooperation from the participant.

By contrast, the larger, touchscreens of smartphones and the growing popularity of tablets has greatly increased the range of research that can be conducted via mobile market research. Similarly, the growth of higher speed internet connections, including 3G, 4G, and Wi-Fi, has enabled mobile devices to be used in a growing number of ways.

Similarly, the standardization of the processes for writing apps, and downloading them from app stores, has opened up a wide range of alternatives for market research.

4. PASSIVE DATA COLLECTION

Mobile devices, especially smartphones and tablets, can collect a wide variety of information as the research participant goes about their normal, everyday life. In most cases, this is based on the research participant downloading an app onto their device. For example, a location tracking app could use a phone's GPS receiver to create a record of the participant's journeys to and from work.

Passive data is very attractive to marketers and market researchers because it can collect a large amount of detailed data about what people do, without burdening participants with research tasks, and without introducing the biases implicit in asking research participants to decide what to report or capture.

A BRIEF HISTORY OF MOBILE MARKET RESEARCH

Table 1.1 provides a timeline giving a brief history of mobile market research.

Table 1.1   A brief history of mobile market research

Date	Description
1990s	The first serious attempts to use mobile phones for market research appeared in the 1990s, most of which used SMS. Questions were sent to participants via text messaging and the participants answered via text, typically by entering a single digit, such as 1 for Agree strongly, 2 for Agree, etc. These surveys needed to be very short. Only a small percentage of market research projects were conducted using this method because of the requirement for surveys to be very short and because the interface was considered so limited.
	This method is still in use today, in cases where it meets specific research needs, for example reaching a broad range of mobile phones in developing economies.
	One early innovation with the SMS method was to utilize its 'in the moment' potential. For example, some businesses put up signs inviting users/visitors to text their satisfaction score to a central location.

(continued)

Table 1.1 (*Continued*)

Date	Description
2000	As phones became 'smarter', acquiring larger screens and some form of internet access (e.g. WAP) researchers began to use these phones for longer and/or more complex surveys. By 2001, researchers were reporting success in Japan by capitalizing on DoCoMo's early lead in advanced services for mobile phones, sending longer surveys and incentivizing participants via telephone credits (Cattell 2001).
	However, mobile market research remained a small percentage of all market research. Studies such as the Confirmit Annual Market Research Survey regularly reported mobile as being less than 1% of all data collected.
	With the growth in the ownership of more advanced phones, market researchers explored two routes to conduct mobile market research. Some researchers preferred to design software that could be downloaded onto participants' mobile devices, while others thought it best to ask participants to connect to the internet via the browser on their device. This dichotomy exists today and is explored in more detail later in this book.
2005	As BlackBerry phones and internet-enabled PDAs became more common, researchers started reporting that a small percentage of participants were completing online surveys, intended for PCs, on their mobile devices. At that time this 'unintentional' or 'accidental' mobile market research (unintentional on the part of the researcher) accounted for a very small proportion of online surveys. In the years since, as phones became smarter/larger and tablets emerged, the proportion of unintentional mobile surveys has grown substantially. It is now often reported as being in the range of 20–30% of all online surveys.
	The qualitative uses of mobile devices expanded with a range of new and interesting approaches being developed, including mobile diaries and mobile ethnography. Researchers began using participants' phones to collect data about their everyday lives – for example by collecting images and recordings. Researchers also began using participants' mobile devices to connect the participants with blogs, bulletin boards, discussions, and communities.
2007	With the launch of the iPhone, mobile market research moved into a higher gear as qualitative researchers sought to use the iPhone's extra features and more participants in surveys tried to complete online surveys via their device of choice.
	In 2008, the appearance of Android phones from companies such as HTC and Samsung helped ensure that the new generation of smartphones established a critical mass.
2010	The release of the iPad led to a major growth in the penetration of tablets (especially Apple and Android-based devices). Tablets provided market researchers with still more features to use and a larger canvas on which to work.
	Mobile phones had become common across both the developed and developing world, and researchers were putting them to ever greater use in both developed and developing markets.
	In developing markets mobile market research tends to focus on feature phones rather than smartphones, and online surveys are often not an option. One of the trends in the developing markets is for research to move from face-to-face to mobile, often as mCAPI.
	Passive data collection, i.e. data collected from a mobile device without the traditional asking of questions and submitting of responses, starts to grow, especially in media and outside conventional market research.

THE INTERNATIONAL DIMENSION

Different countries present different opportunities and challenges for market researchers utilizing mobile market research. This is also the case for other research modes, such as online. In the more developed markets (i.e. richer, more technically developed, and with a more developed market research infrastructure) the default mobile market research options tend to be smartphones and, increasingly, tablets, with an assumption that the devices will be able to reliably connect to the internet.

In the less developed markets (where there tend to be lower incomes per head, technology is less widely distributed and owned, and there is a less developed market research infrastructure) the default mobile market research option tends to be the feature phone. This is accompanied by the assumption that the internet may not be available reliably and/or continuously. This has led to many researchers continuing to utilize technologies such as SMS in these markets. For example, in 2011 Bain reported in Research-Live that Jana (previously TxtEagle) had secured arrangements with 220 mobile operators in 80 countries to collect data via SMS and to use airtime as the incentive.

However, researchers should note that these definitions imply there are developed and less developed countries, and in many cases countries do not fit neatly into this simple division. Some technically advanced countries have relatively weak market research infrastructures and some less developed countries have well established market research infrastructures. Researchers should also note that contexts differ depending on local factors. For example, Australia has a much higher level of internet and smartphone usage, per head of population, than China. However, Shanghai has a population about the size of Australia (a little over 20 million) and has a similar level of smartphone and internet usage. For some target groups, smartphones are an appropriate technology, even in developing markets.

Researchers should note that the prevalence of feature phones in Africa does not mean that every aspect of mobile usage is more primitive than in, say, Western Europe. For example, mobile banking and mobile payments are far more developed in many African countries than they are in Europe.

When planning an international mobile project it is essential to get an up-to-date assessment of the current situation in each market, and this is covered more fully in the chapter that focuses on international research. Key issues that researchers need to focus on include: the quality, speed, and reliability of mobile internet access; the penetration of smartphones versus feature phones (and perhaps tablets); the type of data contracts that are common; and the sort of sample services that are available.

MOBILE QUANTITATIVE RESEARCH

Mobile quantitative research can be divided into two broad categories: surveys and passive data collection. Examples of passive data collection include browsing statistics, systems usage, and a variety of measures specific to mobile devices, such as geographic position.

In terms of surveys, mobile market research can be further divided into:

- *Unintentional mobile*
- *Mobile only surveys*
- *mCAPI*
- *Mixed-mode studies.*

UNINTENTIONAL MOBILE

Most market researchers who conduct online surveys are already using mobile market research, even if they have not decided to, and even if they are not aware of it. Any online survey, even if not designed for a mobile device, runs the risk of being completed on a mobile device by some participants – unless specific measures have been taken to avoid it. This form of mobile market research is referred to as unintentional (or sometimes as accidental) mobile market research, and the prevalence of unintentional mobile market research was one of the reasons why by 2014 it was safe to say that mobile market research had 'arrived'.

Reliable and consistent figures about the prevalence of unintentional mobile market research are hard to obtain. However, the consensus seems to be that in 2014 researchers should expect about 20–30% of online surveys to be completed from a mobile device.

MOBILE ONLY SURVEYS

A mobile only survey is one where the expectation is that all of the participants will complete the survey using a mobile device. This is a broad category and includes:

- *Surveys conducted via the internet using a browser on the mobile device*
- *Surveys conducted via an app downloaded to the mobile device*
- *Surveys conducted via SMS or similar protocols.*

Designing mobile surveys requires an understanding of the implications of using different screen formats and different versions of questions.

mCAPI

CAPI refers to Computer Aided Personal Interviews: interviews that are conducted face-to-face with an interviewer and a computer. Mobile versions (often called mCAPI), for example utilizing mobile phones or tablets, offer a new approach to this 30-year-old method. One of the benefits of using mobile devices for this new form of CAPI is that the device can often be configured to automatically send the results back to a server, for example via Wi-Fi or 3G/4G, either during or after data collection.

mCAPI allows multimedia to be integrated into the face-to-face interviewing process, for example by playing videos or recording video interviews with participants.

MIXED-MODE STUDIES

The terms 'mixed-mode', 'multi-modal', and 'hybrid' refer to studies where more than one mode of data collection is used. In the case of quantitative mobile market research, mixed-mode usually refers to an online survey in which some participants complete it using a PC, some using a tablet, and some via a mobile phone. However, the terms can refer to studies where participants enter some of their data through one channel, and other data through another.

The trend in market research is to move towards a platform agnostic approach, i.e. one where research participants are given as much choice as possible about the sort of device they use when taking part in research activities, for example using a phone, tablet or PC. This means choosing software systems that enable the researcher to design research that works – and produces comparable results – with participants using a wide variety of devices, including PCs, phones, and tablets.

Mixed-mode studies raise two issues: (a) how to ensure that the survey works on multiple platforms and (b) whether and how the data can be combined.

MOBILE QUALITATIVE RESEARCH

Mobile qualitative research is comprised of research that is purely mobile and research that is mixed-mode. The mixed-mode category consists of studies where some of the participants are using mobile devices and others are using other options, and studies where mobile is used for a particular stage of the study and another mode used at another stage (such as PC or face-to-face).

Mobile devices have made major inroads into the collection of personal and ethnographic information from participants in qualitative research projects. This type of mobile qualitative project involves research conducted by the participants, as opposed to research conducted by and in the presence of the market researcher. Enlisting participants as collaborators in the research process is a practice referred sometimes to as WE-research.

The use of mobile devices can be as simple as asking participants to upload images or join an online discussion. Or, at the more complex end of the spectrum, the research may take place over an extended period of time, with the participants collecting a wide range of diary or ethnographic data, and/or personal reflections, utilizing a variety of software packages.

MOBILE DEVICES AND COMMUNITIES

Research communities are (according to the 2013 and 2014 GRIT reports) the fastest growing major new approach to market research (Greenbook 2013b; Greenbook 2014). Research communities are usually private, branded, online communities, often using both qualitative and quantitative approaches. Mobile devices are increasingly being used for research (both qualitative and quantitative) with communities and for the management of the community. Management aspects of communities include: registering and logging in, sending messages to members, newsletters, portal access, and in some cases, incentives. Increasingly, the providers of platforms for research communities are ensuring that they accommodate mobile devices, typically by adopting a device agnostic approach.

The use of mobile devices in research communities is covered later in the book, in a chapter on Panels, Lists, and Communities.

THE MOBILE ECOSYSTEM

The term 'mobile market research' tends to be used to describe research conducted using mobile devices. However, it can also be used to describe research into the mobile ecosystem. The mobile ecosystem encompasses every aspect of mobile devices and uses, for example: the way mobile services are provided, the mobile devices themselves, mobile advertising, mobile shopping, mobile gaming, and mobile social media.

Research into the mobile ecosystem often employs approaches that utilize mobile devices, for example passive data collection, mobile diaries, and mobile surveys. However, it can also use more traditional approaches, including focus groups, usability labs, and conventional tracking surveys.

The mobile ecosystem has produced the tools that are used in mobile market research, and the new techniques being developed in fields like mobile gaming, mobile advertising, mobile marketing, and mobile navigation will in time work their way through to the world of mobile market research. The mobile ecosystem is also challenging lawmakers and regulators, both because of the speed of its development and because of its potential to collect vast amounts of sensitive information, and this issue will also have an impact on market researchers.

THE CHALLENGES OF MOBILE MARKET RESEARCH

Given that the arrival of mobile market research has been predicted and evangelized for several years, and given the importance of mobile phones to modern life, it is perhaps surprising that it has taken until now for mobile market research to take off.

This section looks at some of the factors that have delayed the adoption of mobile market research and some that may present challenges in the future.

SHORTER SURVEYS

There is a widespread belief that surveys on mobile phones need to be shorter than those being conducted via CATI, face-to-face, or PC. This is felt to be because:

- *People using their mobile devices are potentially going about their daily lives; an interruption of 20, 30, or 40 minutes is too long.*

- *The devices, phones in particular, are not suitable for extended exercises like a long survey, although the amount of time people can spend game playing with mobile devices might suggest otherwise.*

- *People's phone signal and/or connection may not last for the full length of a long questionnaire, when using the mobile web for surveys.*

However, it is worth remembering that when online surveys first appeared in the mid-1990s, it was widely assumed that online surveys needed to be shorter than 10 minutes. Since that time, participants have been trained or incentivized to do much longer surveys online, or at least a few of them have. Most researchers who have conducted research-on-research with longer surveys have found few differences between mobile and PC surveys. See the Research-on-Research chapter for more information.

Because most people believe that mobile questionnaires need to be short, many research buyers have been reluctant to move their major studies, which currently employ long questionnaires, to mobile. A number of strategies for tackling these issues, such as breaking surveys into modules (e.g. chunking) are being explored, and these are also covered later in the book.

THE COST EFFICIENCY OF PC-BASED ONLINE SURVEYS

Online surveys, in which participants use a PC, have become highly optimized in terms of speed and cost, and tend to have an advantage over mobile surveys. At the moment, mobile studies typically cost the same as or more than those designed for completion on a PC, and the total time from design to data delivery tends to be similar (the design, sample selection, and checking of mobile surveys often take longer, but the fieldwork can be quicker).

Because mobile research tends to be a little more expensive and because, until recently, the sampling was a little more limited, it has often been relegated to situations where it was believed to provide 'better' data, such as that from 'in the moment' or ethnographic studies.

However, with the improvement in standardized platforms for mobile, and increased range of sampling offers, the price/efficiency barrier is being eroded.

LIMITATIONS OF THE DEVICES

Most of the concerns about the limitations of mobile devices relate to phones, not to tablets. Phones, before smartphones, were seen to have a large number of weaknesses, particularly in terms of completing surveys. However, even with the latest smartphones, the screens are small and it has taken a while for the organizations offering mobile market research to deal with most of the concerns, for example by creating smartphone friendly versions of the full range of their question types.

VARIABILITY OF MOBILE DEVICES

Mobile phones are much more variable in their characteristics than the sorts of PCs that online surveys are typically designed for. In terms of PCs, researchers will usually assume they need to cater for Windows and Mac operating systems, with a screen size of at least 800 by 600 pixels, and a relatively modern browser. With phones, there are more operating systems and more configurations than with PCs, and beyond the smartphones there are tablets, phablets, and feature phones. This complexity makes designing mobile research more complex and problematic.

However, the current growth and dominance of Google Android and Apple iOS is making life simpler for those market researchers who are not dealing with feature phones, although the many variations of Android that are used by different man-ufacturers and devices mean that this is not quite as standardized as it might first appear.

ACHIEVING PARTICIPANT COOPERATION

Most developed research markets have an infrastructure of access panels, customer databases, and even online dynamic sampling services, such as river sampling, from which to source potential participants. This means that participant cooperation is at least predictable and organized.

Mobile market research is at an earlier stage of development, and while many researchers have found people willing to take part in surveys or qualitative research, there has been a less complete infrastructure to support mobile market research.

In around the year 2000, online market research grew because online sampling methods became widely available, and the sampling options grew because online research was growing. The same situation now appears to be well underway with mobile sampling options and mobile market research.

ETHICAL, REGULATORY, AND PRIVACY CONCERNS

Like all forms of research, mobile market research raises a number of ethical, regulatory, and privacy concerns. As with other modes, some of these concerns are general and some are specific. These issues are covered more fully later, but the key points are:

- *The safety of people taking part in surveys (we don't want people driving and filling in surveys at the same time).*

- *Defining and achieving informed consent.*

- *Avoiding annoying people: don't send unwanted or too many messages or send messages at the wrong time of day (very easy with global studies and/or global travel).*

- *Avoiding passing on costs to the participants, or using up a significant propor-tion of participants' monthly data contract.*

- *Ensuring participant privacy and anonymity.*

- *Ensuring that communications to and from participants are secure.*

THE FUTURE FOR MOBILE MARKET RESEARCH

It is clear that mobile market research has arrived. A large number of surveys are being conducted via mobile, some as mobile only, and many as part of mixed-mode online studies. Most of the major survey platforms have mobile options and there is a growing body of research-on-research (RoR) suggesting what works and what does not work in mobile market research.

Mobile market research is having a major impact on some forms of qualitative research and on research communities and is beginning to help create a range of new and innovative approaches, especially in the areas of ethnography, diaries, and data logging.

Passive data collection is already an important part of media consumption measurement and is a major business for some non-market research businesses. A number of industry forecasters expect it to be a major part of the market research mix in the near future.

Mobile market research is not an established method, yet, but it is one that most researchers will be dealing with as part of their regular, everyday work. Mobile market research is no longer a niche, it is a mainstream approach. Many researchers are forecasting that mobile will become the dominant mode of data collection over the next few years, while others forecast that online and mobile will merge to become a single, platform agnostic approach.

2 Mobile Research in Action

INTRODUCTION

This chapter highlights some of the ways that mobile approaches are being applied to different types of market research, and how they are being utilized in the context of different markets and situations.

The areas covered are:

- *Retail research*

- *Customer experience and satisfaction*

- *Advertising testing*

- *Tracking brands and advertising*

- *Product testing*

- *Advanced quantitative research*

- *B2B research.*

The key theme amongst these different strands is that mobile market research is making significant inroads; broadening the range of people who can be contacted for research and increasing the ability of market research to get closer to customers.

RETAIL RESEARCH

Mobile devices are having a major impact on retailing (both through online retailing and the use of mobiles as an aid to in-store shopping) and mobile market research is having a major impact on retail research. The sorts of changes that mobile market research is introducing include: increasing and enhancing the mobility of interviewers (for face-to-face research), utilizing the multimedia functions of mobile devices, collecting passive data, using geolocation to locate participants, and enlisting shoppers to participate as collaborators in research projects.

This section looks at how the following key areas of retail are benefiting from mobile market research:

- *Understanding shopping trips and processes*

- *Face-to-face customer research*

- *Retail audits*

- *Mobile shopping*

- *Mystery shopping.*

The final part of this section looks at the future of mobile market research in the context of retail.

UNDERSTANDING SHOPPING TRIPS AND PROCESSES

Understanding shopping trips and processes has been a major challenge for market research for many years. Methods of trying to research this aspect of retail have included:

- *Surveys and qualitative research that probed participants' memories, asked about their intentions, and sought to interpret their responses to alternative propositions.*

- *Accompanied shops within stores, sometimes augmented with video tracking.*

- *In-store and store exit interviews.*

- *Recruiting shopper panels to record their purchases, initially with paper diaries, and more recently with scanners and online updating.*

- *Big data analytics, in the form of loyalty card, purchase, and lifestyle data.*

Whilst these methods have been useful for some brands, for some types of purchases, and for some types of retailers, they have left many questions unanswered. Mobile market research is providing new solutions to many of the most difficult problems, producing answers that are a combination of better, faster, and cheaper.

One of the key breakthroughs in this area, facilitated by mobile market research, has been to recruit shoppers to be active participants in market research. As active participants, shoppers use their mobile devices, mostly phones, to capture information during and immediately after the shopping process. This form of participant research is being conducted both qualitatively and quantitatively, using both active and passive techniques.

Examples of the sorts of project that are being conducted include:

- *Shopper diaries. Shoppers use a mobile device to keep a diary of their shopping trips. The diary tasks can include: taking photos and/or videos, describing shopping intentions, experiences during shopping, and the outcomes from the shopping. Shopping diaries are typically conducted as qualitative projects. The data collection can include scanning or taking photos of bills/receipts as well as products, stores and so on.*

- *Shopping audits. Instead of research participants logging all their purchases when they reach home, which tends to understate smaller and/or quickly consumed items, participants can use their phones to record purchases 'in the moment'. This can be achieved by scanning, taking photos, or using an app or survey to enter the data.*

- *Quantified shopping. Quantified shopping is the quantitative version of the mobile shopping diary. Participants use their phones to record where they go, what they do, what they buy, and how much they pay – often with a mixture of active and passive data collection. The key differences between shopping diaries and quantified shopping are the sample sizes (quantitative shopping tends to use larger samples) and the type of data collected (qualitative research captures more unstructured data and quantitative research captures counts and survey responses), and the type of analysis (quantified shopping tends to aggregate information, qualitative focuses on individual examples).*

- *Geolocation and geofencing. One of the newer fields in retail research is to track a shopper's location as a record of what they do and to trigger surveys as they approach or leave a specific location, such as a retail outlet, using positioning technologies such as GPS. An even newer development is to utilize short-range location techniques to track shoppers around shopping malls and stores. This topic is covered in more depth in the Utilizing Passive Data chapter and is illustrated in the next case study.*

- *Wearable technologies. Wearable cameras, eye-tracking goggles, and devices like Google Glass provide a more complete, shopper's eye view of the retail process, compared with accompanied shopping. And whereas Google Glass is very much at the exploratory stage, the use of life-logging cameras, such as Memoto, and mobile eye-tracking devices like Tobii Glasses, is much more established.*

Using Location Analytics and In-Store Mobile Surveys to Understand 4th of July Shopping

Locately, a US-based shopper insights firm specializing in location analytics and location-targeted mobile surveys, conducted a study of US shoppers in Summer 2013, timed to coincide with the US 4th of July celebrations. The study included 1152 participants who had opted to share their GPS location via Locately's smartphone app, and generated 918 in-store mobile survey completes.

The research triggered in-store interviews when Locately's location analytics technology detected that the shopper was in a store of interest, which for this study included mass merchandisers, grocery retailers, and warehouse club stores. Location analytics captured data on the shopper journey (passively) and gathered information about what happened inside store (via mobile surveys).

The data and insight generated by the research operate at two levels, the macro and the micro. At the macro level, the data answered questions around the awareness and impact of in-store shopper marketing activations, dollars spent to prepare for key 4th of July events (such as grilling), and location-specific metrics such as stores visited, store drive-pasts, time spent in the store, and distance travelled to reach the store. At the micro level, the data allowed a single participant's journey to be illustrated on a map and annotated with survey feedback from the stores they visited.

The study showed the power of integrating location analytics (e.g. mining passively-captured location data) and of combining the behavioural data with survey responses to gain insight into the 'Why?'

FACE-TO-FACE CUSTOMER RESEARCH

Face-to-face customer research, both inside shops and at store exits, remains a very important part of researching the retail experience. Face-to-face interviews allow the researcher to catch respondents when issues are fresh in their minds, in the context of the retail outlet, and can facilitate speaking to the full range of shoppers, not just those who answer phone calls, answer the door, or agree to do online or mobile studies. Mobile devices, especially tablets, have changed the nature of face-to-face retail interviewing, reducing costs, increasing speed and flexibility, and improving the quality of the research and insights.

For example Tesco, working with market research agency Marketing Sciences, have implemented a scheme using tablets to interview 100 shoppers a week across their over 950 UK stores. This study is reported in more detail in the mCAPI chapter.

RETAIL AUDITS

In the developed markets the process of retail audits is largely automated, in terms of tracking goods from distributor to store to checkout – although there is still a considerable amount of manual stock-taking within stores. However, in the less developed markets retail audits are often slow, expensive, and they are perceived to be of variable quality. Mobile devices are making inroads in the developing markets to facilitate faster, cheaper, more accurate audits.

Audits of point of sale, shelf displays, and promotional material are particularly suitable for mobile research as mobile has the advantage of giving visual proof to the other parameters being collected.

Display audits are popular in the newer economies where large parts of the retail and distribution network are perceived as unorganized. For example, as part of their distribution strategy soft drink manufacturers often give away display coolers to stock and display their products at point of sale. They do this as many outlets couldn't or wouldn't purchase a cooler on their own. However, many of these 'mom and pop' retailers pack the cooler with all their products that need refrigeration, including competing soft drinks. This creates a compliance role where researchers or specialist teams conduct compliance audits, utilizing mobile devices.

MOBILE SHOPPING

Mobile shopping and mCommerce have been a growing phenomenon for a number of years, and the growth looks likely to continue. According to eMarketer (2013), mobile commerce in the US was worth $25 billion in 2012. Deloitte reported that in 2013, in the US, 68% of smartphone owners and 63% of tablet owners planned to use their devices for shopping during the October to December shopping period. Amongst those who planned to use a smartphone or tablet for shopping, the key uses are shown in Table 2.1.

Making a purchase was recorded as 31% for phones and 52% for tablets.

Table 2.1   Comparison of uses of smartphones and tablets for shopping

Smartphone users	Tablet users
Get store locations, 56%	Shop/browse online, 69%
Check/compare prices, 54%	Check/compare prices, 58%
Get product information, 47%	Get product information, 58%

The use of mobile devices in shopping and commerce is hot news, because of its size, its growth, and also its complexity. Mobile devices are used to investigate potential purchases, to navigate to shopping locations, and to make purchases. Some of the information about this process is available from what is often termed 'big data', for example transactional data, loyalty programme data, web-tracking data. However, big data only explains part of the picture, leaving market research to add the 'Why?' and 'What if?' components.

Research approaches being used in the context of mobile shopping include:

- *Usability testing, for example, how easy it is to buy from an online site using a phone or tablet. Usability testing is conducted both quantitatively and qualitatively, in central locations (for example usability labs) and remotely.*

- *Passive data collection, finding out how often people use their mobile device, what they use it for, and where they use it.*[1]

- *Mobile diaries and 'quantified self' research, using qualitative and/or quantitative approaches. These diaries can be combined with a variety of triggers, for example, app triggered, researcher triggered, or triggered by the participants themselves.*

MYSTERY SHOPPING

Mobile devices are making major inroads in the area of mystery shopping, including:

- *Assigning tasks to mystery shoppers.*

- *Facilitating photos and videos being collected, along with time and location information.*

- *Checking the performance of telephone companies offering mobile services, especially broadband.*

- *Helping with the logistics of organizing mystery shopping, for example navigation, and helping monitor the performance of mystery shoppers.*

As with all mystery shopping research, care needs to be taken to conform to ethical and legal guidelines. For example, secretly recording a retail assistant is likely to be illegal in many situations, and unethical in some of the situations where it is legal.

---

[1] Note, passive data cannot be used to track everything that happens on a mobile device, at least not within the OS guidelines, and one of the key restrictions is in the area of tracking commercial transactions.

THE FUTURE OF MOBILE MARKET RESEARCH AND RETAIL

In terms of retail research, some of the key trends appear to be:

- *Integrated/single source data, combining multiple data streams about individuals, to help identify the contribution of different factors to purchase behaviour. The data strands might include mobile passive data, transactional information, internet usage, and loyalty card data.*

- *Wearable technologies, such as life-logging cameras and Google Glass, are only just beginning to be used in retail research. In the near future these technologies could provide a complex and comprehensive 'shopper's-eye' view of the shopping process – especially if integrated with passive data collection.*

- *Geofencing and geolocation are likely to be increasingly important in tracking the routes taken by shoppers (at the wider geographic level, at the within store level, and even at the specific retail fixture level) and in terms of triggering research exercises, for example surveys triggered immediately after shopping at a specific store.*

CUSTOMER EXPERIENCE AND SATISFACTION RESEARCH

Mobile devices have opened up new opportunities for companies trying to find out more about customer satisfaction and/or customer experience. The key to these new opportunities is the 'always present' aspect of mobile devices, particularly phones and phablets.

Traditional customer satisfaction and experience research has been criticized for suffering from several key problems:

1. It tends to be based on people's memory rather than their current or recent experiences, resulting in inaccurate measurements.

2. Halo effects can swamp actual, real-time experiences and distort the recalled evaluations. For example, if somebody likes an experience they are prone to say everything was good. However, if the experience was negative they are prone to describe most of the experience as negative – this makes the findings less actionable.

3. The research is often targeted at phenomena that are of little interest to research participants. For example, questions about how a customer is greeted at the bank or supermarket can result in blunt and hazy measurements if users do not find that aspect relevant to them.

4.   A company's area of interest is often too wide to create a meaningful research instrument. One consequence of the breadth of interest has been the creation of ever longer customer satisfaction surveys, delivering ever lower levels of satisfaction to the users of the research.

5.   Customer satisfaction and experience is a lagged measure; it talks about what happened, not what is happening. The longer the delay between the measurement and the reporting, the more lagged the information is, making it difficult to use proactively in managing a brand or service.

The sections that follow look at several ways that the limitations described here are being addressed via mobile market research. The final section looks at how these developments might be expanded still further.

CAPTURING EXPERIENCES

Because phones/phablets tend to always be with people they are a great way to capture experiences as and when they happen. This type of mobile market research tends to be based on the participant recognizing that they are doing something or experiencing something and initiating the research activity, for example completing a micro-survey, taking a photo, or recording a video.

Whilst this research approach can be used to capture any type of experience, it tends to be particularly helpful when researching phenomena that are not perceived by participants as being particularly important or memorable. The Sweaty Moments study quoted in the Mobile Diaries and Ethnography chapter is a good example of this sort of research. Participants sent an SMS message to their blog every time they felt sweaty, and expanded their comments later, allowing the researchers to identify satisfaction with antiperspirants and deodorants, without having to make these products the overt topic of the research.

BIAS AND CAPTURING EXPERIENCES

The main concern that has been raised about these mobile approaches to capturing experiences is that the research participants are too aware of the process, becoming sensitized to the task, and creating too much bias. Whilst most researchers would agree that this is a concern, the proponents of this type of research make the following points:

- *The alternatives that are currently available are substantially more flawed, typically relying on participants to recall phenomena they barely noticed, and to answer questions about feelings they may not have experienced.*

- *The aim of the research is to collect relative measures, not to assign absolute values to activities and campaigns.*

- *In most projects the research participants are only engaged for between a day and two weeks, which reduces the sensitizing effects.*

EVENT TRIGGERED SATISFACTION SURVEYS

Traditional customer satisfaction studies often look at a broad range of customers' potential interactions with the brand. For example, a bank might seek to review mailings received, online banking, ATM usage, phone calls, and visits to the branch, each of these elements having its own questions in the survey, and its own satisfaction score. This is one of the reasons that standard customer satisfaction surveys are so long. It also means that participants might be asked to remember a letter or phone call from some time ago.

Mobile customer satisfaction surveys focus on capturing feedback 'in the moment', or shortly afterwards. Participants are encouraged to complete a research exercise, usually a survey, when the service or product is used. The survey can be very short because it is linked to a single activity, and the participant's memory and views are fresh and focused.

LOCATION TRIGGERED SATISFACTION SURVEYS

Location triggered satisfaction surveys apply geolocation/geofencing approaches to customer satisfaction research. With location triggered surveys, the researcher uses a location technique to identify that a customer is at a particular branch or location and initiates a survey invitation. This type of research tends to require an app-based approach to the research. For example, the 4th of July shopping study quoted earlier in this chapter used GPS to recognize that participants were in a target store and to initiate a survey, but devices like Apple's iBeacon can achieve a similar result.

ALERT/TIMER TRIGGERED SATISFACTION SURVEYS

Another approach to customer satisfaction or experience is to launch an activity, for example a survey, in response to a message from the researcher or in response to a request generated from a timer. This approach is particularly relevant to services or products that are offered/used/consumed continuously, for example electricity, gas, and local and national government services.

The Mappiness Project (MacKerron and Mourato 2013), summarized in the next case study, is a good example of how an alert can be used to collect data. In a customer satisfaction project the survey would focus on satisfaction with, for example, a bank, a power supplier, a transport system, or a branch of government.

UK Mappiness Project

The Mappiness Project sought to find out what factors affected how happy people in the UK were. The project was based on an app that was signalled twice a day asking people to rate how happy they were. The data was combined with phone coordinates using GPS.

The Mappiness Project was launched in the UK in 2010, and the initial report was based on over 1 million responses, gathered from almost 22,000 participants.

In addition to the happiness rating, the GPS data allowed the project team to determine the weather, whether it was daytime or not, and area (divided into one of nine habitat types, such as 'Marine and coastal margins' and 'Continuous urban'). The app also asked who they were with and what they were doing.

The general findings were not a surprise: being out of urban areas was associated with more happiness than being inside the urban areas, and being by the seaside was best of all.

The published paper is a useful resource in terms of methodology and approaches to analysis.

TAKING EXPERIENCE AND SATISFACTION FURTHER

One picture of the future was set out by Jan Hofmeyr (2013) at the London MRMW (Market Research in a Mobile World) Conference in 2013, where he called for:

- *Short surveys conducted via mobile devices, compatible with SMS or USSD.*

- *Linking surveys to social media data.*

- *Utilizing predictive analytics to move customer satisfaction from a rear view mirror to a forward looking approach.*

Other options about the future are possible and are being explored. These options include: biometrics and other implied measures of satisfaction, increased tracking of behaviour, and utilizing insight communities to have discussions with customers about their perceptions of services.

ADVERTISING TESTING

Advertising testing is one of the oldest forms of commercial market research and it is still one of the most important.

Evaluating Mobile Ad Testing

A number of organizations have been testing and evaluating methods of using mobile devices to test ads. The two cases below are both covered in the Research-on-Research section of the accompanying website.

In 2012 Ipsos ASI with MobileMeasure created and tested AdShout with three TV commercials that had been shown in Australia during the 2012 Olympics. The mobile test concentrated on key measures from the Ipsos ASI standard testing method and produced very similar results.

In 2011 and 2012 Luma and Research Now tested print ads and TV commercials with a slightly modified version of Luma's add+impact test. The results of the TV commercials were highly comparable. The print ad results were broadly comparable, but with one interesting and relevant difference, the mobile results produced lower scores for attention grabbing.

Within advertising testing, the most important element, in terms of money spent, is TV advertising. This is because TV ads (and cinema ads) are very expensive to make, relatively few ads per brand are created, airtime is very expensive, and the consequences of running a poor ad are felt to be very large. Most TV ad testing involves showing the ad as a video – although if early ideas are being tested, the ad might be represented as a series of story boards or even just a description.

The largest impact of mobile research has been in the area of unintentional mobile, i.e. participants with mobile devices taking part in surveys intended for PCs. In the early days of mobile research, unintentional mobile was a potential problem for TV ad testing because the mobile phones had small screens, restricted bandwidth, and were felt to only be suitable for short surveys. Consequently, TV ad testing was an early user of methods to screen out participants seeking to use a mobile device to take part in a survey.

Most of the limitations of using mobile devices for TV ad testing have lessened. Alternative formats for videos are available, bandwidth is better, participants seem willing to spend more than five minutes taking part in a survey, screens are often larger/clearer than they were, and participants can use headsets to listen to the ad if they wish.

Consequently, there are a growing number of testing systems that are platform agnostic, and a few that focus on mobile users.

TRACKING BRANDS AND ADVERTISING

Brand and advertising tracking is one of the largest uses of market research and it is also one that often uses some of the longest surveys – with some tracking surveys lasting longer than 60 minutes! Tracking surveys seek to measure some or all of: brand awareness, brand perceptions, brand usage, and contact with brand advertising. The analysis of the data often seeks to link advertising expenditure to changes in brand beliefs, attitudes, or behaviour.

How Many Cereal Packs?

As an illustration of the difference a picture can make, MMR CEO Mat Lintern highlighted a study they conducted in 2013 with UK housewives. In an online survey the average claimed number of cereal packets stored at home was lower than expected. So to check the accuracy of the online data, around 150 participants were asked to take a photo of the place where they kept their cereal and send this via MMS to the agency. This showed that, on average, people had almost twice as many packs of cereal (9 versus 5) than they had claimed based on recall, and it also showed the proportion of own label was much higher than had been claimed (35% versus 20%).

Mat commented 'The recall of the market leading brands in the survey was reasonably accurate, but consumers consistently failed to recall many of their lesser used cereals – which often tended to be smaller brands and own label products. The use of photos completely removed any ambiguity, providing accurate data with minimal input required by the respondents.'

Because many tracking studies were perceived as being too long for mobile, the movement of tracking studies to mobile agnostic platforms has been relatively slow. However, there is a growing amount of interest in two areas of tracking research:

1. In developing markets, where the majority of tracking studies are conducted face-to-face, there is a move to mobile to increase quality controls and to produce faster turnaround speeds.

2. In the more developed markets there is growing discontent with the large, expensive, and slow tracking studies, with calls to move to more agile solutions, typically ones that are either mobile friendly or in some cases mobile specific.

PRODUCT TESTING

Product testing has adopted mobile market research in a number of interesting ways, partly because the barriers are seen to be lower and partly because of the specific benefits of mobile market research. One of the reasons that mobile research is seen as appropriate for product testing is that the surveys tend to be shorter than tracking studies. The main limits have been where large images or videos were needed, but these restrictions are diminishing.

IN USE TESTING

When the product being tested is something the participant is going to use, mobile research can capture information throughout the usage experience. This information can include survey responses, multimedia, and qualitative feedback. For example, in a face cream test the participant might enter a small diary note every time they use it, along with a picture of the product and/or their own face.

ADVANCED QUANTITATIVE RESEARCH

The main reason to conduct an advanced technique, like conjoint analysis, via mobile devices is to extend the range of people who can be reached and to increase the speed in which the results can be achieved. In Western markets this typically means reaching younger/busier people. In developing markets it can mean the difference between being able to use an advanced technique (such as adaptive surveys) and not being able to, because PC-based solutions may not be available.

The limitations of using mobile devices for advanced quantitative research techniques, such as discrete choice modelling, have tended to be:

- *If the questionnaire requires specialist data collection software, will it run on the devices that participants are likely to have?*

- *If the questionnaire requires a large screen it may not render in a usable way on a small screen, especially a phone screen.*

- *The questionnaires for some advanced quantitative approaches are quite long, so there was a concern that they might not be suitable for mobile.*

CREATING MOBILE FRIENDLY AND MOBILE SPECIFIC ADVANCED QUANTITATIVE RESEARCH

As well as recognizing that most advanced software packages support mobiles and that mobile devices now have larger screens, there have been innovations in the way that research projects are designed and implemented.

Key innovations include:

1. Shorter/lighter forms of advanced methods. For example, some researchers have been utilizing discrete choice studies with just three options per screen and just three screens per participant. This method allows the researcher to reach mobile audiences and still utilize leading edge analysis tools. For example, see the case study from SKIM (Loosschilder & Ashraf), at www. handbookofmobilemarketresearch.com.

2. Alternative evaluations. The fashion for the last 15 years has been towards discrete choice and away from ranking and rating. However, some researchers have shown that they can use ratings-based conjoint to allow concepts to be displayed one at a time on the screen of a phone and capture the information required to analyse the attributes and levels.

3. Implicit Association Testing (IAT). Implicit association testing is a research approach developed from social psychology that measures the association between concepts, based on the time it takes to respond. Social psychologists have shown that concepts that are associated are answered more quickly than dissonant ones. IAT has been available for online surveys via PCs for a few years, but more recently researchers have been using it specifically for mobiles.

B2B (BUSINESS TO BUSINESS) RESEARCH

B2B is an example of a category of research that shares many characteristics with general market research, but which also has some nuances and features that are either unique to its sector, or which need to be designed, implemented, or interpreted differently.

SAMPLING ISSUES

B2B sampling is often more challenging than consumer research. Problems can include:

- *Absence of a sample frame.*
- *Very large differences in the size of businesses.*
- *Deciding who to sample within a business.*
- *Concerns that access panels for B2B research are not as fit for purpose as consumer access panels.*

An example of the challenges facing B2B researchers can be illustrated by the market research industry itself. Although the industry comprises tens of thousands of companies, many of which employ fewer than ten people, over 40% of the revenue of the industry is accounted for by the largest six agencies (Nielsen, Kantar, GfK, Ipsos, Gartner, and IMS Health). The challenge for a researcher is how to sample the industry, who to interview in the large and, in particular, the largest companies, and how to combine the data from the different sized agencies.

However, sometimes B2B studies can be simpler to organize than a consumer project. For example, if the study is being conducted with a customer list, and if the list has email addresses and telephone numbers, and if the client has a positive relationship with their customers, the project might compare favourably with consumer research.

VARIATIONS IN MOBILE DEVICES

Different business sectors and different companies make different choices about the types of hardware and operating systems they use. If a B2B mobile project excluded BlackBerry users, it might introduce significant biases if this resulted in a group of companies that are still using BlackBerry devices being excluded from the study. Information about which companies are using which types of mobile device is often hard to obtain.

ETHICS AND INTELLECTUAL PROPERTY RIGHTS

B2B researchers are usually aware of the need to understand and comply with privacy and competition laws. However, in different countries the boundaries between competitive intelligence and industrial espionage are different, and the legal consequences of the difference can be severe.

The mobile devices used by participants in B2B research (particularly for quantitative research and auto-ethnography) are often owned and paid for by their employers, which raises potential ethical issues about asking participants to use their mobile devices to take part in research projects.

SUMMARY

This chapter has illustrated the many ways that mobile market research is already making inroads into different aspects of market research. The key points that need to be kept in mind are:

- *Mobile market research is becoming a key feature of most market research fields, either through a move towards platform agnostic research or to achieve mobile specific benefits.*

- *The move towards platform agnostic research has reduced the number of types of projects that can only be run via PCs.*

- *In many cases, such as with tracking studies, the main limitation in making studies mobile friendly is felt to be the survey length, especially for surveys over 20 minutes.*

- *The move towards platform agnostic research is the result of a combination of pull and push. The push is represented by researchers looking to widen the range of participants able to take part in research projects. The pull is represented by the fact that something in the range of 20–30% of participants are choosing to use a mobile device to take part in research projects.*

- *The move towards specifically mobile research is particularly relevant when using mobile devices to capture 'in the moment' information and feedback, often by enlisting the participant as a collaborative partner in the research.*

- *In the newer, less developed markets, mobile research is also being used to replace slower and relatively expensive forms of research, such as paper questionnaires, administered via face-to-face interviews.*

3 The Technology of Mobile Market Research

INTRODUCTION

This chapter looks at the hardware and software that define today's mobile world, in the context of what market researchers might want to know. Given the speed that mobile technology is advancing, the book does not seek to be a technical manual; it aims to create a framework of understanding.

Topics covered in this section include:

- *Types of mobile devices*
- *Connecting with mobile participants*
- *The mobile ecosystem*
- *The features of mobile phones*
- *Mobile operating systems*
- *Location-based services.*

This chapter focuses on technologies that are in use currently and that impact the world of market research. Beyond today's technologies there are a variety of new innovations, for example the use of wearable technologies and biometrics. These advances are covered as part of the Evolving Picture chapter towards the end of the book.

TYPES OF MOBILE DEVICES

There are a variety of mobile devices that are of interest to market researchers. Each device has something in common with the other mobile devices, but each also has something unique.

From a research point of view, mobile devices can be thought of as falling into one of three broad categories:

- *Smartphones*

- *Feature phones*

- *Tablets (including PDAs and phablets).*

There are also other devices such as wearable technologies (e.g. Garmin Vivofit and Google Glass) and GPS navigation systems that are mobile, but are not yet part of the standard market research tool kit.

SMARTPHONES

The definition of a smartphone has evolved considerably over the last ten years. Initially, the high-end phones introduced by companies like Nokia, with colour screens and cameras, were considered 'smart'. Over the next few years the features that defined a smartphone expanded to include email, web browsing, business integration, keyboards, and touchscreens. Today, the term 'smartphone' often refers to either an Apple iPhone or a phone with a touchscreen running the Android operating system, or an alternative such as the Windows Phone operating system.

Some key milestones in the evolution of smartphones are shown in Table 3.1.

Table 3.1   Key milestones in the evolution of smartphones

Date	Description	Impact
2002	Colour and larger displays appear on mobile phones. Cameras become common on premium phones.	Arrival of camera phones
2003	More phones with a camera sold than standalone cameras. Launch of BlackBerry, with push email, web browsing, and wireless services.	Arrival of the business phones, driving data usage on mobiles
2007	iPhone appears, creating an alternative definition of 'smart'.	Start of the touch revolution
2008	Android smartphones, such as those made by HTC and Samsung appear. Apple's App Store launched, changing the way apps are accessed.	Android makes 'smart' affordable. Apps go mainstream.
2010	Apple's iPad appears, followed by tablets running the Android operating system.	Start of the tablet revolution
2011	Samsung Galaxy Note launched, a phone with a screen over 5 inches.	Arrival of phablets
2013	Android becomes the most common operating system on new phones.	The rise of a dominant OS?

It should be kept in mind (when designing mobile market research) that a smartphone ceases to be so 'smart' if it does not have a reliable and affordable connection to the internet and if the user of the phone is not familiar with the core features that make it 'smart'.

At the time of writing this book, the majority of smartphones use one of two operating systems, Google's Android and Apple's iOS, which are also the two leading operating systems for tablets. This standardization makes market research easier to organize, compared with a situation where there are multiple operating systems. However, not every web browsing phone uses these two operating systems. The 2013 GRIT Consumer Participation in Research Report (Greenbook 2013a) estimated that about only 55% of its global survey invitations served to mobile devices were to iOS and Android devices.

For most research projects, the question is not about defining what a smartphone is, but determining whether the phones that the research participants have are 'smart enough', and whether they can be cost effectively utilized.

FEATURE PHONES

A 'feature phone' is a term that is used to describe any phone that is not a smartphone, which is not a particularly useful definition as it covers a vast range of devices. A feature phone can be a very basic phone, with little more than the ability to make phone calls and send SMS text messages, or it may be as feature rich as a smartphone. Some use the term 'feature phone' to describe the more sophisticated phones that are not smartphones, reserving the term 'dumb phone' for the more basic types of phone.

One of the complexities of utilizing feature phones for mobile market research is their variability. In the world of feature phones the hardware varies, the range of features varies, their ability to connect to the internet varies, and their operating systems vary.

> **TIP:** *The term 'feature phone' does not really describe a type of phone, it is a collection of everything that is not a smartphone. If feature phones are going to be used for a mobile market research project the definition needs to be more precise, describing the types of phones and features that will be used.*

MARKET RESEARCH AND FEATURE PHONES

When researchers talk about conducting surveys suitable for a feature phone they tend to be referring to one of the following:

(a)   Surveys utilizing SMS

(b)   Surveys using a web-browser on the phone, typically without a large screen, without a touchscreen, and with limited interactivity

(c)   Surveys based on downloading an app.

Globally, there are more people using feature phones than smartphones and this is likely to remain the case for a few a more years, especially in emerging markets. In Q3 of 2013 Gartner reported that 45% of global new phone sales were feature phones. In India, IDC reported that about 80% of new phone sales in Q3 of 2013 were feature phones. Mobile market research projects that try to be broadly representative of a whole market, especially developing markets, must accommodate feature phones.

Although the majority of surveys conducted via mobile devices in the developed markets utilize smartphones (usually as a mixed-mode option with online research), there are tens of millions of surveys being conducted globally via feature phones.

It is also important to note they there are a large number of qualitative projects, for example mobile diary projects, being conducted using feature phones.

TABLETS (INCLUDING PDAs AND PHABLETS)

This section reviews those mobile devices that are not phones and are not considered PCs. This section does not discuss laptops or netbooks, even though some might consider them to be 'mobile devices'.

Tablets

The earliest tablets were introduced before 2000. However, the modern tablet was launched by the introduction of the Apple iPad in 2010. The iPad was quickly followed by other similar tablets, many of them using the Android operating system.

The key features of tablets, in terms of mobile market research, are:

1.   Touchscreens. Tablets have touchscreens, larger than a phone, allowing a wide range of question designs and stimuli to be used.

2.   Size. Tablets generally have dimensions in the range of 7–11 inches.

3.   Internet connectivity. Some tablets have 3G or 4G connectivity, but many of them only have Wi-Fi connectivity. Tablets that only have Wi-Fi connectivity can only connect to the internet (e.g. to complete an online survey) when there is a suitable Wi-Fi service available.

4.   SMS. Those tablets that do not have a SIM (i.e. are not connected to the mobile phone network) cannot easily send and receive SMS messages.

5.   Standard operating systems. Most tablets currently being sold and most of the installed base (installed base refers to devices in use, not just to those bought recently) use one of the two leading operating systems, such as Apple's iOS or Google's Android, which are also the two leading operating systems for smartphones.

PDA (Personal Digital Assistant)

PDAs have been around almost as long as mobile phones, with products such as the Palm Pilot, the Apple Newton, and the Psion range. The concept behind PDAs was to provide miniaturized PCs, typically, designed for specific uses. These days PDAs tend to be used for highly specialized tasks, for example courier or delivery staff sometimes use PDAs to record and track shipments. One area where PDAs may continue to have an advantage is where security is critical. In these cases, the fact that the PDA has no other use, and is not a phone, can be an advantage – such as staff conducting meter readings for utilities like water, electricity, and gas.

As smartphones have become more powerful, and with the introduction of tablets, PDAs have become less relevant to the world of market research.

Phablets

A recent phenomenon has been the arrival of the so-called 'phablet' (occasionally referred to as a padphone). The phablet is a fusion device that combines the attributes of a phone and a tablet. Phablets may be loosely defined as a mobile phone with a screen size of between five inches and seven inches. Anything larger than seven inches is usually referred to as a tablet.

THE LINK BETWEEN DEVICES AND MOBILE MARKET RESEARCH

Within the context of mobile market research the term 'mobile device' mostly refers to feature phones, smartphones, tablets, and phablets. Different mobile devices have different characteristics that influence how they are used in market research projects. For example, a feature phone is unlikely to have a large touchscreen and a large tablet is not typically carried everywhere by its owner.

The design of a specific mobile project needs to balance the needs of the research with the mobile devices available. Researchers have to match the research to the devices the participants have, or select participants who have the right types of mobile devices. If the research plans to use high-end functions, for example those found on smartphones, phablets, and tablets, then the users of feature phones will have to either be screened out or offered a version of the study that will run on their device. In either case, the researcher may be introducing biases into the results. The researcher needs to ensure that whatever research applications are used in the study work correctly on all device types likely to be used by study participants.

CONNECTING WITH MOBILE PARTICIPANTS

There are four key methods that market researchers use to connect with participants:

1.   Mobile web or mobile internet

2.   Short Message Service (SMS/Text), and to a lesser extent USSD

3.   Voice

4.   Mobile applications.

MOBILE WEB OR MOBILE INTERNET

The mobile web, or mobile internet, works like the 'normal' web where a URL or web address gives access to an internet web page. Participants use their mobile device to go online via a browser to take part in research activities such as discussions or surveys. Mobile devices come in multiple sizes and screen resolutions, and web pages can render poorly on mobile screens (particularly small screens). As a result, it is important that online research applications are optimized for smaller screens.

Since different participants are likely to be using devices with different screen sizes, research applications often use techniques such as auto-detection of the operating system and screen size to render correctly for each specific device. One key element of this optimization process involves ensuring that the mobile version is 'big finger' friendly, making objects large enough to tap easily.

On touchscreen devices there are a number of elements that have become intuitive to users, such as tap and swipe. For example, swiping right to move to the next page and swiping down to reveal more of the page. A key part of making a research platform mobile friendly is to ensure that it uses these mobile intuitive elements.

If the research participants are using feature phones, then the available options are more limited. Most feature phones have smaller screens than smartphones and usually feature phones do not have touchscreens. This means that some of the more engaging types of questions and activities that might be used on a smartphone or PC either do not work or function very differently on feature phones.

SMS/TEXT

SMS, Short Messaging Service, or simply 'text', is a mobile protocol that allows users to send and receive text messages. In its traditional format, SMS has a maximum of 160 characters for single byte languages (e.g. English, French, and German) and 70 characters for double byte languages (e.g. non-Roman script languages such as Mandarin and Japanese).

There is an enhanced form of SMS called MMS that can carry photos and videos as part of the SMS message. However, MMS is not as standardized as SMS and is not accessible to all consumer mobile phones, and not all users have a suitable contract or knowledge to use MMS.

Before the advent of the mobile web, SMS was the core of mobile market research surveys, and it is still used for some research projects, amounting to millions of interviews every year. SMS can also be used to initiate an activity, for example the link to a survey can be sent via SMS, allowing the user to take part in the survey when they have access to the mobile web, or reminding users to participate in a research activity, such as a diary or online discussion.

SMS is very limiting for market research, with researchers often restricting question-naires to fewer than six questions and the questions usually need to be very simple. For example, an SMS questionnaire might just consist of Yes/No questions or scales with single code answers.

Another protocol that is being used with basic phones is USSD. USSD allows a partici-pant's phone to be connected to the researcher's computer via a gateway, allowing for messages of up to 182 characters to be sent backwards and forwards. Some agencies have had success using this method for research surveys, particularly in countries where smartphones and/or internet access are relatively rare, such as many countries in Africa.

MOBILE VOICE

Mobile voice is a protocol allowing users to make and receive voice calls on mobile phones and phablets, but is not always practical on tablets. Mobile voice is widely used for phone-based interviews such as CATI (Computer Assisted Telephone Interviewing) or depth interviews on mobile phones. Mobile voice is covered in the mCATI chapter.

Mobile voice can be an important support element in mCAPI and mobile qualitative projects. Voice can also be offered as a support line for participants in quantitative projects, subject to not overloading the support team and taking into account the cost implications.

Another use of mobile voice is via VOIP systems and conferencing systems, such as Skype, Google Hangouts, and GoToMeeting.

MOBILE APPLICATIONS

Mobile applications, or simply 'apps', are small programs stored on a mobile device. Apps make it possible to extend the range of tasks a mobile device can offer or support. Apps can offer something as simple as showing the time as an analogue image, or they can support more complex tasks such as playing games or collecting data for a research study. Apps may be pre-installed on a mobile device or they can be downloaded onto a mobile device from an app store.

Apps designed for mobile market research have some important advantages over the mobile web. For example, they can prompt the user to take a survey (perhaps triggered by a time alert or GPS information) and they do not necessarily require the device to be linked to the internet at the time the data collection is taking place.

Organizations creating apps can embed code from analytics companies, such as Flurry and comScore, that can be used to collect data from mobile devices and transfer it to the analytics company.

There are two key disadvantages to apps:

1.   They require participants to download the app (introducing issues of confidence and competence).

2.   They need to be specifically written for each type of device used in the research.

These two limitations are less of a concern for qualitative research, where the samples are smaller (so more support can be offered to help download the app).

THE MOBILE ECOSYSTEM

The mobile ecosystem is complex and dynamic; however, it can be broadly divided into three key players/providers:

1.   Mobile service providers

2.   Device manufacturers and brands

3.   Third-party service providers.

The details within each of these three headings change rapidly, so the facts, figures, and names quoted in this section reflect a moment in time. A more up-to-date picture is available from the internet, for example from the ITU (www.itu.int).

MOBILE SERVICE PROVIDERS

The mobile service providers are the organizations that connect mobile devices to the telephone network and to other mobile devices. Mobile service providers are also known as wireless service providers, mobile network operators, mobile network carriers, and other similar names.

The key mobile service providers have access to a radio spectrum licence, a network of radio masts, and a business model for selling access to the network. If a mobile service provider does not own its own radio spectrum licence or infrastructure (e.g. if it buys or rents these from other companies) then it is known as a 'mobile virtual network operator'. From a researcher's point of view, there is little difference whether an organization is a mobile service provider or virtual provider.

The services provided by the mobile service providers include voice calls, data access (e.g. 2G/GPRS, 3G, and 4G), SMS messaging, and a range of additional services. The pricing models and rules for connecting to a network differ from country to country, and usually from one provider to another.

The prices charged and the way contracts are organized varies widely by country. In some countries the receiver of a call pays part of the charge, in many countries the receiver pays nothing. In some countries SMS and data are built into the typical contract, in others, they are considered 'extras'. In some countries some services are limited to 'within network' connections, i.e. the user can only connect to people who are with the same mobile service provider, or the price for within network connection is very different from an out of network connection.

Mobile service providers, typically, charge on either a prepay system (where the user buys credit) or a contract basis (where the user pays a fixed amount and/or an amount for services used). Many service providers offer both types of pricing models.

In many markets, subscribers obtain their handset directly from the service provider. Service providers in these markets often keep prices low by absorbing some or all of the initial costs for the handset, but they thereby tie the customer into a 12-, 18-, or 24-month contract. In other markets, subscribers buy a handset from a retail source and the phone services from a mobile provider.

The key issues for mobile market research include network coverage, reliability, and cost of access to the mobile web. One key question is whether it will cost the participant money to take part in the research, and if that cost is not trivial, how to reimburse the participant. In markets where people tend to have comprehensive contracts, SMS contact and mobile web usage may effectively be free (if the participants do not exceed their monthly quota). But, if the participants are on a 'pay as you go' contract, there will be costs, especially if large amounts of data are moved (e.g. if videos are downloaded or uploaded).

DEVICE MANUFACTURERS AND BRANDS

The mobile device manufacturers and brands are the consumer electronics companies that provide the phones and tablets that people use. This is a highly competitive area and each brand has invested heavily in the technology, branding, and positioning of their mobile phones and other mobile devices. Over the last few years there have been major changes in which brands are the most popular, for example Nokia, BlackBerry, Motorola, Ericsson have all had periods when they were world beaters, and times of trouble. Brands like Samsung and Apple are currently in the ascendency.

In terms of mobile phones, innovation has been a key driver of the market since the introduction of digital networks in the early 1990s. Handset manufacturers vying for consumer sales introduced cameras, QWERTY keyboards, large screens, colour screens, games, music, GPS, and much more.

Different handsets, even from the same manufacturer, can have different features and functions. For example, one handset may have a large touchscreen with 4G capabilities; another handset may have a small screen, a numeric keypad, and limited access to the internet. Indeed, except for the manufacturers who focus solely on smartphones, providing a wide range of handsets has often been seen as a key part of a mobile handset marketing strategy.

The data on current sales of handsets is of interest to mobile market researchers, but it is only part of the story. The key to designing mobile research is knowing what phones are in use, a number referred to as the installed base. Sales data only reflects a small proportion of the installed base. For example, in 2013 the global sales of Android phones exceeded that of Apple iPhones. However, the GRIT Consumer Participation Report suggested that in 2013 researchers were more likely to encounter an iPhone than an Android phone when conducting global market research.

From a mobile market research point of view, knowing about the sorts of handsets that research participants are likely to be using is key to designing mobile research that is going to work. If most of the phones are feature phones, the research needs to be designed for feature phones.

THIRD-PARTY SERVICE PROVIDERS

The term 'third-party service provider' refers to a company that provides a variety of goods and services to mobile consumers via other companies' mobile networks. These goods and services are delivered via the mobile web and/or are downloaded onto the mobile device as an app. Examples of these third-party services include health and exercise services like RunKeeper and MyFitnessPal, games such as Angry Birds, and location services like Glympse.

Third-party services can come preloaded or embedded as part of a network's service offer. For example, in Kenya, a mobile money transfer service called M-Pesa comes preloaded and accessible to mobile customers using the Safaricom network.

Table 3.2   Features of mobile phones (early 2014)

Mainly Smartphones	Smartphones and Feature Phones
GPS	SMS
Full QWERTY touch keypad	MMS
Dual camera [i.e. front and back facing]	Colour screen
Enhanced cameras and video recording	Camera with video recording
3G/4G	Apps (e.g. games)
Tethering/portable hotspot	Bluetooth
Large screen	Web access
Touchscreen	Speaker
Gyroscope	Audio recording/microphone
Accelerometer	
NFC [Near Field Communication]	

Mobile surveys and discussions, whether accessed via mobile browsers or apps, are examples of services from third-party providers. In the world of market research, these services are often third-party in two senses of the term. They are third-party in the sense they are not provided by the mobile service providers or handset manufacturers, and they can be third-party in the sense that a market research company may have obtained them from another organization, such as a panel company or market research software platform provider.

THE FEATURES OF MOBILE PHONES

This section looks at the features of mobile phones and the key ways that market researchers use phones as a mode of data collection.

Mobile phone features vary between one device and another, and the list of features is continually evolving. Some core components like voice calling, SMS, colour screens, and cameras have become standard across handsets. But other features appear and sometimes disappear, such as radio receivers in phones, which are less common in smartphones than in modern feature phones.

Table 3.2 shows a list of some of the commonly found features of mobile phones in early 2014 – focusing on those relevant to mobile market research. The features are divided into those that are mainly found in smartphones and those found across a broader set of both smart and feature phones. Note that the terms used in Table 3.2, and elsewhere in this chapter, are explained more fully in the glossary.

Market researchers usually use one of three channels to conduct their research with participants:

1.   SMS

2.   Mobile web; or

3.   Apps.

1. STUDIES VIA SMS AND MMS

SMS was the first method used to conduct mobile market research, but it is now the least used channel. However, it is still used for some types of projects and in some regions. Studies that use SMS are able to communicate with participants using all types of phones, not just those with the more sophisticated phones.

SMS surveys are normally conducted via a market research platform, which can be based on the researcher's computers/servers, or quite often accessed as SaaS (Software as a Service, i.e. a service running on somebody else's computers, often via The Cloud) and connected to an SMS gateway. The researcher designs and deploys the survey via a research platform, which deals with sending the survey to the participants as a series of SMS messages. The survey platform needs access to the mobile phone numbers of the participants in order to conduct the research, just as online studies often use email addresses.

SMS can be used in some types of qualitative research, for example a simple diary study could be conducted via SMS. If the project requires participants to see or upload images or videos, MMS (a variant of SMS) can be used. However, not everybody is able or willing to use MMS, and MMS can create higher costs for participants.

2. STUDIES VIA MOBILE WEB

The mobile web can be reached from any mobile device that has a browser and a connection to the internet, either via a data service or Wi-Fi. A modern research platform should have the capability to detect the configuration of the participant's device (e.g. the type of phone, the operating system, and the screen size) and render its pages appropriately.

Features of the device that may be important to the researcher include:

- **The size of the screen.** *If small screens are going to be used, the survey design and platform need to accommodate this.*

- **The presence of a touchscreen.** *If the device has a touchscreen then options such as drag and drop are easier to use than they are on a non-touchscreen device.*

- *How images and recordings are downloaded and played.*

- *How images and recordings are uploaded.*

- *How other information from the phone can be shared, such as information about the phone's location.*

3. STUDIES VIA APPS

In order to use apps for research it is usually necessary for participants to download the app onto their device. This can raise issues of willingness and competence, for example, not everybody is happy to download a research app and not everybody is able to.

When using an app for research, all of the features of the phone or tablet are potentially available, including:

- *GPS to locate the participant, or to initiate a survey.*

- *Using the camera to capture photos or video.*

- *The sensors on the phone like its gyroscope, accelerometer, microphone, and environmental sensors can be used to collect additional information.*

- *Tracking the phone's usage, for example, calls made, locations visited, websites viewed, and apps used.*

When using apps, a variety of triggers can be employed to improve the quality of data being collected. For example, apps can initiate reminders to do specific tasks or request a specific activity to be undertaken. Apps can allow the research to use features on the phone to create a gamified or interactive experience.

A key benefit of app-based research is that some of them can function with or without a connection to the internet. However, a connection to the internet will usually be required at some point in order to upload the data.

When using a research app there tends to be a trade-off between a standardized research app that can be used without much setup time or costs and a custom built app that can access more of the phone's features and deliver precisely what the researcher wants, but typically at a higher cost and requiring a longer development period.

MOBILE OPERATING SYSTEMS

All mobile devices have an operating system or OS, just as all computers have an operating system. However, unlike PCs, where the majority of computers use either Microsoft

Windows or Apple OS X, the mobile world has been highly fragmented with a much larger number of operating systems.

Before the rise of smartphones, the operating systems of phones were less visible and more closely linked to a specific manufacturer. However, in terms of smartphones and tablets, the operating systems are more visible and a more widely discussed feature of device choice and status.

The sections that follow provide a brief overview of the key mobile (phone and tablet) operating systems.

ANDROID

Android was created by Google as their entry into mobile operating systems in 2007. In just a few years, Android has successfully overtaken Nokia's Symbian to become the most commonly installed operating system on new mobile devices.

Android was the first major mobile operating system to be offered free to handset manufacturers. Being free, coupled with Google services like maps and email, it became an almost overnight success. Several manufacturers who were building and selling handsets using their own in-house operating systems abandoned their own solutions and adopted the Android platform. Being a new operating system, Android was able to learn from the market and was able to build a system that is widely seen as user friendly and technologically superior to most of the other options.

Android is a leading operating system for both smartphones and tablets, which has helped increase the level of standardization in the market. However, the standardization of Android is not complete, and there are a wide variety of versions of Android in use, both because manufacturers can implement variations and because users tend to have a wide variety of generations of Android. Android is updated frequently; with the versions having quirky names like 'Gingerbread', 'Ice Cream Sandwich', and 'Jelly Bean'. Many users of Android devices do not update their operating system and others only update it occasionally.

APPLE'S iOS

Apple's entry into the mobile world came in 2006 via the iPhone, running its own operating system called iOS. The iPhone launched the touchscreen revolution. Although touchscreens were in use before the iPhone, Apple was the first to successfully build a user friendly operating system solely based on touch. In addition, Apple integrated their iTunes store to distribute content exclusively to iOS users. In 2008, they opened up content creation for third parties, which rapidly expanded their library of content, making it a valued and envied asset of the iOS platform.

The Apple iPad and iPad Mini also use the iOS operating system, providing standardization across the Apple phone and tablet range.

MICROSOFT MOBILE PHONE OS

Windows Phone was launched by Microsoft as the successor to Windows Mobile in 2012, in partnership with Nokia. Microsoft, which has now acquired Nokia's handset business, is looking to this operating system to help them revive their fortunes in the mobile world.

The Windows Phone operating system works in conjunction with the Windows 8 operating system, which covers PCs and tablets, providing another strand of standardization.

BLACKBERRY

BlackBerry OS was one of the outstanding success stories in the otherwise Nokia dominated world of the first half of the 2000s decade. BlackBerry phones were marketed as a business phone, with a secure business operating system and software. BlackBerry offered secure communication for email, a full QWERTY keyboard, and strong business integration. BlackBerry became the dominant phone system for enterprises and executives through most of the 2000s. Like Nokia, BlackBerry missed out on the touch revolution and saw its dominant position eroded.

In 2013, BlackBerry launched the QNX operating system, as the platform of the future for its tablets and smartphones. However, QNX has seen limited success in the market.

SYMBIAN

Symbian was an alliance of handset manufacturers who planned to use the Symbian OS as the core operating system for their phones. The dominant player in Symbian was Nokia and over time the company became synonymous with the Symbian OS.

In the 1990s and through the first decade of the twenty-first century, Symbian was the dominant operating system, with Nokia controlling over 70% of the global handset market. Most of the handsets that still use Symbian are Nokia phones. Broadly, there are two Symbian operating systems in common use, the S40 series and S60 series.

The S40 series is the older and less powerful of the two systems. The S60 series was intended for the next generation of Symbian phones and smartphones in particular. However, even Nokia is phasing out Symbian and moving to Windows Phone as its operating system.

Table 3.3   Mobile and Tablet Operating System Shares. Data sourced from StatCounter (http://gs.statcounter.com/)

Operating Systems Shares for Phones Intercepted on the Web	StatCounter Oct–Dec 2013, Global	StatCounter Oct–Dec 2013, North America	GRIT 2013 Participation Study Global	GRIT 2013 Participation Study North America
Google Android	38%	32%	25%	25%
Apple iOS	32%	59%	33%	51%
Other	30%	9%	42%	24%

OPERATING SYSTEM OVERVIEW

The overall global picture is fragmented in terms of handsets and operating systems, with substantial variation from country to country. In terms of smartphones and tablets, the picture seems, currently, to be stabilizing on Google's Android and Apple's iOS. However, at a global level, researchers who cater only for iOS and Android are excluding some smartphone users and most/all feature phone users.

The data in Table 3.3 looks at how often a researcher might expect to meet users of Apple's iOS and Google's Android when conducting market research via the internet. The two sources are both based on intercepting visitors, rather than sales or research data. The figures are not verified and should only be taken as an indication of a moment in time, but they do make the point that relying on just iOS and Android will exclude people.

> **TIP:** *When assessing whether a market is ready for smartphone only research, care should be taken to assess the installed base (what phones are in use) rather than just recent sales.*

LOCATION-BASED SERVICES

Some phones and tablets have location-based services that can be utilized for a wide range of uses, for example, satellite navigation. These services are often referred to as geolocation services, and some of these services are known as geofencing. These terms are explained more fully next.

In broad terms, location services can be used in the following ways:

- *To tell a device/user where the device/user is, for example, by locating the phone via GPS.*

- *To tell other devices or people where the device is, for example, via apps such as Glympse. This process is known as geolocation. More geolocation uses are covered below.*

- *To tell the user how to get from their current location to another location, for example, using the device as a satellite navigation system.*

- *To keep a record of where the device has been. For example, the app Run Keeper tracks a device whilst its carrier runs, cycles, walks and so on, allowing a map to be produced at the end of the exercise, along with statistics on distance, speed, height gained and so on.*

- *To trigger some action based on the location of a device, for example an app could be configured to trigger a survey every time somebody arrives at a specific location, for example, a retail park or train station. This triggering by location is known as geofencing.*

GEOLOCATION USES

There is a growing range of services that utilize geolocation, including:

- *Adding location to photos or videos taken by the phone/tablet.*

- *Apps that can tell the owner where the phone is, if it has been lost or stolen.*

- *Social mixing apps, such as Grinder, which tell users whether other members of Grinder are in the area.*

- *Apps that will search for local services, for example, nearby restaurants.*

DIFFERENT WAYS OF FINDING THE LOCATION OF A MOBILE DEVICE

There are a variety of ways of locating a device and the key ones are described next.

GPS – Global Positioning System

GPS location is a system that allows a GPS-enabled device to locate itself in terms of longitude and latitude. The positioning is achieved by the device locating the signal from three or more GPS satellites and using these to triangulate its position.

The use of GPS is free and anonymous, the mobile device utilizes the signals from the satellites, but does not register with them or send a message. Only devices that have a GPS receiver as part of their hardware and suitable software can use GPS location. This tends to mean smartphones and the more powerful feature phones.

Researchers should remember that people do not always have GPS turned on, even when they have it on their phone. Reasons not to turn it on include: conserving battery charge, not interfering with the device's performance, not wishing to record the device's geographic position, and not wishing other people to be able to locate the phone.

GPS can only be used when the device has a 'line of sight' to at least three satellites. In this context, line of sight means the ability to receive the microwave signals from the satellites. It is not possible for clouds to block the signal, but being inside a building or basement can (and so can putting the phone into a large bag or briefcase).

Cell tower tracking

The towers, masts, and units (also known as base stations and cell towers) used to connect mobile phones to the phone network are capable of locating a phone. This location can happen anywhere the phone can receive a signal, including inside most buildings. The main limitation with network location services, from a market research point of view, is that they are only available to the mobile network companies. Any access to this form of location information needs to be via the mobile networks.

Wi-Fi

Wi-Fi has become a very common way of wirelessly connecting computers, phones, tablets and other devices together and to the internet. Wi-Fi can be used to identify devices that connect, or try to connect, to it. The identification can be relatively generic and passive, or, if the connection is bundled with a registration process, the information can be more personalized and detailed. Since Wi-Fi is typically restricted to a limited geographical area, it is possible to log the location of a device connected to a particular Wi-Fi network.

NFC – Near Field Communication

NFC, or Near Field Communication, is a method of connecting smartphones to each other or to a fixed sensor point. The communication is based on radio technology and is restricted to very short distances, either contact or a gap of at most about 20 centimetres.

In the wider business world, NFC is being used to develop new initiatives such as payment systems. In terms of market research, experimental projects are being run in conjunction with activities like competitions in order to collect information from consenting participants. When used in geolocation, NFC requires the cooperation of the participant to place their device in contact, or near contact, with a sensor, for example as they move from one booth to another at a conference or trade show.

NFC refers to a specific protocol. There are also other developments that are seeking to create similar benefits and characteristics, for example, extremely short range Wi-Fi.

Bluetooth

Bluetooth is another wireless protocol and can be used to pass information from one device to another. Bluetooth can be used for a wide range of uses, for example, to connect a tablet to a PC or to connect an earpiece to a phone.

Bluetooth, in practice, tends to have a short range – typically about 10 metres.

Many mobile devices do not have their Bluetooth connectivity turned on, reducing its usefulness for market research, other than in situations where participants are sufficiently involved to be interested in changing the settings on their device. One interesting development in the area of Bluetooth is Bluetooth LE (low energy). Because Bluetooth LE uses less power it can be more readily used in 'always on' contexts.

iBeacon

iBeacon is an indoor positioning system from Apple that uses Bluetooth LE. iBeacons can be positioned inside stores to work with apps on phones to record where people are and to send tasks or messages to the phones. In early 2014 InMarket announced that they had fitted iBeacons to 150 grocery stores in the US, with the aim of pushing announcements and coupons to people as they arrive in the shop (McCormick 2014).

RFID – Radio Frequency Identification

RFID is most typically used as a method of identifying that something is passing a sensor and of reading the information from the RFID device. Many RFIDs do not have their own power source; they are simply a very small chip that uses the energy from a broadcasting unit to be able to send a response.

RFID tags can be used to track packages through a system, people around a factory, or shopping carts around a supermarket. They can also be used to read information from ePassports.

Audio signals

Apps can be built to either emit or pick up specific audio signals, using a microphone and/or speaker. ShopKick uses an app, on the mobile phones of people who have signed up to their scheme, to track them entering participating retail outlets and locations. This is how the ShopKick participants earn shopping coupons. The stores have speakers emitting a high frequency (i.e. non-audible) signal that is recognized by the app and uploaded to the ShopKick system.

Market researchers are using audio frequency systems to experiment with locating participants within target sites, for example learning about their route around the aisles in a supermarket.

THE LIMITATIONS OF OUTDOOR GEOLOCATION

Whilst there are several interesting and useful possibilities created by following people's movements there are also some significant barriers and limitations to overcome.

Key barriers and limitations include:

- *The need to download an app onto participants' phones and for GPS to be turned on and for a signal to be available.*

- *GPS via mobile phones can lack accuracy and there is a risk that the battery will be run down.*

- *Large amounts of geographic tracking data can be hard to convert into market research information.*

- *In some countries there are limitations to the collection and use of location information.*

- *Location via cell towers and networks is normally only available to the telecommunication companies, not to third parties.*

Most of the developments for indoor location or positioning do not use GPS or cell tower tracking. They tend to use beacon and app approaches and these may become relatively common over the next few years.

KEY ISSUES AND STRATEGIES FOR MOBILE MARKET RESEARCH

In terms of market research and mobile technology the key issues are shown in Table 3.4:

Table 3.4   Key issues for mobile market research

Question	Examples
Are feature phones going to be used?	Since the term 'feature phone' is not well defined, a decision to make a study suitable for feature phones needs clarifying. Exactly which sorts of phones will be included? With what sort of features and connections?
Is the study going to use the mobile web or apps?	If apps are going to be used, how will participants download them? If the mobile web is going to be used, what is the availability and reliability of the internet?
What are the implications for the participants involved in the study?	Will they have to download anything? Are there any potential costs, for example data charges? What impact might the research have on battery life?
Are Android and iOS enough?	If the research is restricted to tablets, probably. However, even if the research is focused on mobile devices using the internet using only Android and iOS operating systems would currently exclude large numbers of people in some countries.
What is the installed base?	Check what devices participants are likely to have. Don't just check recent market shares based on sales.
Are location based services going to be used?	Check that the design is feasible. Phones generally can't use GPS indoors. Most people can't access cell tracking data. Many participants don't have the location services turned on.

SUMMARY

The mobile ecosystem refers to all of the elements in the mobile landscape, for example, the handsets, the apps, the operating systems, the mobile service providers, patterns of use, the number of phones per person, the degree to which tablets are genuinely mobile, and the cost implications of using these devices. The mobile ecosystem has a major role in determining who can participate, the type of research that can be conducted, and the potential biases that may be introduced into the data.

PART II

Qualitative and Quantitative Research

This part of the book looks at the main two methods or paradigms used by market researchers, namely qualitative and quantitative research, and how mobile approaches are being used in both.

The key differences between qualitative and quantitative market research relate to the analysis of information and the researcher's belief about their role in the research process.

The first three chapters in this part of the book look at qualitative research and the next two look at quantitative research.

Part II covers:

4.   Mobile Qualitative Research
5.   Mobile Forums and Online Focus Groups
6.   Mobile Diaries and Ethnography
7.   Mobile Quantitative Research
8.   Designing and Conducting Mobile Surveys

4 Mobile Qualitative Research

INTRODUCTION

Qualitative market researchers were initially faster and more creative, than quantitative researchers in incorporating mobile market research in their toolkit. The growth in qualitative mobile market research has often been in newer and more collaborative areas of research. For example, market researchers have recruited participants to be active collaborators in research projects by using their phones to capture pictures and recordings from their everyday lives – a form of ethnographic data. Many qualitative researchers have also been quick to use mobile devices as part of pre and/or post tasks around conventional qualitative exercises or as stimulus material during conventional sessions.

This chapter provides an overview of the current uses of mobile qualitative market research, highlighting the main topics, opportunities, challenges, and practices. The following two chapters look at two key forms of mobile qualitative research in more depth, mobile online discussions and online focus groups, and mobile ethnography and diaries.

THE BENEFITS OF MOBILE QUALITATIVE RESEARCH

Market researchers have highlighted a number of benefits that they are gaining by using mobile devices in qualitative research projects. Key mobile benefits include:

- *Participants are able to enter their responses, thoughts, and observations during the day, as they go about their normal lives. This 'in the moment' recording of experiences is in contrast to traditional research that asks participants to recall much later what they saw, what they thought, and how they felt. This in the moment feedback from participants is not filtered by subsequent experiences and not diminished by a failure to remember.*

- *The material collected can include pictures, videos, and audio recordings of what the participants see and do. This diversity of material can enrich the insights generated.*

- *The use of mobile devices can change the relationship between the researcher and the participants, empowering participants to become true collaborators in the research.*

- *Mobile devices enable researchers to use technology-enabled research with people who do not have access to the internet via PCs, particularly in countries where mobile phones are much more common than PCs.*

- *Mobile devices can be used by participants to access online moderated qualitative research approaches, such as online focus groups and discussions. Meaning that participants can join from a wider range of places, and in the case of discussions, contribute when they wish.*

- *Mobile devices can add passive data to a qualitative project. Passive data can be used to add an observational element to projects, for example by recording location, journeys, or activities.*

- *Tablets, can add substantial depth to qualitative projects, including the collection of a wide range of data, their use in online focus groups, and as a medium for collaborative and creative tasks in face-to-face settings.*

DIFFERENT TYPES OF MOBILE QUALITATIVE RESEARCH

Mobile qualitative research can be thought of as having four broad components, as shown in Figure 4.1.

Connecting from Mobile
Participants use their mobile devices to take part in online or remote activities, such as:
- Online focus groups
- Online discussions and forums
- Online depth interviews
- Insight communities.

Participant Research
Participants are active collaborators in the research, using their mobile devices to record information. For example:
- Diaries
- Ethnography
- WE-research
- Mobile blogging.

'On the shoulder'
Researchers sharing the moment via mobile technologies, approaches being trialled include:
- Quantified self
- Passive tracking
- Google Glass and similar.

Conventional
Utilizing mobile devices for a variety of purposes, including:
- Stimuli in face-to-face groups and depths.
- Homework, for example collecting photos from their kitchen to share in the group.
- Communication with participants.

Figure 4.1 Broad components of mobile qualitative research

Participant research includes those approaches where people are recruited to be active collaborators in the research, using their mobile devices to collect information. Connecting from mobile describes the ways that existing remote research approaches, mostly online approaches, have been modified to enable them to take advantage of mobile devices.

'On the shoulder' research is by far the least developed of the four themes and utilizes mobile technologies to watch, track, or see what the participant sees. Conventional is simply the label we have used to group together the many ways that qualitative research is utilizing mobile devices and mobile connectivity to improve existing processes.

The rest of this section reviews the methods and approaches described in Figure 4.1. The following sections cover the relationship between different types of devices and qualitative research, key issues surrounding mobile qualitative research, and designing and implementing mobile qualitative projects.

The next two chapters focus on specific areas of mobile qualitative research.

CONNECTING FROM MOBILE

The key driver for this aspect of mobile qualitative research has been to add mobile connection to existing online qualitative options, and where appropriate to extend what online is able to do. The three key reasons to do this are:

1.   To reach people who do not have PC access to the internet.

2.   To enable participants to take part in activities when it suits them, not just when they are at a PC.

3.   To add mobile specific benefits to the research, such as the ability to upload in the moment images and videos.

This type of research is explored fully in the next chapter. However, the key components of connecting from mobile are shown in Table 4.1.

PARTICIPANT RESEARCH

Participant research represents a major shift in how research is typically conducted, away from simply observing or questioning participants and towards working collaboratively with participants. Participants are enlisted to capture information and images from their lives and in some cases to help interpret this information. This form of research is covered fully in the Mobile Diaries and Ethnography chapter.

The key elements of participant research are shown in Table 4.2.

Table 4.1 Using a mobile device to connect to existing forms of qualitative research

Category	Description
Mobile focus groups	Online focus groups are a well-established qualitative research technique, and mobile devices enable participants to join in from a wider range of locations and situations. Mobile devices can also be used for voice only group discussions and in some cases video chats.
Discussions and forums	Discussions and forums are a popular online qualitative technique where moderators post questions and participants post their replies and comments. Mobile devices broaden the range of who can take part and enable participants to post from a wider range of locations and situations. Mobile devices can greatly enrich the sorts of materials that participants upload, such as in the moment feedback, photos, and video. They also enable participants to be set mobile tasks, such as contributing their thoughts during a commuting journey or shopping trip.
Online depth interviews	Mobiles are being used in voice and video depth interviews, and as an alternative to a PC in online parallel depth interviews.
Insight communities	Communities are one of the fastest growing new research approaches. Communities make extensive use of online discussions and online focus groups, and – as outlined previously – mobile devices have a contribution to make to both of these. The other contributions mobile connectivity can make to communities are covered in the Panels, Lists, and Communities chapter, later in the book.

Table 4.2 Key elements of participant research

Category	Description
Mobile diaries and blogging	The terms 'mobile diaries' and 'mobile blogs' are often used interchangeably, although some researchers give them different meanings. Mobile diaries have substantially updated the paper-based model for diaries. Instead of asking participants to write down what has happened based on their memory, mobile diaries travel with the participant, capturing in the moment experiences, in the form of notes, images, and recordings. Uses of mobile diaries and blogging include: in-home product tests, product experience, paths to purchase, and activities as varied as shopping, commuting, and holidays.
Mobile ethnography	Mobile ethnography takes the diary methodology and moves it to the next level to explore participants' lives to produce an ethnography, with the participants as active collaborators in the process.
WE-research	WE-research involves enlisting participants to be the ears, eyes, and reporters on behalf of the research project. Examples include asking participants to record every interaction with a new advertising campaign, or public service, or type of product.
Shopper studies	Shopper studies combine many of the approaches outlined above, along with things like passive data collection, to create a much richer picture of the shopping process, including planning, the journey, the in-store experience, and post-purchase phase.

'ON THE SHOULDER'

'On the shoulder' research is much less developed than the other types of mobile qualitative research mentioned in this chapter and uses some of the newest technologies. 'On the shoulder' research is observational research, taking what people do as its most important element, rather than focusing on what people say they do.

Until recently 'on the shoulder' techniques were restricted to accompanied shopping and CCTV approaches. However, mobile devices are creating a wide range of exciting new options for 'on the shoulder' research.

Three interesting areas are:

- *The 'quantified self'*
- *Passive tracking*
- *Wearable technologies.*

Utilizing the 'quantified self'

A growing number of people are recording different aspects of their lives. They might be pursuing fitness or diet goals, while others are simply interested in recording their lives in terms of people, places, and experiences. Together, these activities are referred to as the 'quantified self'.

The 'quantified self' is producing a wide array of new products and services, from apps on phones, to websites, to wearable monitors and devices. In combination these devices and services provide a rich and detailed picture of what people do, some of which will be of great interest to market researchers.

The qualitative use of 'quantified self' information usually involves the participant and the researcher reviewing the data together, so that the participant can articulate what was happening when the information was collected.

Qualitative tracking

Qualitative mobile tracking involves working with passive data and small groups of participants (unlike quantitative passive research, which typically uses larger samples). The analysis of qualitative tracking is normally conducted collaboratively with the participant. For example, by showing their routes on a map and exploring the significance of the route options selected.

A full review of quantitative and qualitative uses of passive data is provided in the Utilizing Passive Data chapter.

Wearable technologies

One group of technologies that specifically enables researchers to see what the participant sees are those wearable technologies based around cameras and images. Devices such as mobile eye tracking glasses have enabled researchers in test situations to see what participants saw, but the advent of wearable devices, such as the Memoto lifelogging camera (worn like a pendant and taking a picture every 30 seconds), GoPro (a high definition wearable video camera), and most recently Google Glass mean that ordinary citizens can be recruited to capture what they see.

This form of 'on the shoulder' research raises a large number of ethical and legal concerns, most of which have not yet been resolved.

USING MOBILES IN CONVENTIONAL QUALITATIVE RESEARCH

Market researchers have found a wide range of uses for mobile devices within their existing toolkit.

As a tool in qualitative sessions

Mobile devices can be used in a variety of ways as part of a conventional qualitative exercise. For example, tablets can be used in focus groups or in one-on-one interviews, to show images and video, or to allow the participant to access materials and to take part in activities such as sorting exercises or creating collages.

Mobile homework

Many qualitative projects benefit from assigning tasks before (or after) the main session, for example participants might keep a diary or collect images before a face-to-face focus group or a depth interview. These tasks can be sent to participants via their mobile device and may require that participants use their device to capture information as they go about their daily lives, for example asking participants to take pictures of the food and products in their pantry or kitchen cupboards.

Mobile devices can also be used for post-session tasks, for example joining an online discussion or sending photos and/or ideas back to the researcher.

OTHER USES OF MOBILE DEVICES FOR QUALITATIVE RESEARCH

Mobile devices are also used to organize and coordinate qualitative activities, ensuring people receive instructions, helping them find locations, and generally communicating with participants. Mobile devices also are commonly used in conjunction with research communities as part of the overall method of communication with members for qualitative, quantitative, and administrative purposes.

THE ROLE OF DIFFERENT MOBILE DEVICES IN QUALITATIVE RESEARCH

This section of the chapter reviews the key characteristics of the leading types of mobile devices, in the context of qualitative market research (i.e. feature phones, smartphones, and tablets). More information on the devices and their uses is available in the chapter on The Technology of Mobile Market Research.

FEATURE PHONES

The term 'feature phone' does not refer to a specific type of phone, it is a catch-all phrase for anything that does not meet the current definition of a smartphone.

Some feature phones are limited to phone calls and text, although a camera is almost universal. Other feature phones support email, internet access, video recording, and the ability to download apps. Therefore, feature phone-based qualitative mobile market research can refer to a continuum of approaches.

One common use of feature phones is to ask participants to record events in their lives, using texts, photos, or videos as data for the types of research described earlier as 'participant research'. The data can be sent to the researcher in a number of ways, including SMS, MMS, via a downloaded app, or via a face-to-face meeting with an interviewer.

Phones at the 'smarter end' of the feature phone spectrum, particularly those with internet access, can be used for a wider range of qualitative projects, including accessing blogs or communities, and for taking part in online focus groups. Some of the smarter phones can also be used for types of tracking research and for the testing of mobile advertising/marketing.

Feature phones are also used to help with the logistics of research projects, for example to book focus group sessions or depth interviews, to send reminders, and to deal with queries.

SMARTPHONES

The power and portability of smartphones makes them very attractive to qualitative market researchers for a wide variety of uses. In situations where it can be assumed that smartphones can connect to the internet an even wider range of online qualitative research is possible, including online discussions, online focus groups, and virtual in-depth interviews. Indeed, most forms of online qualitative research can be conducted via smartphones.

In addition to being a mobile option for traditional online qualitative research, smartphones can be used for research that is specifically mobile, and in some cases, specifically smartphone. This use of smartphones relates to the term 'participant research' used earlier in the chapter and described in full in the Mobile Diaries and Ethnography chapter. The smartphone equips the collaborative participant with everything they need to be an active partner in research projects, capturing slices of their lives, the lives of people around them, and information about their interactions with the surrounding world.

The key to the usefulness of the smartphone include its ability to play and record multimedia, to connect to the internet, to download apps, and to record passive data, including location data. Because people tend to have their smartphone with them 24/7, it is available to capture things when they happen, rather than relying on participants recalling and describing events at a later date.

TABLETS

Tablets are capable of more, in some ways, than either feature phones or smartphones. They are typically configured to access the internet, and their screen is much larger than a smartphone – and therefore capable of displaying more than a phone. However, tablets are not as portable as phones and so they are less likely to always be with the participant. These key differences tend to impact the way tablets are used for qualitative research, making them less useful in the context of things like shopping trips, but very valuable in the context of the home and on some sorts of journeys.

The larger screen on a tablet makes it a good alternative to a PC for online focus groups, online depth interviews, video chats and so on – provided the software being used is suitable, and assuming there is a good connection to the internet. The larger touchscreens on tablets make them an interesting option for more innovative qualitative approaches such as sorting, drawing, creating collages and so on, both remotely and in face-to-face situations.

Tablets are, typically, used less than smartphones in the collection of ethnographic type data, because tablets are less likely to be carried all the time, even though the data collection tools typically run equally well on both smartphones and tablets. However, when the focus of a study is images and photos from around the home, tablets can be as suitable as smartphones.

KEY ISSUES SURROUNDING MOBILE QUALITATIVE RESEARCH

Mobile qualitative market research is a new field, and key issues are still being identified and ground rules established. This section reviews some of the key issues.

ANALYSIS

Mobile qualitative research creates some interesting challenges in the area of analysis, because:

- *It can create more data than can be easily processed, particularly with respect to images, video, and passive data.*

- *There are relatively few tools to help with the processing of images, video, and passive data.*

- *Because the data collection tools for approaches like online focus groups and mobile ethnography are widely available, people with little training in the design and analysis of these approaches are being tempted into conducting projects without adequate support or resources.*

DATA OVERLOAD

Mobile devices are capable of producing large amounts of data, including pictures and videos. Analysing images and especially video can be very time consuming. Much of the attraction of mobile qualitative market research is that it can leverage the power of the many and reach into the nooks and crannies of everyday life, but care needs to be taken to avoid data overload.

Steve August, founder and CEO of Revelation, has said:

'Researchers need to think carefully about study design, and understand the volume of the data they have built into their studies. In some ways this flies in the face of more data is always better. Until analytic tools evolve further, researchers may increasingly have to actively limit the data they collect. For example, consider when video is truly important or a "nice to have".'

PRACTICAL TIPS FOR WORKING WITH VIDEO

The following tips from practitioners can make processing video easier:

- *Tag and code videos as they are collected, don't wait until the end of the project.*

- *Sorting video clips by attributes such as time of day, user, and length can make working with video easier.*

- *Ask participants to supply tags for their videos, for example children, breakfast, school day (the tags will be more consistent if you supply the participants with a list of suggested tags).*

- *To assemble a view of, say, breakfast habits, restrict the initial viewing to videos shot between 7am and 10am, or to videos tagged with 'breakfast'.*

- *Request participants to keep their videos short, for example 30 to 60 seconds.*

- *When searching for a particular activity, for example frying, videos can be skimmed at higher than normal speed until frying related items are found.*

- *As the analysis progresses more codes and tags should be added.*

ANALYSIS SKILLS SHORTFALL

One of the great things about the new mobile tools is that they bring the potential to collect ever more varied qualitative data to a wider range of people. Whilst at one level, this is a democratization of the research process, it also raises the issue of people collecting information they don't know how to analyse.

Good examples of this challenge are ethnography and online discussions. There is little difficulty in collecting ethnographic data, for example pictures from a variety of kitchens at mealtimes, or of conducting online discussions. However, the real value of this sort of information often derives from the analysis. One common criticism from clients is that too much of the material presented to them is a description of what happened, rather than what it means, or better still, advice about what the client should do next.

People new to the field of qualitative research are encouraged to seek support, tuition, or advice before undertaking the more advanced projects, and to perhaps start with one of the more straightforward approaches, such as mobile diaries, before embarking on online focus groups and mobile ethnography.

MOBILE COSTS

The use of mobile devices can generate higher costs for participants and/or researchers. Researchers need to be aware that taking part in many mobile qualitative research approaches is not necessarily free to participants. If participants are collecting images, videos, and audio recordings, then care must be taken to ensure that they do not incur data costs when transferring these to the researcher. This may mean reimbursing participants as part of their incentive, or it might mean finding alternative ways for the participants to transfer data, i.e. ways that incur zero or minimal costs, for example via Wi-Fi.

One of the potential advantages of app-based approaches is that they can be designed to make much less use of the internet than browser-based approaches, something that might need to be factored into the project design.

> **TIP:** *In markets where mobile costs are a major issue and where the internet is not widely available, some researchers have found it advisable, for mobile qualitative projects, to recruit users who have access to Wi-Fi, for example people who have Wi-Fi at home or who can access it at convenient locations.*

RECRUITING AND BRIEFING PARTICIPANTS

Most mobile qualitative projects use the same recruitment methods as other forms of qualitative research, in particular professional recruiters, panels, client lists, and communities.

Participants need to be recruited who have the right sort of devices, the right sort of connectivity (e.g. internet connection), and so they understand what is being asked of them in terms of number and types of tasks. This recruitment needs to be conducted without introducing factors that will overly bias the research.

In terms of briefing participants, the key elements to consider are:

- *Will the briefing be managed by the researcher or a third party, such as a fieldwork company?*

- *Will the briefing be face-to-face or remote?*

- *If the briefing is remote, will it be via video, paper, webcast etc.?*

- *How will support be provided to participants if they have questions after the briefing?*

FOCUSING ON A TECHNOLOGY SUB-GROUP

When conducting mobile qualitative research, researchers need to avoid the risk of focusing on people who are so tech savvy as to be poor representatives for the issue being researched.

The risk of focusing on the tech savvy early adopter is all the greater if the research is being conducted in several countries, with differing economic and technological considerations. For example, using smartphones to explore the use of commuter trains might be appropriate in London, but somewhat less appropriate in somewhere like Jakarta or Mumbai.

Some of these concerns can be addressed by making the appropriate technology available to people who don't have it. For example, in much of the developing world doing 'rich world' mobile research often means giving the sample, or part of the sample, a smartphone or tablet device and providing training on how to use it.

ETHICAL AND LEGAL CONSIDERATIONS

Mobile market research is a dynamic field and the guidelines, regulations, and laws are regularly updated and changed, so it is important that researchers keep themselves informed about what is and is not allowed, and what actions and procedures are required. This book has a chapter specifically on ethics and guidelines, and comments are added throughout the book where relevant.

Researchers are advised to consult the ESOMAR guidelines, local regulations, and advice from bodies such as the MMRA.

In terms of mobile qualitative research, some of the key issues to consider include:

- *Participants*
- *Third parties*
- *Clients.*

PARTICIPANTS

Market researchers take the interests of participants very seriously and participant welfare is written into market research codes of conduct and regulations. As well as the issues common to other forms of data collection (such as the need to protect anonymity and the security of personal information) mobile market research approaches create some areas of special interest.

Physical safety. Participants should be advised not to put themselves at risk. For example, participants should be advised not to take part in research whilst driving or using machinery. Participants should consider the danger factors around them, for example, not standing in a road to take a picture, approaching wild animals, or taking videos of people in a rowdy bar.

Legal safety. In many countries, there are places where mobile phones should not be used, especially to capture images, and there are people who should not be videoed or photographed. In places such as immigration halls, civic buildings, courts and so on, bans on the use of cameras and video recording is not uncommon. In many countries, taking photos or videos of other people's children is illegal. It is not unusual, around the world, for it to be illegal to photograph police officers or soldiers.

Data costs. As mentioned earlier, taking part in mobile qualitative projects can incur costs. Market researchers need to ensure that participants are briefed about the risks, told how to avoid costs, and reimbursed if they are out of pocket.

THIRD PARTIES

When using participants to collect information, researchers may find themselves in possession of information about people who have not consented to be part of the research, or who may not even be aware of the research. This raises a variety of informed consent issues.

The advice that has been offered to researchers includes things like:

- *Not accessing the contacts file of a participant's mobile phone.*

- *Pixelating the faces of third parties captured in photos and video.*

- *When conducting research with a household, it is a good idea to request the permission of all members of the family.*

Participants should be advised about the sort of data they should not collect about other people, the sort of information/images that they should not transmit, and the research team should monitor what is being uploaded.

CLIENTS

Care needs to be taken not to compromise client's intellectual property or information. Mobile devices are easily lost or stolen, so care should be taken to ensure that the information on them is regularly backed up to servers, and nothing on the device could cause a problem or embarrassment for the client.

DESIGNING AND IMPLEMENTING MOBILE QUALITATIVE PROJECTS

Table 4.3 highlights the key steps and considerations in designing and implementing a mobile qualitative project.

Table 4.3   Key steps and considerations when designing and implementing mobile qualitative

Consideration	Options
What is the role of mobile?	Does it need to be platform agnostic, with some people using mobile, some using PCs, and some using a mixture, for example, online focus groups. Or, should it focus on mobile, such as collecting images and recording throughout the day?
What sort of mobile device do you need?	If people need it with them all day it might need to be a phone, if the focus is home or office then a tablet might work. Do you need a smartphone, or will a feature phone give you what you need? The more types of phones you are willing to include the more potential participants you will have to choose from.
Browser or app-based?	Browser-based solutions are often easier to set up and do not require the participant to download anything. But apps give access to more features of the mobile device, can prompt the participant, and can work when the internet is not available.
What sort of mobile device is available?	In a developed market you might find smartphones and/or tablets are widely available. In a less developed market insisting on smartphones might bias the study.
How are the participants going to be recruited?	Do you know of a recruiter with experience in recruiting for mobile qualitative research? If not, you will need to put in extra time for communication and quality checks.
What systems/ software are you going to use?	Creating custom built solutions is less necessary now than a few years ago. There are a wide range of systems available and using these will tend to be cheaper, faster, and sometimes more reliable. However, a custom built solution might give you exactly what you need, rather than having to adapt your design to what is available.
How much data are you going to collect?	With mobile qualitative research it is very easy to collect more data than is necessary and more than you can actually use. The more information you collect per person, the fewer people you should probably use. In-depth ethnography style projects are often conducted on 10 to 20 people for this reason. Limit the length of videos that participants are asked to collect, for example to 30, 60, or at most 90 seconds.
How is the data going to be analysed?	Photos, audio recordings, and video take time to organize and even longer to analyse. The analysis plan should be created before the project is finished and the time and resources allocated.
How are the insights going to be presented?	If images and recordings from the research are going to be used then permission should be obtained before the data is collected, not retrospectively. The material collected is not the insight; the insights should determine what material is used in the presentation.

SUMMARY

Although mobile qualitative market research is a small part of the total qualitative picture, it has opened up new and interesting opportunities. This process is likely to continue to develop as mobile devices become more powerful, as smart devices become more common, and as researchers create new opportunities and approaches.

Some of the key points to keep in mind:

- *Enabling mobile access to existing forms of online qualitative research broadens the range of people able to take part, and allows participants to take part from more locations and situations.*

- *Mobile devices have enabled participants to be recruited as collaborators in the research process, collecting slices of their lives, the lives of people around them, and their interactions with the surrounding world. New research approaches such as mobile diaries and mobile ethnography have been developed to take advantage of these opportunities.*

- *New technologies are allowing researchers to capture observational data, seeing what the participants see, and collecting passive data that describes their movements and actions.*

- *One of the key challenges for researchers is to handle the potentially vast amount of information collected from participants, including video, photos, and passive data.*

- *Key strategies to control the amount of data being collected are to limit: the length of a project, the number of participants, the number of images they are asked to upload, and the length of video they capture (typically to 30 or 60 seconds).*

- *One of the key challenges facing mobile qualitative research is in the area of analysis, including how to analyse ever larger amounts of information and how to ensure newcomers to the discipline understand what is needed.*

- *Key ethical challenges include ensuring participant safety, obtaining informed consent, ensuring costs do not fall on participants, and avoiding compromising the privacy and rights of third parties.*

5 Mobile Forums and Online Focus Groups

INTRODUCTION

The previous chapter provided an overview of mobile qualitative market research, dividing the topics into four broad categories: participant research (where participants use their mobile devices to help gather research material), 'on the shoulder' research (using mobile technologies to see what the participants see), conventional uses (such as using mobile devices to communicate with research participants), and a category termed 'connecting from mobile'. The two key approaches in the connecting from mobile category are mobile forums and online focus groups.

This chapter covers the 'connecting from mobile' category in more depth and focuses on approaches such as online forums, discussions, and focus groups. These approaches tend to have two things in common:

1.   They are moderated by a researcher.
2.   The participants are remote from both the moderator and each other – for example they are in different parts of the country, connecting to the research process via their mobile devices.

MIXED-MODE RESEARCH

Whilst some forums, discussions, and remote focus groups are purely mobile, the majority are mixed-mode, with some participants connecting via mobile devices and others connecting via PCs. The projects can also be mixed-mode in the sense that participants use a mobile device some of the time and a PC some of the time.

Mobile focus groups and online discussions can also be used in conjunction with other types of research, for example as a follow-up to a face-to-face focus group or after a quantitative exercise such as an online survey.

In this context, describing projects as 'mobile' refers to ensuring that they are at least mobile compatible and in some cases ensuring that they use the opportunities created by some of the participants using mobile devices.

Synchronous and Asynchronous Online Qualitative Research

The terms 'synchronous' and 'asynchronous' are used to describe whether the moderator and participants have to be connected at the same time (as in a focus group), or whether they have the option to be online at different times, as in a forum. **Synchronous** means people have to be online at the same time as each other. **Asynchronous** means that people do not have to be online at the same time as each other.

FORUMS AND DISCUSSIONS

'Forums' and 'discussions' are terms that are often used interchangeably and describe unstructured or semi-structured, asynchronous conversations with a group of people online. Because forums and discussions are asynchronous, participants can log in, check what the moderator and the other participants have said, make their own contribution, and leave, all at a time of their own choosing.

Market research discussions and forums are almost always private discussions. The participants to the discussion are invited and some form of private login is used to ensure that the discussion remains closed.

In the context of market research, an online discussion is most typically a question posted by a moderator or researcher, and a series of replies from the participants in the discussion, usually with additional questions or probes from the moderator.

A forum, in market research, is often a virtual location where several discussions can take place. However, different software platforms have different terms, and some even choose to have forums within discussions.

MOBILE DISCUSSIONS AND FORUMS

At present, most mobile discussions and forums are actually 'online' rather than purely 'mobile'. They have been designed with the internet in mind, and use tools that create forums and discussions that depend on browsers to access them. The terms 'mobile discussions' and 'mobile forums' tend to mean one or more of the following:

- *An online discussion/forum that is suitable for mobile devices.*

- *An online discussion/forum where some of the tasks are intended to be completed via a mobile device.*

- *An online discussion/forum where the purpose of the research relates to mobile (either about mobiles or the mobile ecosystem).*

In most cases, mobile discussions and forums are accessed via internet browsers, which means their use is restricted to internet-enabled phones and tablets.

MARKET RESEARCH DISCUSSIONS AND FORUMS

If somebody posts a comment on Facebook or starts a discussion in LinkedIn and nobody responds, that is typically the end of it – although they might try posting it elsewhere to get a response. Market research forums and discussions are created for a purpose, which tends to make them different from naturally occurring forums and discussions.

Market research forums and discussions tend to have the following characteristics:

- *The discussion platform will be private/closed (i.e. not searchable by Google and only accessible to people with a login and password).*

- *The intended participants will have been specifically recruited to take part in the discussion.*

- *The participants are usually incentivized, typically with extrinsic rewards (such as a prize or cash), but sometimes with intrinsic rewards, such as recognition or praise.*

- *The researcher will have a research question (usually in the context of a business question) and will have specific things they want to explore, often in the form of a discussion guide or scripted questions.*

- *Depending on the researcher's style and choice of method, the discussion on each point posed by the researcher will continue until either:*

  - *Every participant has answered.*

  - *The researcher feels the point has been sufficiently answered.*

- *In most market research discussions and forums the majority of the posts and comments from the participants will be in response to and directed at the researcher or moderator.*

  - *This is not normally a problem. Quite often the participants are taking part because they want the brand to hear their views, not necessarily because they want to talk to other users or customers.*

- *When participants are posting their own questions it can be a clue that the researcher does not understand key issues of concern to the participants.*

- *When participants are responding to/disagreeing with each other it may be a clue about segments, for example manual versus automatic cars or organic versus value food.*

● *Many market research forum or discussion platforms have tools to aid the researcher, for example:*

- *The ability to pre-load questions into the platform, potentially with automated/timed release.*

- *Tagging or coding facilities to help analyse the contributions – which may include a facility for participants to tag/code their own contributions and/or the contributions of other participants.*

- *Tag clouds or links to text analysis software.*

● *Many platforms support a facility for the moderator to require that participants post a reply before they can see the replies posted by other members of the discussion.*

LOCATING DISCUSSIONS AND FORUMS WITHIN THE WIDER SOCIAL MEDIA CONTEXT

Both forums and discussions grew out of bulletin boards and message boards, which is where some of the jargon related to this approach was developed, such as threads and moderators. Since the explosion of social media, particularly Facebook, the expectation of most participants is that online discussions will broadly follow the conventions of social media – even though market research discussions and forums are generally private.

Common conventions/expectations are:

● *People making posts will have some sort of online persona or avatar. This might be a made up name, or it might be their real name. Participants will often be represented by an image, which could be their photo, but might be an image they have chosen, or one they have been assigned.*

● *A single conversation, for example a question from the moderator and a series of answers, is often called a thread (but it can also be called a discussion).*

● *The posts and answers in a thread will be laid out so that people can understand the sequence that they were added in.*

- *There are two main approaches to laying out posts and comments in a thread. Firstly, from the most recent to oldest (or vice versa), or secondly, with answers embedded next to the comments they were a reply to. Examples of these approaches are in shown in Figures 5.1, 5.2, and 5.3.*

- *Participants are often given the chance to 'Like' a post or comment. Sometimes, there might also be a facility to 'Not like' a post or comment. Thumbs up and down are often used as symbols for 'Like' and 'Not like', as are smiley and sad emoticons.*

The examples in Figures 5.1, 5.2, and 5.3 are based on examples from the *Handbook of Online and Social Media Research* (Poynter 2010). Figure 5.1 shows a simplified discussion with the oldest comment first, Figure 5.2 shows the same conversation with the newest comment first, and Figure 5.3 shows the same discussion with comments embedded next to the item they were replying to.

When the oldest comment is at the top, the flow of the comments tends to be relatively natural, but the latest comments may require a reader to scroll through several pages of comments before seeing them. This can result in the conversation running out of energy when the posts fill more than one page.

When comments are sorted with the newest entries at the top, it is easy for readers to see the latest comments, but the discussion flow is less natural to read and responses tend to focus on the last point, and less on the whole conversation.

What is the best food to take on a long walk?
I always like to take an apple, cheese and bread. <div align="right">Starman, 5 December 2009, 12:15</div>
I think nuts are a great food when out for a walk. <div align="right">HappyGal, 5 December 2009, 14:21</div>
What about if somebody on your walk is allergic to nuts, might it be dangerous? <div align="right">FreeBird, 5 December 2009, 19:42</div>
I think it depends on the time of year. In the winter I always take a flask with hot soup in it. But in the summer I am more likely to have something like fruit. <div align="right">WanderFull, 5 December 2009, 20:22</div>
Hmm, that's a good point I had never thought about before <div align="right">HappyGal, 5 December 2009, 21:51</div>

Figure 5.1   Discussion sorted with oldest comment at the top

What is the best food to take on a long walk?
Hmm, that's a good point I had never thought about before *HappyGal, 5 December 2009, 21:51*
I think it depends on the time of year. In the winter I always take a flask with hot soup in it. But in the summer I am more likely to have something like fruit. *WanderFull, 5 December 2009, 20:22*
What about if somebody on your walk is allergic to nuts, might it be dangerous? *FreeBird, 5 December 2009, 19:42*
I think nuts are a great food when out for a walk. *HappyGal, 5 December 2009, 14:21*
I always like to take an apple, cheese and bread. *Starman, 5 December 2009, 12:15*

Figure 5.2   Discussion sorted with newest comment at the top

What is the best food to take on a long walk?
I always like to take an apple, cheese and bread. *Starman, 5 December 2009, 12:15*
I think nuts are a great food when out for a walk. *HappyGal, 5 December 2009, 14:21*
What about if somebody on your walk is allergic to nuts, might it be   dangerous? *FreeBird, 5 December 2009, 19:42*
Hmm, that's a good point I had never thought about before *HappyGal, 5 December 2009, 21:51*
I think it depends on the time of year. In the winter I always take a flask with hot soup in it. But in the summer I am more likely to have something like fruit. *WanderFull, 5 December 2009, 20:22*

Figure 5.3   Discussion with replies inset

Discussions that allow replies to be inset, and which allow replies to specific elements in the conversation can be the most natural for participants. However, they can render badly on mobile phones, so this should be checked before selecting this layout.

> **TIP:** *Do not create your own discussion protocols (even if you think they are better than traditional options). People expect research discussions to follow the conventions that are currently popular.*

CREATING MOBILE FRIENDLY DISCUSSIONS AND FORUMS

Most online research should be done in a platform agnostic way, allowing users to choose whether to contribute via a mobile device or a PC, unless there are strong research reasons why a discussion or forum should be mobile only or PC only.

Steps that need to be addressed to make discussions and forums mobile friendly include:

- *Recognizing that mobile participants may have less bandwidth than participants using PCs, so there should be options to reduce the size of images/videos.*

- *The platform should optimize for mobile, especially for phones, stripping out unnecessary elements and re-organizing the material so it can be browsed in a convenient way. Platforms based on HTML5 tend to be the best for this sort of optimization, including the ability to add dynamic animation.*

- *Not using Flash. Flash was a popular tool in making PC-based online tools more engaging, but it does not work on the leading smartphone and tablet operating systems. Flash is no longer being developed and is being phased out.*

Most of these steps are the responsibility of the platform provider, not the researcher. The researcher's role is to select an appropriate system and within that to choose mobile-enabled options.

CREATING MOBILE TASKS FOR FORUMS AND DISCUSSIONS

There are a wide range of mobile tasks that can be created to enrich mobile forums and discussions, for example:

- *Capturing photos and images and uploading these to the forum. These can be as varied as photos from the participants' bathroom cabinets or images* of brands in the wider world. Three ways of uploading media should be facilitated:

-     *Directly from the mobile device's camera*

-     *From the mobile device's memory*

-     *Copying the media to a PC and uploading from there.*

- *Capturing and contributing slices from the participant's life and adding them to the discussion. For example, if the discussion is about clothes, making contributions from a clothing store, talking about the moment while in the moment.*

- *Time critical posts. PC-based forums require people to be at their desks to respond, mobile contributions can be made across a wide range of times and places.*

- *During journeys or trips, for example, asking commuters to take part in discussions during their commutes.*

> **TIP:** *Participants often have problems when first uploading photos or videos, so be prepared to help them. The researcher should have been through the process themselves, to make sure the advice is genuinely helpful and easy to understand. It can also be a good idea to get someone who is not familiar with the process to pilot or trial the instructions to see if they can follow them and perform the action.*

CREATING MOBILE SPECIFIC FORUMS AND DISCUSSION

A mobile specific forum or discussion is one where the members can only access the platform using their mobile device, i.e. they cannot use their PC. Just as there are few situations that justify excluding mobiles, there are relatively few situations where participants should be prohibited from using PCs. However, there are a few situations where mobile specific discussions or forums may be appropriate, including:

- *If the target group are all mobile users and the platform is app-based.*

- *Where the research topic is the mobile device or some function of the device and the intention is to focus the conversation on the experience of using the device.*

- *When the research centres around an event, and the respondents are expected to take part from the event, for example a festival.*

INCLUDING NON-INTERNET ELEMENTS IN FORUMS AND DISCUSSIONS

Whilst there are few discussions or forums that operate entirely without the internet, a number of them allow participants to post comments, answers, images, or videos using basic services such as SMS and MMS. Participants can be primed to send a text or image every time a specific action happens. Typically, this approach is combined with participants using the internet later to expand on text they sent or explaining more about the context for an image.

ANALYSIS OF FORUMS AND DISCUSSIONS

Forums and discussions can generate a large amount of material, and if mobile devices are being used, this can include images and videos. The forum and/or discussion might last just 24 hours, or it might last weeks, so the analysis needs to be carefully planned to avoid the researcher being overloaded and to avoid the risk of missing key insights.

Strategies that can help with the analysis process include:

- *Starting the analysis when the discussion starts, rather than at the end. Quotes and images can be selected and/or tagged, and the moderator can use probes to triangulate their findings.*

- *Matching the tasks to the number of people in the discussion. If there are 20 people in the discussion, then asking them to upload 10 to 20 images each results in a reasonable research task. If there are 100 people in the community, 10 to 20 images each would require a large amount of analysis and are likely to create a large amount of redundant repetition. If video uploads are being used then they should, normally, be kept to a short length, for example, 30, 60, or at most 90 seconds.*

- *The members of the discussion can be asked to help with the analysis. At the simplest level this might mean asking people to highlight their most and least preferred comments, but it could also include asking participants to tag, group, or even code comments, photos, or videos.*

If any of the images uploaded by the participants are going to be used in reporting the research, or by the end-client, then permission needs to be obtained early in the process, usually when the participants are being recruited.

FOCUS GROUPS

Face-to-face focus groups date back to the 1940s, and online focus groups date back to the 1990s. Focus groups are a synchronous method, i.e. all the people are present (or online) at the same time.

The majority of online focus groups are text-based, typically using specialist market research software. But there are approaches and platforms that incorporate sound and sometimes video in the process. Text-based online focus groups make few demands on bandwidth, which make them very suitable for mobile participants. If video groups are planned, then the platform should be checked to see what its requirements are and the recruitment of mobile participants matched to these requirements.

Another use of the term 'online focus group' is to describe conventional, face-to-face focus groups where the internet is used to stream a video feed from the group, such as the service offered by companies like FocusVision.

As with other forms of market research, the trend is for online focus groups to be platform agnostic, especially for participants and observers. At present, the systems for the researcher or moderator are more likely to require a PC as they are often used in combination with other tools, for example access to corporate servers, email, analysis programs, or messaging systems.

ENSURING ONLINE FOCUS GROUPS ARE MOBILE FRIENDLY

In order to be mobile friendly, an online focus group platform should avoid using non-mobile features such as Flash, be capable of using lower bandwidth images where appropriate, and be written using web technologies that render correctly for mobile. To make the platform mobile friendly, care must be taken to scale controls and buttons so that they are easy to manipulate on a mobile device. These issues are largely the responsibility of the company creating the platform. The researcher's responsibility is to select an appropriate platform and then to select the mobile friendly options.

In terms of tablets, the mobile experience is relatively similar to the PC experience (provided that the platform is written properly). However, some people find that typing on a tablet is slower than via a keyboard, which may impact the quantity of contributions from tablet users.

In terms of phones, more attention needs to be made to ensure that participants can see the moderator's prompts, the responses of other participants, any stimuli being displayed, and that they can easily enter their responses. Entering comments on most mobile phones is slower and less accurate than on a PC or tablet.

> **TIP:** *Tell participants not to worry about spelling and typing accuracy. Mobile slang can be encouraged, if all the participants are familiar with it.*

A typical online focus group lasts 60 to 90 minutes. Making an online focus group mobile friendly, especially for phones, involves making sure that mobile participants are warned about the length of the session, or breaking the session into two or three shorter sessions.

VOICE ONLY FOCUS GROUPS

Although voice only focus groups are relatively rare, they are very suitable for mobile devices. If voice only focus groups are utilizing mobile devices the researcher has the choice, and should ideally offer the participant the choice, of using telephone or some form of VOIP (e.g. Skype).

ANALYSIS OF MOBILE FRIENDLY FOCUS GROUPS

The analysis of online focus groups, including mobile friendly online focus groups, is similar to the analysis of traditional focus groups. The moderator loses the advantage of seeing the body language, but gains instant access to a full transcript.

When analysing groups where some participants were using mobile devices and some were using PCs, the device usage should be flagged next to participants' IDs, and it should be one of the factors taken into account during the analysis.

DEPTH INTERVIEWS

Depth interviews are, traditionally, one-on-one, face-to-face interviews between the researcher and a participant. However, there has been a long tradition of conducting some depth interviews, particularly in B2B research, via the telephone.

In terms of mobile market research, phones and tablets can be used in a number of ways, including:

- *In face-to-face interviews mobile devices can be used to record or even video the interview. One popular option is to record the voice interview and at the end of the interview to return to a key item in the interview and re-ask the question capturing the answer on video.*

- *Ringing people on, or from, mobile phones, which means the depth interview can be conducted in a wider range of situations. For example, a depth interview can be conducted during business or shopping trips.*

- *Using VOIP, for example, or Skype or Google Hangouts, to avoid phone costs especially for long distance or international studies.*

- *Using web services such as Webex or Citrix to allow the participant to connect from their device (PC or mobile) to take part in an interview, to record sound and/or video, and to show stimuli.*

PARALLEL DEPTH INTERVIEWS

Parallel depth interviews utilize modified forms of discussion or forum software, to create text-based, remote, asynchronous depth interviews. The researcher posts a question that is sent to each participant, the participant enters their reply (from a PC or mobile device), but the participant can't see the other participants in the study. The key benefits of making parallel depth interviews mobile friendly are that they can speed up the responses, as well as broadening the range of people willing and able to take part.

ETHICAL AND LEGAL CONSIDERATIONS

As well as the general ethical considerations that relate to all market research, there are some considerations that are particularly relevant to forums, discussions, and online focus groups. For example:

- **Safety.** *Participants should be reminded not to do anything that puts them or others at risk. For example not putting themselves at risk to try and get an interesting or provocative picture.*

- **Anonymity.** *In order to protect participant anonymity the trend is away from allowing participants to use their own names and photos, in favour of made up names and images.*

- **Intellectual property.** *It is normal for the terms and conditions for a discussion or group to specify that the end-client owns the rights to all the ideas generated during the research.*

- **Acceptable behaviour.** *The terms and conditions usually specify that the moderator will determine what is acceptable and what is not (usually including a statement that profane, sexist, racist, and homophobic language will not be accepted), and assigning the moderator the authority to edit or remove comments, and suspend or ban members who break the acceptable behaviour guidelines.*

- **Rules for the incentives.** *The terms and conditions should specify what participants have to do to qualify for incentives. For example, do they have to respond to every post/question?*

SUMMARY

The key points to note in the context of mobile forums, discussions, and online focus groups are:

- *Moderated qualitative market research approaches, such as focus groups, forums, and discussions, can normally be made mobile friendly.*

- *Extending mobile market research into the area of moderated qualitative research does not typically mean creating a mobile only form of research; it typically means giving participants more choice.*

- *Key reasons for making forums and discussions mobile friendly include increasing the range of people willing to take part and enabling faster responses.*

- *Mobile friendly forums and discussions can leverage the power of mobile – for example by asking participants to upload photos and videos.*

- *When recruiting participants to mobile forums, discussions, and focus groups, participants' attention should be drawn to the requirements, terms, and conditions that apply.*

- *When trying to attract mobile participants to online focus groups, consider breaking the discussion into more than one session, rather than trying to keep people online for 90 minutes.*

6 Mobile Diaries and Ethnography

INTRODUCTION

This chapter looks at several mobile qualitative approaches that involve working with participants to collaboratively explore their lives, the lives of people around them, and the environment they come in contact with.

The topics covered in this chapter are listed below:

- **Mobile ethnography:** *where participants capture slices of their lives and/or the lives of people around them, as an input to an ethnographic analysis.*

- **Mobile diaries and blogs:** *where participants record their activity in relation to a specific topic, for example during the purchase of a mortgage, or whilst trying a new household product.*

- **Shopper studies:** *where participants use their mobile device, in effect, to take the researcher along on their shopping trip.*

- **WE-research:** *where participants seek out and record their interactions with the subject of the research, for example every time they see an advert for a particular category.*

- **Passive tracking:** *Passive tracking uses the phone or tablet features and sensors to record where the participants go, what they do, and so on. It does this without any moment-to-moment intervention from participants. These traces are then reviewed by the researcher as an input to their qualitative analysis.*

To some extent, there is a degree of overlap between some of these approaches. For example, in mobile ethnography, mobile diaries, shopper studies, and WE-research, participants might be asked to take a specific action when a specific event happens. They might be asked to take a photo or record a video, or to record how they feel. The difference tends to be the balance between the various activities, the reason for the research, and how the data will be analysed. For example, in a mobile diary project, the participants' descriptions may be the key deliverable; in an ethnography it is the analysis and write-up that are the key elements of the project.

Several of these mobile qualitative approaches use data collection methods that are similar to mobile quantitative techniques. For example, a qualitative mobile diary project might be used to follow 16 participants for a week, capturing information about everything they drink, including images, feelings, and consequences. A quantitative mobile diary study might have a sample of 400 participants and be based on the answers to closed questions; captured every time the participants drink something.

> **TIP:** *The key difference between a qualitative and quantitative market research project is often how the information is analysed, which in turn helps determine the sample size and the nature of the information captured.*

MOBILE ETHNOGRAPHY

In mobile ethnography, participants are recruited to use their phones and/or tablets to collect material about their own lives and surroundings, and the lives of people around them. This process can be as straightforward as participants taking photos of some aspect of their lives (e.g. the contents of their wardrobes or kitchen cupboards) through to enlisting participants in collaborative ethnographic studies where the participants collect an extensive amount of information and are involved in the analysis of the material collected.

The main developments in mobile ethnography have come through the use of participants' phones, although there are examples of tablets being used, and it might be expected that more use will be made of tablets in the future. During the last few years, a number of specialist market research apps, which allow researchers and participants to collaborate in capturing and interpreting data via phones, have been developed, for example Revelation and Ethos.

Collaborating with participants to conduct research focused on the collection of ethnographic data has a number of names. Some of these names relate to variations in what is being done, others are simply alternative names for the same thing. Amongst the variations are:

- *Mobile ethnography*

- *Auto-ethnography (the word auto relates to about oneself)*

- *Smartphone ethnography*

- *Mass anthropology (anthropology has more of a flavour of watching other people, but in terms of qualitative research the term 'mass' can be a misnomer as it often refers to numbers as small as 20 to 30 participants)*

- *'WE-research' (a term we come to later in the chapter).*

> **TIP:** *Because mobile ethnography is still developing and because of the variety of names being used, researchers, vendors, recruiters, and buyers should ensure that everybody involved in a project has a shared understanding of what is planned.*

This section on mobile ethnography covers the following topics:

1.   A definition of ethnographic data

2.   The difference between ethnography and ethnographic data

3.   Collaborative ethnography

4.   Compensating for differences in device familiarity

5.   Mixed-mode approaches to mobile ethnography.

1. A DEFINITION OF ETHNOGRAPHIC DATA

In the context of mobile market research, the term 'ethnographic data' refers to material collected about people's everyday lives by research participants, using their mobile devices. Terms like 'trace data' and 'artefacts' can also be used to describe ethnographic data. Examples of ethnographic data, in the context of mobile market research, include:

- *Photographs*

- *Videos*

- *Audio recordings*

- *Location data from a phone*

- *Text descriptions of what the participant can see or is experiencing.*

Ethnographic data (like most qualitative data) tends to be unstructured and not immediately suitable for structured analysis. Research and analysis tools that can store and manipulate a wide range of unstructured data, such as images, posts, and recordings, can help considerably. In a mobile ethnography project it is very easy to collect more data than can be cost-effectively analysed. For example, most researchers allow a time ratio of 3:1 to analyse video (three hours to analyse one hour of video). Therefore, the amount of data collected by a mobile ethnography project is normally controlled in some way. Methods of limiting the amount of data include:

- *Restricting the number of participants*

- *Limiting the duration of the project*

- *Limiting the size of material collected (e.g. restricting the length of videos to 90 or 60 seconds, or even 30 seconds).*

Some forms of ethnographic data, such as video, can require a substantial amount of storage space and the cost and logistical implications of transferring ethnographic data from participants to market researchers can be significant. These issues need to be taken into account when designing a project that will collect ethnographic data.

> **TIP:** *Don't collect more data than can be analysed with the resources available.*

2. THE DIFFERENCE BETWEEN ETHNOGRAPHY AND ETHNOGRAPHIC DATA

Ethnography is the analysis of the lived experience, not simply a description of it, and certainly not just a collection of ethnographic data. Ethnographic data can be interesting in its own right, but it only becomes an ethnography when it is written up in a way that captures something useful or informative about the lives of the people being researched.

The difference between ethnographic data and ethnography does not mean that there is no value in only collecting and sharing ethnographic data. Clients can gain insight by looking at collections of images, and researchers may find videos or images that help express their broader findings.

3. COLLABORATIVE ETHNOGRAPHY

Different collaborative ethnographies require different levels of involvement from the participant. For example:

- *Collecting ethnographic data about the participant's own life, usually about one specific activity, for example shopping, cooking and so on. This type of project requires informed consent, but is the easiest type of ethnography to achieve – from a logistical and ethical point of view.*

- *Collecting ethnographic data about people with whom the participants interact. This process can raise a number of logistical issues, and certainly raises more ethical concerns (e.g. to what extent have the third parties consented to the research). Participants should be given advice on what to do and what not to do. For example, do not take photos in restricted areas or of other people's children.*

- *Being involved in the analysis as well as the data collection. At a minimum this might include 'member checking', where the researcher shares their interpretation of the data with the people supplying the data, to check that it appears coherent and plausible. More fully, this collaborative approach can include involving the participants as active parties to the analysis process.*

One of the key elements of most collaborative mobile ethnographies is that it is a two-way process, between the researcher and the participants. Researchers can, typically, access the material being recorded by the participants and can update the instructions and requests to the participants.

Collaborative projects are particularly suited to ongoing research communities, where the project becomes part of the long-term discussion.

4. COMPENSATING FOR DIFFERENCES IN DEVICE FAMILIARITY

In situations where different participants have very different degrees of familiarity with the devices being used, for example if conducting a project that combines urban professionals and rural poor, there is a risk that the data from the less experienced will be less complete and informative.

Strategies to compensate for differences in familiarity focus on those who are less familiar, for example:

- *Providing a more detailed briefing.*

- *Conducting depth interviews to supplement the data they collect.*

- *Using co-capture techniques if somebody in the household or extended family is more familiar with the technology.*

5. MIXED-MODE APPROACHES TO MOBILE ETHNOGRAPHY

Mobile devices, such as phones or tablets, might be central to an ethnography project, but they do not necessarily need to be the only technology used. Other modes and devices can be combined with the use of mobile devices to make the process easier, richer, or deeper.

The most common option is to use PCs in addition to mobile devices. If the participants are posting comments they might find it easier via a PC, and they might also find downloading requests, reading training notes, or collaborating on the analysis easier via PC. Other channels, modes, and devices that can be used in a mobile ethnography include: telephone calls, face-to-face meetings, digital cameras, audio recorders, and if any of the participants collect 'quantified self' information, this can be included too.

MOBILE DIARIES AND BLOGS

The purpose of mobile diaries and mobile blogs is for participants to record a specific aspect of their life. This aspect can be a naturally occurring one, such as how they travel to work, or their lunchtime choices, or it can be an activity created by the researcher, such as an in-home product test.

The term 'mobile diary' is more typically applied to the use of an app to record participants' activities, and the term 'mobile blog' is more typically applied to the use of a website to record activities. However, many people use the terms interchangeably, while others ascribe a variety of specific meanings to one or the other. In this section the term 'mobile diary' will be used in cases where both terms are applicable.

Mobile diaries have revolutionized the research diary model and have produced both quantitative and qualitative approaches. The key improvement is that mobile devices, particularly phones, are with people all the time, so recording takes place when something happens. With traditional, paper-based diaries, the participant had to remember to fill them in, and they had to try and recall what happened.

Another benefit of mobile diaries is that they can capture more than just words and numbers, they can capture images and video, and they can record time and location.

In many cases, the data collection platforms/systems for qualitative and quantitative diary studies are the same. The differences arise from factors such as: number of participants, the depth of the responses they are asked to collect, and the type of analysis the information is subject to. In its quantitative form, mobile diary studies typically collect mostly closed answers and utilize larger sample sizes. Qualitative studies, typically, use smaller sample sizes, collect more open-ended and visual material, and the analysis focuses on individuals rather than averages and totals.

Qualitative mobile diaries and blogs can take a number of forms, including:

- *In-home use tests.*

- *Recording a specific type of activity or situation, for example every time they feel hungry, when they put fuel in their car, when they consume something, or when they buy something with cash.*

- *Recording reactions to some activity, for example how they feel every time they shop, or travel on public transport, or view the news.*

- *Recording the performance of some activity, for example how they were served in a shop, how well their detergent cleaned their clothes, or the quality of a bought meal.*

- *Recording a multimedia representation of an aspect of their lives, for example photos of their breakfast, clothes, or a coffee bought when out and about.*

- *Time initiated responses, for example, a phone can be set to prompt for input every X hours, at some random interval, or in response to a central request (e.g. via SMS, IM, email, or directly from the app). The request could be, for example, 'How do you feel?', 'Where are you?', or 'What are you doing?'*

Because the projects are mobile, it is very simple, and is usual practice, to send/push reminders to participants to help participants keep the project top of mind.

METHODS OF RECORDING ACTIVITIES

There are many ways for participants to record their activities in a mobile diary or blog. Participants can send their responses directly to the researcher via SMS, IM, or email. If the internet is available, the participants can enter their information directly into a website. If the research is using an app, the participants can enter their information into their device, and it can be uploaded immediately by the app, or at a later date.

SMS to Blog Capturing 'Sweaty Moments'

This project was conducted in the UK in 2007 on behalf of a leading deodorant brand by UK agency Join the Dots, to find out more about women's 'sweaty moments'. Sweaty moments are those times of the day when women become aware they are sweating. The research needed to be in the moment, as recall has been shown to be a poor method of researching sweaty moments in terms of issues such as: how many times it happens, what the main causes are, how it made women feel, what they did as a consequence.

The project utilized SMS as the core triggering element for the study. During the first week of the project, the participants (20 women, aged 20 to 40 years old, with a mobile phone, and home PC access to the internet) were asked to send a text every time they experienced a sweaty moment. This text was logged on each participant's personal blog, which had been created for the research project. Participants were encouraged to access their blog later in the day to expand the short text message, to add some context and further information. The participants edited their blog via a PC.

At the end of the week, the SMS phase was complete and a second phase, based on asking the women to review and comment on each other's blogs, took place.

The research captured quantitatively the number of times the participants experienced sweaty moments and the times of day those moments happened. The research captured qualitatively descriptions of the triggers for the moment, how it made the women in the study feel, and the sorts of strategies they employed to deal with these moments, for example 'headed home for a shower', 'popped into an air conditioned shop', and 'sprayed on some deodorant'.

The format of the material recorded can be as varied as the researcher's imagination and the power the chosen device allows. Common options for recording information include: text, voice (recorded), video, and pictures. With the right system it is possible for the time and the location to automatically be added to the data.

The process of recording activities and reactions can be made easier in a number of ways, for example by assigning common responses to key strokes or using QR codes to initiate aspects of an app or to enter a specific response.

RESEARCH OVERSIGHT/SUPPORT

One key difference between most paper-based diaries and most mobile diary projects is that the researcher tends to be aware, in real time, of what the participants are recording and is able to update requests and provide support and guidance.

THE DIFFERENCE BETWEEN MOBILE DIARIES/BLOGS AND MOBILE ETHNOGRAPHY

The key difference between a mobile diary or blog study and a mobile ethnography is the analysis, although this is often a matter of degree rather than an absolute difference.

The results of a mobile diary or blog often concentrate on what was happening, rather than a narrative of the underlying context and motivation. Mobile diaries and blogs are particularly useful:

- *For people who may not have the training and experience to conduct a mobile ethnography.*

- *For projects that do not have the budget for the level of design and analysis required by ethnography.*

- *Where the research problem is not sufficiently complex to need the power of ethnography.*

SHOPPER STUDIES

Although this category has been termed 'shopper studies', the same approach could be applied to a wide range of activities, such as commuting, holidays, or sports events. The key element of this approach is to find out as much as possible about a specific activity, for example shopping.

Shopper studies can be qualitative or quantitative, and again, the difference between the two tends to be the sample size and the sort of material collected. Qualitative studies tend to use smaller samples, engage the participants for a longer period of time, and collect less structured information.

RESEARCH TOPICS

There are a wide range of topics that a shopper study can focus on and a wide range of material that can be collected. Typical ones include:

- *The journey to and from shopping, particularly for those using options other than a car. In the case of cars, parking and the logistics of getting shopping to the car can be useful topics to research.*

- *The sequence of stores/shops visited, particularly in a mall or high street.*

- *Reactions to point of sale and in-store promotional material.*

- *Shelves viewed, perhaps including topics such as 'things I hate', 'looks really cool', 'confusing'.*

- *Products purchased. Including where they were in the store, the sequence within the trip around the store/shop/market, photos of the shopping trip, from the car parking through to the receipt/bill.*

- *Reactions to the shopping environment, including how it made the shopper feel.*

> **TIP:** *The rules about taking photos and recordings in shops/stores (and even within malls) vary from country to country and even store to store, so the researcher should check what is allowed and brief participants.*

TRIGGERING PARTICIPANT ACTIVITY

The simplest option is to ask the participant to initiate the activity when they go shopping. For example, they may turn on an app, or log into a website at the start of their shopping trip, or at some point during their shopping trip. If the activities only require them to use their camera (or video) they can do this as and when appropriate.

If the project is being conducted in conjunction with specific stores then the trigger can be put in the store, for example messages, QR codes, or via location based/geofencing techniques such as GPS or iBeacons (which are explained in more detail in the Utilizing Passive Data chapter).

APPS OR BROWSER-BASED?

In terms of shopper research, apps give a greater range of possible activities, for example geofencing, tracking movement, and additional ways of initiating activities. An app may have the advantage of not requiring the internet to be available when data is being entered. Browser-based solutions avoid the need for participants to download an app onto their device and allow participants to sign in from more than one device.

Shopper studies may use a combination of an app and browser-based techniques, with the app focusing on the 'in the moment' data collection and the browser used for techniques such as online discussions.

WE-RESEARCH

The term 'WE-research' was coined by John Kearon and Mark Earls (2009) to distinguish it from ME-research (by which they meant ordinary research, conducted by the researcher on the respondent). The term 'WE-research' echoes the way that Charles Leadbeater (2009) uses the term 'WE' in his book WE-Think. In WE-research participants are asked to make a record every time they encounter a particular stimulus or activity. For example, participants might be asked to make a record every time they see an advert for coffee, hear a particular song, or see a particular product in use.

Like mobile diaries, WE-research can be applied as either a quantitative or qualitative method. In its quantitative guise the number of participants is larger and the data that is collected tends to be closed responses, typically using a questionnaire or similar. Qualitative WE-research uses smaller sample sizes and captures qualitative data, for example photos and/or open-ended comments.

The difference between WE-research, shopper studies, and mobile diaries, and between all of them and mobile ethnography, is again a matter of degree, intent, and analysis. In a typical WE-research study the participants are acting as proxies for the researcher, watching for specific events and reporting on what they find. A mobile diary, typically, reports on what the participant does, and how he or she feels or thinks. And, a mobile ethnography takes both the WE-research and mobile diary approach to the next level of depth and complexity.

Gatorade, Real-time Tracking of Interactions with Experiential Touchpoints via Mobile Phone

Gatorade is a global sports drink brand owned by PepsiCo, which has a strong heritage and position in Latin America. In 2011 Gatorade G-Series was launched in Mexico, creating more of a specialist sports nutrition position. PepsiCo had a substantial amount of research on the global messaging associated with this move, but the decision to spend money on sports related experiential touchpoints, such as parks and gyms, was supported more by market experience than specific research, which meant that Gatorade were keen to estimate the value of their channel investment.

One of the problems that faced Gatorade is that the sort of activities they wanted to research are not easily picked up by traditional research, for example surveys asking people to think back over the last week and recall marginal, fleeting events. Gatorade turned to a MESH Planning and their mobile phone-based Real-time Experience Tracking.

Gatorade's study involved 400 participants, 200 each from two key target segments. The study measured interactions with Gatorade and benchmarked the results against three other brands, a sports drink, a brand of bottled water, and a sports brand.

The MESH Planning method is a mixed-mode approach, with the project starting with a survey, then utilizing SMS for a week, followed by a survey at the end of the week. The SMS phase identified interactions with branded experiential touchpoints such as material positioned in gyms. Later in the day the participants can expand on their SMS entries via an online access point. The interface has been optimized so that participants can typically enter their feedback in just a few key presses. The table shows the sort of schema a project might use to allow participants to enter their encounter with experiential touchpoints (note, for commercial reasons this is NOT the schema that was used in the Gatorade study):

Example from MESH Planning's Website

Category	Codes	Description
Brand	A	Nescafé
	B	Kenco
	etc.	etc.
Occasion	A	TV
	B	In store
	etc.	etc.
Feeling	5	Very positive
	4	Fairly positive
	etc.	etc.
Choice	5	Much more likely to choose
	4	Slightly more likely to choose
	etc.	etc.

A participant might text BB54 to say they saw a store promotion about Kenco, which was very positive and made them slightly more likely to choose it. The system records the time of day of the entry.

Results

The research showed that experiencing a brand touchpoint was associated with shifts in the educational image statements Gatorade were aiming to shift. The research also showed that the two segments responded to experiential touchpoints differently. One group was more influenced by messaging and communications in places like gyms and fitness centres, the other group were more impacted by social messaging.

The research identified the interaction between TV advertising and experiential touchpoints and as a consequence Gatorade shifted some of its funding from TV advertising to experiential touchpoints. The research also provided guidance on the balance of messages between the three varieties of the G-Series: Prime, Perform, and Recover.

In summary, the research enabled Gatorade to spend more on experiential touchpoints, tailored outdoor advertising, and more on the Prime variant, and to spend less on traditional media, generic outdoor materials, and on the Perform variant. The research and product have been rolled out to other markets, including Brazil.

Key General Learning Points

1.   'In the moment' research can reveal information and detail about events that occur during participants' busy lives, which would tend to be invisible to traditional, retrospective surveys.

2.   SMS is a good medium for this sort of real-time, high frequency feedback. For participants, it is typically always available and users are familiar with it.

3.   SMS can be made more useful by making it easier for participants to respond.

4.   The study benefits from combining mobile with different elements; capturing depth via one mode and 'in the moment' with mobile.

PASSIVE TRACKING

With the right apps and smartphones it is possible to collect a substantial amount of information about what participants do. For example, in terms of shopping, passive tracking can collect the route to and from shopping (with GPS), movement patterns within the shopping trip (e.g. how long it took, how many times the shopper stood still etc.), and the use of the phone during the shopping trip.

With some of the newer, developing technologies, and with the cooperation of the store, it is possible to track the shopper around the store, sometimes down to locations within aisles and shelves. With the use of devices such as Memoto's life-logging camera, the passive data can be extended to collect images of an activity or trip, subject to having the appropriate permissions.

In terms of mobile diaries and ethnography, passive data can be used to enrich the data entered by the research participant. Passive data is particularly useful when co-analysed with the participants, allowing the participants to explore the observational data with the researcher.

The use of passive data is the subject of a more detailed chapter.

PRACTICAL ADVICE

Mobile specific qualitative research is a highly dynamic field and the rules are still evolving, however, the following advice, sourced from practitioners, should be of assistance when designing and implementing a mobile participant research project.

ETHICS AND SAFETY

Ensure that all the relevant permissions have been obtained. This topic is discussed in more detail in the Ethics, Law, and Guidelines chapter, however, the key points are listed here:

- *Check what you are doing is legal in the country where you are doing it.*

- *Check what you are doing is in line with industry codes of good practice.*

- *Evaluate if there are any ways the participants, clients, local partners, or researcher, could come to harm (anything from physical danger through to financial loss) and deal with it.*

- *Keep a record of what people have agreed to and ensure that everybody involved in the project knows the limits of what has been agreed to. For example, clients can only distribute images if that was agreed to by the participants.*

- *Make sure that the participants are left feeling that the process was worthwhile.*

In many countries pictures of people (and videos) are considered personally identifiable data and their use is governed by data protection laws and market research codes of conduct. Care should be taken with all personally identifiable data – informed consent must be obtained and data should be protected.

RECRUITING PARTICIPANTS

When recruiting participants for a mobile qualitative project, two key dimensions are:

- *Finding participants who match the needs of the project. This might be in terms of demographics, product usage, attitudes and so on. The choice of participants will be defined by the research design, which in turn is defined by the business needs that are being met by the research.*

- *Finding participants who have the right sort of mobile device (in terms of technology and operating system). The issue of having the right devices can be broadened to include either participants who are (a) already sufficiently competent with their device to be able to take part in the research, or (b) capable of being taught/trained in how to use their device for the research.*

A further consideration, which some researchers add to the mix, is to recruit participants who are likely to be comfortable with the research tasks. For example, if the tasks include uploading blogs, the recruitment process might seek to find people comfortable writing and uploading comments from their phone.

When considering whether to screen respondents by the type of device they use and/or their comfort levels with using the tools of the research, the researcher should determine whether this would introduce an unacceptable level of bias into the results. Qualitative research designs need to ensure that they do not ignore or miss key findings because of how the recruitment was organized.

In many cases, researchers use a profiling survey at the start of the project to gather background information in a structured format. At the end of the project researchers often use another survey to collect information that the project has revealed as being of interest.

Sources of recruitment

Many researchers use exactly the same recruitment channels for mobile ethnographies and diary projects as they use for more traditional qualitative projects, including professional recruiters, panels, client lists, and communities.

THE DURATION OF PROJECTS

There are no hard and fast rules about what is 'best practice', in terms of the length of a diary or ethnography project, and different researchers report different experiences. This is not surprising since researchers may be working in different countries, with different sample structures, researching different product categories, with different methods, and with different incentives.

However, it is fair to say that, in general, the more onerous the task that participants are asked to complete, the shorter the timeframe for the study needs to be. Higher incentives can lengthen the timeframe a bit, but many researchers find that higher incentives soon show diminishing returns. If a topic is more engaging then it is easier to find participants who will complete more tasks for more days.

For example:

- *If a participant is expected to do something six to ten times a day, many researchers will focus the study to cover a single day.*

- *If a participant is going to be making one or two entries a day, then two to five days is a popular option.*

- *If the project is intended to cover two weeks, then asking participants to enter something every other or every third day is popular. This can be combined with sending reminder prompts to the participants to help them remember to complete the tasks.*

- *If the project is going to last weeks or even months, the level of activity needs to be low, perhaps weekly, or sporadically, initiated by reminders or events.*

- *Tasks should be as short as possible, for example asking people to record a 60-second video, or to answer two or three short open-ended questions.*

- *Tasks should be as engaging as possible. For example, collecting photos of what is in a participant's pantry is more fun than typing out what is in the pantry/kitchen cupboard, even though it makes more work for the researcher.*

In terms of using incentives, many researchers use some sort of completion criteria for the payment of the incentives. Two common forms of this are:

- *Participants are paid an agreed amount per day and a bonus if they take part every day.*

- *Participants are only paid if they take part every day.*

In both cases, the researcher may be faced with cases where the participants were unable to take part on a particular day because the research software/platform/connection failed, which raises issues about whether they should receive their incentives. Whilst there are different opinions on this point, the most important thing is to be clear, at the outset, about the terms and conditions.

> **TIP:** *The more onerous a task the shorter the duration of the research should be, and the higher the required incentive is likely to be.*

BRIEFING PARTICIPANTS

Participants have very different degrees of familiarity with the phones and tablets they own, and with research processes, so care needs to be taken to ensure that participants are adequately briefed and supported. In a quantitative study, the briefing process is often handled by the fieldwork provider. However, in many qualitative projects this role is much more in the hands of the researcher, sometimes with the software provider playing a role too.

Example Briefing for a Mobile Diary (being Used to Record Participants' Experience with a New Product during an 'In Home Usage Test' Diary):

1. There are no right or wrong answers so feel free to express your true feelings.

2. Please be as expressive as possible in your answers. Be as descriptive as possible so we can imagine we are right there with you. Please feel free to share your thoughts and feelings whether positive or negative.

3. Please remember to complete all tasks for the day. If you feel like sharing something extra, even if you have completed the number of tasks required for the day, please feel free to enter more. There is a minimum number for each day, but there is no limit to the maximum number of entries.

4. Your entries are spread over different topics and days. So, please follow the day-wise and topic-wise schedule for each day.

5. Please ensure that when you are taking photos and videos that the area has enough light and the photos and videos are clear in the preview. If not please take another photo or video before moving on.

6. While taking photos and videos it can be a good idea to request someone in your family or in your home to help take the photo or video, on your behalf, especially when you are showing how you use the product.

7. Please note that all the samples have to be returned, including empty packaging and unused samples of the product. Please ensure you return the products to the research team and DO NOT discard or throw anything away.

8. Remember, if you have any questions or queries, please contact the research team via. . . .

Example supplied by MobileMeasure Consultancy Ltd.

The researcher needs to determine whether the briefing is going to be face-to-face or remote. If the participants are few in number and closely geographically located, then a face-to-face briefing can make sense. However, in many cases the briefing is going to be remote, because of costs, time scales, and distances. Researchers have reported success in using techniques such as downloadable videos to make the briefings more effective.

If participants are expected to produce written summaries of what they have seen, or of their own data, supplying them with examples of what is wanted will help the participants.

SUPPORTING PARTICIPANTS

Participants should be provided with an easy way to request support if they are having problems or have questions about the technology, the tasks, or the process. The type of support offered will vary depending on the logistics of the project. The ideal option is to provide the participants with a variety of choices, including a local phone number, SMS, and email. If the project is running over a weekend, then the support should, ideally, be provided over the weekend too.

However, with multi-country projects, it may not be practical to provide local phone numbers for voice or SMS, and the support may need to be via email, IM, or the research platform.

ANALYSIS

The type and depth of analysis conducted in mobile qualitative projects will vary depending on the needs of the project, its design, the timeframe, the budget, and the experience and preferences of the researchers. For some diary projects the analysis may be little more than a coherent organization and presentation of the material collected, allowing the material to largely tell its own story. For other projects, such as an ethnography, the analysis will be the construction of a rich and thick narrative.

All of the normal rules and advice about qualitative analysis apply to data collected via mobile qualitative research, such as grounding the findings in the data and seeking to triangulate with other sources. However, there are some points that are worth special mention, given that the data is likely to be rich in photos and video material:

- *Start the analysis when the project starts. Look at the data, generate hypotheses, and check these with the participants.*

- *Tag and code information as it is collected.*

- *Try to avoid collecting too much data. More is not more if it is repetitive and if it is more than can be properly analysed with the resources available.*

- *Seek out tools for organizing the text, photos, and videos.*

- *Try to ignore the quality of the material – a participant who writes well or who uses their camera well is not more important to the analysis than somebody whose typing is full of errors and who produces pictures that are dark or a bit blurred.*

- *Avoid the temptation to use the funniest or most eye-catching material. The material used in the presentation of the findings should be that which best conveys the narrative of the analysis, not that which will amuse the most.*

- *When including photos and video in the deliverables, edit them to increase their ability to add to the narrative being created – this usually means shortening them and adding captions.*

Table 6.1   Key issues to consider when selecting a platform

Question	Issues to consider
Single or multiple projects?	Are you going to use the platform for one specific project or for several projects? If the platform is going to be used for several projects, then the learning curve can be steeper, but it needs to be more powerful/flexible in terms of types of projects it will support, languages supported, and scalability.
Scalable?	Can the system cope with larger numbers of participants (say 100 instead of 10), can it deal with multiple projects, can it deal with extended research teams?
Devices supported?	What sort of mobile devices are participants going to be using? Smartphones, feature phones, tablets?
App, browser, or both?	Many of the diary and ethnography projects are based on apps, to ensure that participants can enter data any time they want to. However, it is not unusual for the platforms to also have a browser-based element, for example to maintain a blog or to interact with the moderator.
Languages?	What languages will the participants be using, what admin languages does it support?
Field supplier experience?	If you are using local fieldwork suppliers or recruiters, are they experienced with the platform, do they have a preference for a particular platform?
Ease of use?	How easy to use is the system for participants, recruiters, and researchers? For researchers, how easy is it to create, manage, and update projects?
Analysis?	One of the key differences between non-research tools and research-based solutions is how they support the analysis process. A researched-based system can help with sorting, coding, tagging, organizing, searching, exporting, and creating a report.

SELECTING A RESEARCH PLATFORM

It is possible to conduct most of the types of research mentioned in this chapter without specialist software. It is possible to assemble a solution of your own by using software tools freely available, and it is certainly possible to work with a technology partner to create a customized solution. However, it is easier and potentially more reliable to use an existing platform.

Key issues to consider when selecting a platform are shown in Table 6.1.

SUMMARY

Mobile devices are developing rapidly and qualitative researchers are engaged in a widespread process of experimentation and adaptation, identifying the many ways that mobile devices can be utilized in qualitative research. Some of these uses are in the context of existing research approaches, or in conjunction with other modes, and these are explored in the two previous chapters. However, the rapid development and adoption of powerful and easy to use mobile devices is ushering in new approaches to qualitative research, in particular new forms of participant mobile research.

The key points that need to be highlighted are:

- *Participant mobile qualitative research is focused on participants using their mobile devices collaboratively to create the material for the research.*

- *There are a variety of participant mobile qualitative research approaches, for example mobile ethnography, mobile diaries, and shopper studies. The difference between them is usually a matter of degree, and often comes down to the objectives for the research and the method of analysis, rather than the way the data is collected.*

- *Because the data is going to be processed qualitatively, and with the tools currently available, it is usually necessary to limit the amount of information collected.*

- *Methods of limiting the amount of information gathered include: restricting the number of participants, restricting the duration of the research, and by limiting the number of photos and the length of the videos the participants are asked to capture and upload.*

- *In general, the more onerous the task (e.g. the more times per day the participant has to record something) the shorter the duration of the project will need to be, and the higher the incentive will need to be.*

- *Good research is more about good design and good analysis than it is about good software, but good software can make the researcher's life easier.*

- *Passive data is often thought of as a quantitative tool, but used in combination with user-entered data it can greatly enrich a mobile qualitative picture, particularly when analysed collaboratively with the participant.*

7 Mobile Quantitative Research

INTRODUCTION

This chapter provides an overview of mobile quantitative research, providing a context for many of the later chapters, such as those covering CATI, CAPI, passive tracking, and in particular the chapter on designing and managing mobile surveys.

The chapter covers:

- *Defining mobile quantitative market research*
- *Mobile specific research*
- *Mixed-mode projects*
- *Connecting with research participants.*

MODES OF DATA COLLECTION

When reviewing mobile quantitative market research the wider context of market research needs to be considered. Most market research, by spend, is quantitative market research. The ESOMAR Global Market Research report for 2013 estimated that, by spend, 77% of market research is quantitative, 17% qualitative, and 6% other (ESOMAR 2013).

It is important for market researchers, especially researchers from the more developed markets, to remember that the majority of global data collection is currently not yet online. Online is currently the most popular research mode for survey research; however, only approximately 50% of survey research globally uses the online mode. Figure 7.1 shows the share of spend allocated to the leading data collection methods in 2012 (ESOMAR 2013).

While online market research has become the leading methodology in developed countries, the low levels of internet penetration in many emerging markets have slowed its global growth. By contrast, mobile phones have very high levels of penetration in most

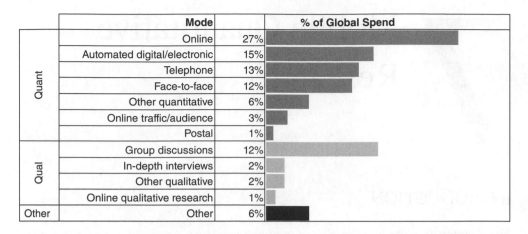

	Mode		% of Global Spend
Quant	Online	27%	
	Automated digital/electronic	15%	
	Telephone	13%	
	Face-to-face	12%	
	Other quantitative	6%	
	Online traffic/audience	3%	
	Postal	1%	
Qual	Group discussions	12%	
	In-depth interviews	2%	
	Other qualitative	2%	
	Online qualitative research	1%	
Other	Other	6%	

Figure 7.1   Global spend by mode, from 2013 ESOMAR Global Market Research Report

of the world, which increases the potential for mobile to be a truly global research mode. However, the uneven adoption of more advanced phones and tablets, and data packages, may still present major challenges for a unified 'one world' research approach.

MOBILE IS BIG BUSINESS

By 2014 mobile devices were already being widely used by participants to take part in market research, with about 20–30% of online studies being undertaken by participants choosing to use mobile devices and a large proportion of CATI interviews being completed on mobile phones (Poynter 2014a). The expectation is that over the next few years the trend will continue and about 50% of online surveys will be conducted via mobile devices and most CATI will be via mobile (Poynter 2014b).

These two categories of mobile usage are in addition to the growth in mobile devices used in media measurement, mobile 'in the moment' projects, other types of mobile market research.

DEVELOPED AND EMERGING MARKETS

In the more developed markets, it is increasingly possible to assume that the majority of people in most target groups will have access to smartphones. In September 2013, the Pew Research Center estimated that 55% of US adults had a smartphone (Pew Research Internet Project 2013).

In less developed markets, the picture is more complex. In many of the less developed markets the penetration of mobile phones is often high. However, a significant proportion of these phones may be older, or more basic, phones, with fewer functions.

In developing markets many of the more modern phones are not accompanied with connection contracts that include access to the internet, and the internet coverage can be unreliable. The options for mobile research in countries where members of the target sample for the research are unlikely to have mobile phones with internet access is covered in the chapter on International Mobile Research.

In some of the less developed markets literacy rates can be an issue for any type of self-completion research, however, this can often be addressed by mobile equipped interviewers (which is covered in the chapter on mCAPI) and by the use of innovative approaches to mobile surveys (Williams 2014a).

However, researchers need to be aware, as Hans Rosling (2013) has pointed out, that the differences between the developed world and developing world are disappearing. The majority of the world have a mobile phone – smartphones are on their way to being the new normal. When planning research in different countries researchers should certainly find out what is possible, but their starting assumption should be that it is probably possible.

DEFINING QUANTITATIVE MOBILE MARKET RESEARCH

Mobile quantitative research is a new and emerging field that has created its own characteristics, some of which are quite different from established modes, such as CATI or online. This section of the chapter provides an overview of the following three key elements:

1.   The relationship between devices and research

2.   Apps versus browser-based solutions

3.   Active versus passive data collection.

THE RELATIONSHIP BETWEEN DEVICES AND RESEARCH

The key devices used in quantitative market research are phones and tablets, and the term 'phone' is normally sub-divided into feature phone, smartphone, and phablet. The distribution of these devices amongst the people to be researched is a major determinant of the sorts of research that can be conducted.

In addition to these mobile devices, there is a growing level of interest in devices such as wearable technology, for example life-logging cameras, GPS tracking devices, and a range of fitness related devices. The impact of these devices in covered in later chapters, especially in the Utilizing Passive Data and Evolving Picture chapters.

Table 7.1   Key devices, descriptions, and their uses in quantitative market research

Device	Description	Role in quantitative market research
Non-internet feature phone	Not a smartphone, no internet browsing.	SMS (and USSD where available) only.
Internet-enabled feature phone	Wide variety of devices, they can usually download applications, have some but not all of the features of a smartphone, may have Wi-Fi.	SMS. Web surveys, but fewer options. App-based research. Some passive data collection.
Smartphones	Mostly large touchscreen, modern operating system, in terms of 2013 sales, mostly Android devices and iPhones. However, the installed base is the key issue.	SMS. Web surveys, almost same as PC. App-based research. Passive data collection. 'In the moment' research. mCAPI (mobile CAPI).
Phablets	Phones with a larger touchscreen, typically more than 5 and less than 7 inches.	SMS. Web surveys, almost same as PC. App-based research. Passive data collection. 'In the moment' research. mCAPI (mobile CAPI).
Tablets	Typically with screen size of 7 inches or more. May not have a SIM, i.e. no link to services like 3G or 4G, but has Wi-Fi.	Web surveys, almost same as PC. App-based research. Passive data collection. mCAPI (mobile CAPI).

Table 7.1 outlines the key devices, descriptions, and their uses in quantitative market research.

Note, Table 7.1 contains quite a few technical terms. Most of these terms were introduced in the first two chapters, the key terms are covered in more depth in the glossary, and the concepts and terms are covered further in later chapters, for example The Technology of Mobile Market Research, Utilizing Passive Data, and The Evolving Picture. However, the following sections cover the key points that are essential to an overview of quantitative mobile market research.

MOBILE PHONES

Mobile phones have become almost ubiquitous. By the end of 2013 there were about as many mobile phones in the world as people, although many people had multiple phones and about one-third of adults did not yet have a phone. The abundance of phones means that for many projects, in most countries, a mobile phone is a viable method of connecting with participants.

Phones are of interest to quantitative researchers for the following reasons:

- *More people have a mobile phone than a PC, and more people have a mobile than a landline, which offers the opportunity to reach more people than most other modes.*

- *People tend to have their mobile with them, which facilitates 'in the moment' research.*

- *The combination of always being available and multimedia (e.g. taking photos and recording videos) means that participants can be recruited to be active collaborators in the research process.*

- *Many phones are capable of collecting passive data, tracking such things as location, activities, and media consumption.*

- *Many phones are capable of triggering research activities, for example at a specific time of day, when in a specific location, or in response to a signal from the researcher. For example a store satisfaction study could be triggered when somebody visits a coffee franchise, or a breakfast study triggered at breakfast time.*

Types of phones

This section very briefly reviews the main categories of phone in the context of quantitative mobile research; more information is available about the general picture elsewhere in the book.

1. **Basic feature phones.** These tend to be phones that do not have internet access, so they cannot be used for web surveys and they cannot be used to download apps from the internet. These phones might not have internet access because of the hardware, or they may simply not have access to a contract that provides access to the internet. In 2014 these were still the most common type of phone and were being used for SMS-based studies and in a few cases USSD studies.

2. **Feature phones internet access.** Most of these phones do not have a large touchscreen, which means that online surveys tend to render differently on PCs and smartphones – and a number of multimedia question types may not run on them. Because there are a wide variety of phones and operating systems within this category, creating downloadable apps can be time consuming and expensive. These phones are used for SMS, USSD, web surveys, and app-based research.

3. **Smartphones.** Smartphones (and phablets) are an established market research device. Most of the survey platforms support smartphones, although some question types are rendered differently on smartphones. Smartphones are also used for anything a feature phone can be used for, and are often used in passive tracking projects and with app-based research.

SMS

In the early days of mobile market research the most widely available mobile option for surveys was via SMS, and some researchers are still using it, especially in the developing markets. SMS is a mobile only method as the questions it can ask are strictly limited. SMS questions tend to be in the format of a short question, asking the participants to type in a digit for the answer, for example, 1 for Yes, 2 for No, or 3 for Don't know.

SMS is widely used as a trigger for mobile research, for example sending an SMS message to participants with a link to a web-based survey.

USSD (Unstructured Supplementary Service Data) is used by a few suppliers in some of the developing markets to conduct market research, but is not available in all markets. USSD is similar to SMS in that it is text-based (182 characters), but unlike SMS it connects a phone and computer synchronously (they are both connected to each other at the same time). In places where USSD is popular it is used for a variety of uses, for example financial transactions.

Web surveys on smartphones

Touchscreen, large screen phones running powerful operating systems such as Google's Android, Apple's iOS, and Microsoft's Phone have narrowed the gap between what can be asked on a PC screen and a phone. The main differences between a PC-based study and a phone are the size of the screen and potential bandwidth differences (a phone using 3G will tend to be slower than a device using Wi-Fi or a direct connection).

Most of the differences between a PC and smartphone can be accommodated by changing the way a question is displayed, something that is typically handled by the survey platform.

Intentional and unintentional mobile web surveys

Mobile surveys can be thought of as existing on a continuum from intentional at one end, for example where the survey was designed for mobile and where the participants were selected because they had a mobile device, through to 'unintentional mobile'. If a researcher designs a survey for online, expecting participants to use a PC, and some of the respondents answer the survey on their phone, that is 'unintentional mobile'.

Device agnostic

The term 'device agnostic' or 'platform agnostic' is used by survey platforms to demonstrate that the surveys they produce are capable of being run on a range of devices, for example PCs, smartphones, tablets, and in some cases internet-enabled feature phones. What this typically means is that the survey authoring system allows the user to specify that a survey should be rendered appropriately on different devices by detecting the type of device being used.

However, this does not mean that every available question will run on every device, when using a standardized survey platform. And, it does not mean that every question will appear in a similar way on each device, which may or may not impact on the results. This topic is covered in greater detail later in the book.

An all smartphone future?

In 2014 market researchers were still dealing with a variety of categories of phone, for example basic feature phones, more sophisticated feature phones, older smartphones (such as BlackBerry), and smartphones. However, the future for most market researchers appears to be focused on smartphones (and phablets), running a very small selection of operating systems (Williams 2014b)

TABLETS

Participants in online surveys are already using tablets to take part and many research agencies and fieldwork suppliers have equipped their face-to-face interviewers with tablets as data collection devices (which is covered in detail in the mCAPI chapter).

Compared with smartphones, tablets have the advantage of having a larger screen, but also a couple of limitations:

1.   Tablets are not carried everywhere with most people in the way their phone is, so they present fewer opportunities for 'in the moment' research.

2.   Many tablets do not have a SIM, so they only have an internet connection when they are connected via Wi-Fi, which can limit their usefulness in 'on the move' web surveys.

APPS VERSUS WEB

There are two main ways of connecting mobile devices to research exercises such as surveys: these are referred to as browser-based and app-based approaches.

Web-based surveys on a mobile device work in the same way as online surveys work via a PC. The participant uses a browser on their phone to access a hosted survey via the internet. For this approach to work, the mobile device has to have an internet connection and the survey has to render (display) correctly for their phone/tablet.

Apps are pieces of software that are downloaded onto people's phones or tablets. Although an app usually uses the internet to transfer data back to the researcher, some research apps do not have to be connected to the internet while the survey or activity is taking place. The ability to run without an active internet connection greatly increases the range of situations when the survey or activity can take place.

An app can respond to a request from a participant to start a survey, but it can also be configured to initiate a survey, which is described as a 'push' approach. For example, a timer can be set to ask a survey at specific intervals or, at a specific time of day, for example asking breakfast related questions in the morning. If the device has geolocation enabled, a survey can be initiated when the participant is near a specific location (such as visiting a store), something often referred to as geofencing.

Apps have many advantages, but two key disadvantages.

The advantages include not needing the internet to be connected all the time, being able to store multiple surveys, being able to collect passive data, and being able to trigger surveys or research activities in a variety of ways.

Being able to collect information when the internet is not currently available is particularly relevant when collecting 'in the moment' data, such as surveys when somebody is shopping, especially in locations or countries where the internet may not always be available, and when used in mCAPI.

The two key disadvantages of apps are:

1.   Apps have to be written for each major platform that participants might be using. The move towards Android and Apple operating systems for modern phones and tablets could mean that this will be less of a problem than it was in the early days of writing apps.

2.   Prospective participants have to be willing and able to download apps onto their mobile devices. However, this process is becoming more common and more streamlined.

However, despite these two challenges the use of apps for market research appears to be growing, especially in the context of panels and communities (Poynter 2014b).

ACTIVE VERSUS PASSIVE DATA COLLECTION

Quantitative mobile market research can be divided into two broad categories, active and passive:

1.   Active research requires the active involvement of participants in the research process, for example, by completing a survey.

2.   Passive market research studies do not involve asking participants questions. In passive data collection the mobile device records information, for example the participant's location, actions, or device usage.

Studies can combine active and passive. For example a location-based app might track a participant's journey, using GPS and when the participant visits a specific location, perhaps a mall, the participant might be asked to complete a survey.

Passive Mobile Market Research

Passive data collection is the topic of a later chapter, but its key features are:

- *Passive data collection usually requires the participants to download an app.*

- *There are some limits to what passive data can be collected, both in terms of the operating system rules and in terms of things like the system limitations, such as GPS.*

- *Most areas of market research are not making extensive use of passive data collection, yet.*

- *One area that is well advanced in terms of passive data collection is media measurement, whose long heritage of automating the collection of television viewing and radio listening have helped develop mobile-based solutions.*

- *Some non-research organizations are making extensive use of passive tracking, from uses as varied as app usage (e.g. Flurry) to location-based marketing (e.g. ShopKick).*

Two common concerns about passive data collection are privacy and running down the participant's battery. Privacy is covered in the Utilizing Passive Data chapter and in Ethics, Laws, and Guidelines.

The issue of battery life stems from the fact that if an app is used consistently then it can make a mobile device's battery run down faster. This was a major problem in the early days of apps, but app developers are getting better at managing battery life.

MOBILE SPECIFIC PROJECTS

This section looks at the types of quantitative market research studies that are designed specifically for mobile devices, i.e. they are mobile only.

WHY MOBILE ONLY?

In reviewing mobile only studies it is useful to consider why a researcher might want to conduct a mobile only research project, given that the trend is towards being device agnostic and giving participants a choice.

Typical reasons for a project being mobile only include:

1.   To collect passive data, as people go about their everyday lives.

2.   The data needs to be collected, or is better if it is collected, 'in the moment', where 'in the moment' typically means as people are using something or imme- diately after using something. For example, interviewing somebody whilst they are commuting or immediately after they finish shopping.

3.   When mobile gives a more appropriate sample than other similar methods. For example, in a country where 80% of economically active adults have a phone and 50% have internet access, mobile may potentially provide access to a better sample.

4.   In order to move from CAPI to mCAPI, a topic that has its own chapter in this book.

5.   To add items like photos and videos to traditional survey responses.

6.   When researching the mobile ecosystem, for example mobile advertising. Researching the Mobile Ecosystem has a chapter of its own later in the book.

7.   To conduct research-on-research about mobile data collection.

The sections that follow illustrate cases where some or all of the previous points apply and where the research tends to be mobile only.

'In the moment' data collection

'In the moment' research capitalizes on people's tendency to have their phone with them all the time. 'In the moment' involves enlisting the participant as a collaborator in the research project. Traditional research is usually based on participants having to recall events, remembering what happened and how they felt. 'In the moment' captures the details and the responses when the experience is fresh, as some of the examples in the following sections will illustrate.

'In the moment' studies can be triggered in a variety of ways, for example:

- *The participant launches the activity when appropriate. In the restaurant example the participant would launch the survey after each relevant meal.*

- *An app might trigger the action, based on a timer, or location, or some other factor.*

- *The researcher may send a message when the activity should take place.*

'In the moment' studies with mobile devices also offer the opportunity for the participant to capture photos and video. Although in the context of a quantitative study, this needs to be handled with care to avoid data overload.

More appropriate samples

An example of mobile devices providing a more representative sample is provided by the French company Elipss, who have created a panel of 6000 people. The panel were selected via random probability and were all given an internet connected tablet. This created a sample source that is both internet-enabled and broadly representative of the group they are seeking to represent.

Quantitative diaries

Consumption tracking is used to explore people's purchasing behaviour, especially for impulse products, where the consumption is often not planned or happens 'on the fly'. For example, a drinking study might request participants to log every drink they consume in a 24-hour period. Items recorded might include:

- *What was the drink?*
- *What brand, if relevant?*
- *Where was it consumed?*
- *Was it bought and if so from where?*

Studies into drinking conducted this way have revealed, for example, interesting differences in where at home people drink their first hot drink of the day, and the use of energy drinks at different times of the day. Details like time of day can be collected automatically, and in some cases location can be collected automatically.

In-home product placement testing

In-home placement tests can utilize both phones and tablets. For example, when conducting in-home placement tests for products such as face cream, the participants can capture pictures of their faces as different stages of the day, and in different stages of product usage, in addition to quantitative information.

In the more developed markets, online, PC-based in-home tests are common, but in the developing markets, using mobile devices can greatly extend the range of participants.

Real-time brand or media monitoring

Mobile data collection can be useful for monitoring people's interactions with brands, advertising, or promotions, especially for low attention products and services. Participants are recruited to log product or service experiences, as and when they happen.

Participants can also be recruited to monitor and record their interactions with media channels, using a combination of active and passive data collection.

Mystery shopping

Mystery shopping is used to evaluate a wide range of phenomena, including customer service, the implementation of campaigns, and product placement/presentation. Mobile surveys make it easier for the mystery shopper to record observations during the shopping experience, or immediately afterwards. With GPS-enabled phones, real-time geotagging can be added to give potentially accurate readings for outdoor advertising research. QR code readers or barcode scanners can be used to track and identify specific products. A mystery shopper can also use a mobile device to add photographs or video to the task.

However, these tools also require that the researcher understand and observe the ethical issues that arise with recording or photographing of anything, including customers, displays, and store personnel. These are discussed in a later chapter on Ethics, Laws, and Guidelines.

Customer experience/satisfaction

Mobile surveys are ideal for fast, non-intrusive feedback immediately after or even during a purchase or service experience. For example participants might be recruited to complete a research activity every time they eat a meal in an agreed set of restaurants. Because the data is entered straight away and in the context of a specific location the survey can be short, the memories will be fresh, and the data can be supplied to the client far faster than a traditional customer satisfaction tracker.

There are a growing number of ways of triggering experience surveys, such as QR codes, barcodes, geofencing (using options such as GPS or iBeacons). Triggering mechanisms are covered in more depth in the Utilizing Passive Data and The Technology of Mobile Market Research chapters.

Passive data collection

Mobile phones and tablets contain a large number of features and sensors and these are increasingly being used to collect passive data, such as the routes taken by participants on shopping trips. Utilizing Passive Data is the subject of a later chapter.

Passive tracking raises a large number of ethical and legal issues, and these are covered in a later chapter, Ethics, Laws, and Guidelines.

Adding multimedia to a quantitative survey

If a quantitative project needs, or would benefit from, photos, videos, or audio recordings, then the logical data collection device is a mobile device. This approach is likely to become even more attractive when techniques for handling large amounts of multimedia information improve.

Retail measurement

In developed markets, retail measurement is increasingly automated, with large format stores dominating sales channels and online channels growing rapidly. However, in the developing world, the 'mom and pop' stores still dominate in many key and emerging markets.

Traditionally, in these developing markets retail measurements have been very labour intensive and potentially error strewn. The last 20 years have seen a move towards automation, based on mobile devices. The initial steps were to use handheld devices, such as PDAs. However, more recently the move has been towards mobile devices, i.e. both phones and tablets.

MIXED-MODE STUDIES

Mixed-mode, or hybrid, studies can be divided into two broad categories:

1. Studies where some participants use one form of data collection, whilst others use another form of data collection. For example, some participants might use a PC to take part in an online study, and others might use internet-enabled phones.

2. Studies where more than one device is used by each participant, at different stages of the project. For example, participants might use their phone to keep a mobile diary for a week, before attending a face-to-face depth interview.

Later in the book there is a chapter specifically on mixed-mode research, but the section below covers the key points that quantitative researchers need to keep in mind.

DIFFERENT MODES CAN CREATE DIFFERENT DATA

If some participants see a survey on their PC, some on a large tablet, some on a smart-phone, and some on an internet-enabled feature phone the results could be impacted by the different modes. As the Research-on-Research chapter illustrates, in most cases the differences found to date are small, but whenever different participants use different modes the researcher needs to check for mode effects.

INTENTIONAL AND UNINTENTIONAL MIXED-MODE STUDIES

As mentioned earlier in the chapter, estimates are that 20–30% of online surveys are being completed via mobile devices, which means most researchers conducting online research are already conducting mixed-mode research. For some researchers this will be the result of an active decision to use device agnostic research, this is intentional mixed-mode research.

Researchers need to check if there are mode effects, otherwise the scale of any problems will go unnoticed.

The next chapter, Designing and Conducting Mobile Surveys discusses best practices for handling this sort of mixed-mode project.

PASSIVE DATA COLLECTION AND MIXED MODE STUDIES

If the researcher wants to collect passive data it is unlikely that the research can combine PCs and mobile devices because the procedures for including passive recording software tend to be different between PCs and mobile devices. The main exception is studies looking at media or internet usage and consumption, where the ability to measure both PC and mobile data is considered vital.

MULTIPLE MODES PER PARTICIPANT

If the researcher wants the participants to use different devices at different stages, they need to make this clear and monitor compliance. For example, if one part of the project is supposed to be collected 'in the moment' it is worth checking that it is not being entered at the end of the day via a PC.

CONNECTING WITH PARTICIPANTS

Until recently the process of finding participants for mobile research has been less developed than those for online, CATI, and face-to-face, but that is changing fast. In particular, there are a growing number of panels available. Some of the key methods of connecting research projects with mobile participants are outlined in the next section.

MIXED-MODE ONLINE STUDIES, VIA PC AND MOBILE

The most common reason for this type of mixed mode study is to offer the participants the choice of device, to increase convenience to the participants to ideally increase cooperation rates and the range of people who are able to take part. Therefore, in most cases, when conducting a mixed-mode study via PC, tablet, and phone, there are no particular quotas for the proportion of participants answering via each device.

In terms of decreasing order of popularity the methods of recruiting and connecting with participants are:

1. Via an online access panel, research community, or similar. The panel emails a survey link and invitation to suitable panel members, describing the range of devices the survey is suitable for. The survey should also check that it is being viewed on an appropriate device.

2.   Via members of a client customer list. With this option the client or the researcher defines an appropriate sample to invite, and the invitation includes a link to the survey, and information about the range of devices suitable for the study.

3.   Through links placed on websites, QR codes on products, URLs included in letters, via links on pop-ups, through social media, or as part of a newsletter. Again, the invitation needs to alert participants to the requirements of the study, and the device should be checked when the survey is commenced.

MOBILE ONLY, ONLINE SURVEYS

Key options include:

1.   Access panels. A growing number of access panels have mobile samples available.

2.   Research communities. Some communities are mobile only, but the majority are centred on either PC usage or an online device agnostic approach. Community members with suitable mobile devices can be recruited for mobile only studies. Ensuring members are profiled in terms of devices owned and willingness to do mobile projects is an important part of this process.

3.   Client lists. With client lists the key issue is to ensure that they are up to date and that the recipients of invitations realize they need to use their mobile device. The invitation and URL can be sent via email or SMS.

4.   Via traditional recruiters or recruitment approaches. This route is more common in the less developed research markets, and can include door-to-door recruitment, telephone, and even postal recruitment.

5.   Through links placed on websites, QR codes on products, URLs included in letters, via links of pop-ups, through social media, or as part of a newsletter. Again, the invitation needs to alert prospective participants to the requirements of the study, and the device should be checked on the commencement of the study.

MOBILE ONLY, APP-BASED SURVEYS, AND PASSIVE DATA

When connecting with mobile participants for an app-based study whether for surveys, passive data collection, or some combination of these, there is often a need for a higher degree of contact between the researcher and the participant (or between the provider of the survey and the participant). This is because there is often a need to brief the participants on how to download and activate the app, ensuring that there is informed consent, and helping the participant to remove the app after the study is complete.

All of the recruiting and connecting routes outlined for web-based surveys are suitable for app-based research, provided that the appropriate level of support can be achieved. However, some panel companies might be reluctant to facilitate the download of apps on their members' devices, and the response rates from routes such as links on websites can be much lower when prospective participants are required to download an app from an organization with which they have not had a prior relationship.

PANELS AND COMMUNITIES WITH APPS

A growing number of panels and communities have their own research app and will have members who have already downloaded the app. If the panel or community app is suitable for the proposed research there is no need for participants to download anything and the process can be relatively seamless for the researcher.

SUMMARY

Most observers expect mobile market research will become a major mode of quantitative data collection over the next few years, perhaps even the dominant method. Key issues that will shape the future of mobile quantitative market research will include:

- *The balance between apps and web-based solutions*

- *The balance between active and passive research*

- *The growth of ever more powerful smartphones*

- *The growth of tablets and phablets*

- *The global increase in data connection speeds, declining cost of data connections, and the growing penetration of devices connected to the internet.*

Key issues about mobile quantitative research include:

- *The need to know what sort of mobile devices the participants are likely to have and to design the research accordingly.*

- *The types of devices available, the options for recruiting the sample, and the likelihood of the internet being available will guide the decision about whether to use browser-based or app-based approaches.*

- *If passive data is going to be collected, then apps are probably going to be necessary.*

- *Most online research is already mixed-mode, with about a quarter of online participants using mobile devices, so researchers should be accommodating them and checking for mode effects.*

- *The key benefits that mobile brings are: 'in the moment' research, a wider range of potential participants, and the potential for passive data collection.*

- *In the newly emerging markets mobile research offers the chance to skip technologies, potentially bypassing CATI and PC-based online.*

8 Designing and Conducting Mobile Surveys

INTRODUCTION

In order to provide a clear and relevant focus to this chapter the majority of the chapter looks at mobile surveys conducted via smartphones and tablets, utilizing web-based approaches and samples sourced from panels and communities. In particular, the context is:

- *The research will be conducted via a mobile survey using a self-completion approach.*

- *The survey will be completed on a smartphone, tablet, or phablet.*

- *The survey will be online and browser-based.*

- *The survey will be created via a survey platform or software system, using the features of the platform, i.e. it will not be custom-built.*

- *The survey will be fielded via a customer list, or from an access panel, or via an insight community.*

Other forms of recruitment and the use of apps are included where appropriate and, in particular, toward the end of the chapter. It should be noted that many of the design principles that apply to smartphone mobile research apply to other forms of mobile research.

This chapter draws heavily on the research-on-research reported at the end of the book for the advice presented.

ONLINE MOBILE SURVEYS

Online mobile surveys are surveys that are hosted on the web and accessed from mobile devices via browsers. This type of research can be mobile only, i.e. all the participants are using mobile devices, or they can be mixed-mode, with some participants using mobile devices and some accessing the survey from a PC. It is claimed that about 20–30% of all online survey participants are using mobile devices.

This section of the book focuses on online mobile surveys conducted via the main sample sources, with participants using smartphones and tablets. In many markets feature phones are still a major part of the online mobile survey picture, and in many markets the organized sample options are fewer.

PANELS, LISTS, AND COMMUNITIES

In many cases the sample for online mobile surveys comes from the same three sources as online surveys, i.e. panel companies, client lists, and online communities. This is the subject of a whole chapter later in the book.

Working with organized providers of sample reduces the need to focus on invitations, incentives, and participant support. However, most panels and communities are currently more online than mobile focused, which means care needs to be taken in countries where the relevant mobile population is larger than the online population. This is a topic covered in the Panels, Lists, and Communities chapter.

SURVEY PLATFORMS

A survey platform is a software system that allows the user to create surveys using a survey language or a graphical interface. The sorts of platforms focused on in this chapter will host the survey on the internet and participants use a browser on their mobile device to access it.

Key elements in using a survey platform for mobile online surveys are:

- *Creating the survey. Many of the survey platforms operate as software as a service (SaaS), instead of having the software installed on the researcher's computer.*

- *Making the survey available on the internet, often referred to as deploying.*

- *Making the survey available to the participants, for example by using email or SMS to send a link to the survey – this stage is often called fielding the study.*

- *The survey platform stores the completed surveys and provides a range of management statistics, for example completes, quotas, and top line results.*

- *Once the study is completed, the platform allows the researcher to export the data, as a file, for analysis and reporting. Some survey platforms have analysis and reporting options as part of the platform.*

One important feature of some survey platforms is the ability to detect the sort of device a participant is using, and to ensure that the right version of the survey is presented to the participant. For example, if a participant is using an iPhone they will see a survey rendered for an iPhone and if they are using a PC they will see a survey suitable for a PC.

The advantage of using a survey platform is that it makes the survey creation process cost-effective, efficient, predictable, reliable, and it allows people with a limited knowledge of technology to create and deploy surveys. The majority of online mobile surveys are conducted via software platforms specializing in market research software.

The alternative to a standardized survey platform is to create custom-built surveys. The advantage of a custom-built solution is that the researcher does not have to fit their research design into what the standard systems offer. The disadvantages are that custom-built solutions are often slower to create and more expensive.

ONE STOP SOLUTIONS

Many of the sample providers, especially access panels, provide a one stop solution where they script the survey, provide the sample, host the survey, and deliver data and in some cases tables and analysis. Even when outsourcing the scripting of the survey, the researcher still needs to be aware of the design implications for mobile surveys.

DESIGNING FOR MOBILE

This section of the chapter looks at the core design issues for mobile surveys, in the context of the assumptions stated above. However, many of the points made in this section will be equally true of apps, custom-built solutions, and research via feature phones.

The key design issues are:

1. The length of the survey
2. Whether to optimize for mobile or for comparability
3. Fitting questions onto the screen
4. Fitting the style of the device
5. Fitting the available bandwidth
6. Data about the survey process.

THE LENGTH OF THE SURVEY

There is a broad consensus within the market research community that mobile surveys should be shorter than the length that has become the norm for online and telephone surveys. There is no definitive view on how long mobile surveys should be, but recommended ranges seem to vary from two minutes to about 12 minutes. However, there are some much longer surveys being conducted, both as unintentional mobile and even as mobile only studies. This issue is covered further in the Research-on-Research chapter.

Mobile surveys sometimes take longer

When working with mobile surveys, researchers need to consider that a mobile survey can take longer to complete than the same survey completed via a PC, especially when the survey is one designed for a PC, and rendered by the survey platform as a mobile study.

The data reported in the Research-on-Research chapter suggests that when a survey is designed for a PC, it often take 1.5 times as long to complete on a smartphone and about 1.25 times as long on a tablet.

But mobile is not always longer

However, the comparison between the time taken to complete a survey on a PC and a phone potentially misses a key point about designing mobile surveys. A well-designed mobile study can be faster than a standard PC survey. In this case 'well-designed' means using approaches such as shorter, more intuitive questions, reducing the length of answer lists, and reducing the amount of text used for each of the answers.

Designing shorter surveys

Shorter surveys are felt to be good because they reduce satisficing (Chudoba 2011), reduce dropouts (Chudoba 2010), and provide a better experience to the research participant.

The approaches in Table 8.1 can make a contribution to shortening surveys.

OPTIMIZING FOR MOBILE OR FOR COMPARABILITY?

A mobile study has the opportunity to make the most of its benefits, being 'in the moment', on the move, able to include passive data, able to use new types of questions, and potentially including the capture of photos and video. However, against those opportunities there is sometimes pressure to make the results comparable with either

Table 8.1   Approaches that can make a contribution to shortening surveys

Approach	Description
Develop a narrative flow for the survey.	Questionnaires should be like a conversation, the participant should be able to see where they go next, which reduces the cognitive load on the participant, and makes it more engaging.
Is every question really necessary?	Review the questionnaire against the research and business objectives, ensure that each question links to at least one of the business and research questions. Even if a question links to the objectives, consider if it is adding something unique or useful.
Shorten the questions.	Shortening questions often makes them less ambiguous and more intuitive. For example, instead of saying '*Which of the following cars is your favourite? (Please select one)*', just ask '*Favourite car?*' followed by the answer list. With a good narrative flow and the right question type and text the meaning should be clear.
Shorten the number of answers.	In many cases the number of answers relevant to a respondent is quite limited. If 80% of people are picking the same four options, perhaps, four options in an answer list are enough, supported with an 'Other' option or a method for the participant to see an extended list of options? A more sophisticated method of shortening answer lists is to tailor them to specific participants, for example creating consideration lists based on earlier answers, meaning different participants see different lists.
Shorten the length of the answers.	Shorter answers make the survey easier to read, quicker to interpret, and help the study fit on a small screen, reducing scrolling.
Can you answer the question without asking it?	Access panels and insight communities store profile information and other information. If age, gender etc. can be read from the data source they do not need to be asked as questions.
Remove irrelevant visuals.	Irrelevant visuals can include things like: the logo of the survey platform and/or the client. Irrelevant visuals can slow down the load and make reading the screen slower.
Ensure that visual elements load quickly.	When images are needed, ensure that they load as quickly and easily as possible. Don't send large images to a small screen across 3G connections, utilize smaller/lower resolution images.
Consider 'chunking' the survey.	Chunking a survey means breaking it into segments and asking participants to complete the survey one segment at a time. This is also referred to as modularizing (OnDevice Research).
Use shorter, more frequent surveys.	This is a useful approach in general, and particularly true when the sample is from an insight community.

historic data, or with data collected via PCs, if the study is being collected via both mobile device and PC.

The owner of the research project has to make the final call about the risks of losing comparability against the benefits of optimizing the mobile survey.

FITTING QUESTIONS ONTO THE SCREEN

In most cases, mobile survey questions should fit on the screen without the participant having to scroll left and right, and only requiring intuitive up and down scrolling. The questions should be designed either for the smallest screen likely to be used, or the question should be rendered differently on different sized screens.

Many of the processes necessary to make a standard market research question fit on a small screen have to be dealt with by the software platform, but some are in the hands of the researcher.

Fitting to the screen – the researcher's role

Key steps that the researcher can take to help the questionnaire fit on the screen include:

- *Many of the shortening approaches mentioned previously, e.g. shorter questions, shorter answers, and shorter answer lists.*

- *Choosing layouts, skins, designs that maximize the space for the questionnaire, and reduce branding, logos, footers etc.*

- *Checking what options the survey platform offers; sometimes, for example, there may be two or more ways of rendering a grid or a slider – choose the one that works best for the questionnaire being created.*

- *Think about asking questions in a different way. Could that 10-point scale just as easily be a 5-point scale? Could a grid question be asked as five separate questions?*

Fitting to the screen – what the software can do

Many of the processes required to make a standard market research question fit on a small screen are handled by the software. In this case, the researcher may be able to influence this through their choice of survey platform, but if that is not an option, the researcher at least needs to know how the question will be rendered on different devices.

Figures 8.1, 8.2, and 8.3 show comparisons of how the same question might appear on different mobile devices.

Online Survey

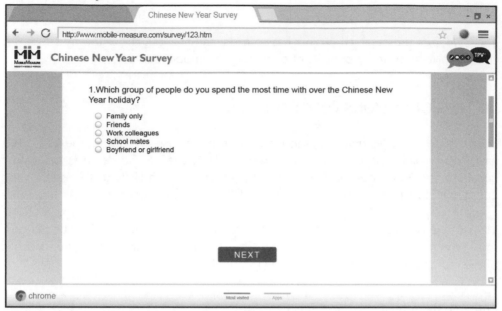

Mobile Web Survey

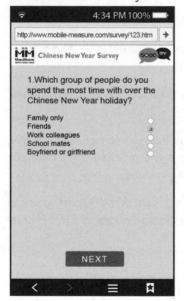

Mobile App Survey

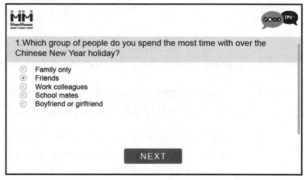

Figure 8.1   Example of a single response question displayed on different devices. Example supplied by MobileMeasure Consultancy Ltd.

Online Survey

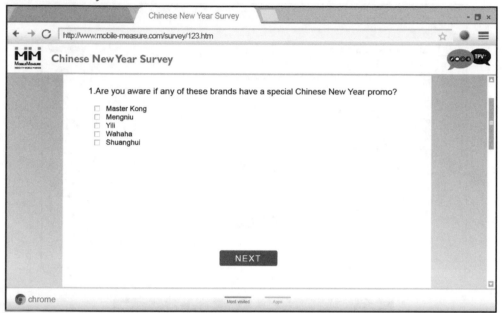

Mobile Web Survey

Mobile App Survey

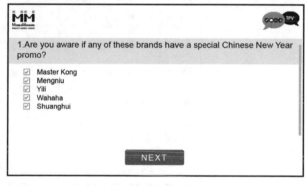

Figure 8.2 Example of a multiple response question displayed on different devices. Example supplied by MobileMeasure Consultancy Ltd.

Online Survey

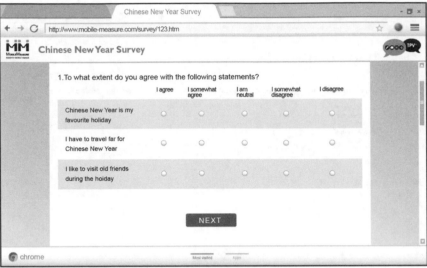

Mobile Web Survey

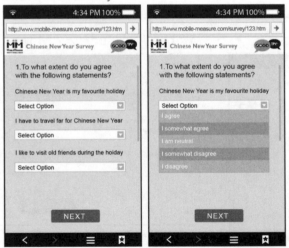

Mobile App Survey

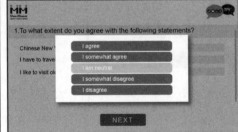

Figure 8.3 Example of a grid question displayed on different devices. Example supplied by MobileMeasure Consultancy Ltd.

FITTING THE STYLE OF THE DEVICE

As well as fitting on the screen, a mobile survey should fit the style of the device. If a survey is on an iPhone it should look and behave like an iPhone app behaves. Most of this is the responsibility of the software, but there are things the researcher should remember to do, such as asking the participant to 'tap' rather than 'click', and 'pinch' to 'zoom' in or out.

FITTING TO THE AVAILABLE BANDWIDTH

Bandwidth is the capacity of a network to transfer data. If your survey includes lots of downloads (e.g. high resolution images or videos) it might run very slowly or even time out for some participants. If the survey is going to be conducted in a market where high speed (e.g. 4G) mobile is the norm (such as Singapore or South Korea) then the survey can make greater use of uploads and downloads. However, in most markets (both developed and less developed) mobile coverage is variable and speeds are often slow.

For the researcher the main way of fitting a survey to the bandwidth is to minimize the number of images, the size of images, and the size of videos that are going to be downloaded as part of the survey. With some platforms the researcher can specify more than one image (e.g. a high and low resolution image) and the system will use the appropriate option.

If an app is being used, or if the survey is being custom built, then some more options are possible, such as downloading media files at the start of the survey, in the background, so they are ready when needed. And, if media uploads are being used, allowing them to be stored on the device until the internet and sufficient bandwidth are available.

DATA ABOUT THE SURVEY PROCESS

'Paradata' is a term used to describe data about the data collection process, and is used to help understand how a survey is working. For example, the survey platform can determine how long surveys are taking, what questions are causing the biggest delays, and where dropouts are occurring.

Mobile devices can provide a considerable amount of information, such as the model and make of the device and in some cases location. This sort of information is called 'passive data' and is covered in the Utilizing Passive Data chapter.

The researcher should determine what paradata can be collected, decide what should be collected, and ensure that permission to collect this data has been obtained. At a minimum, the researcher should normally seek to collect the screen size, the operating system, the browser, and the mobile device model and make.

The data about the data collection process can be used to improve the survey and it will enable the researcher to test for mode effects (described later in this chapter).

MANAGING MOBILE STUDIES

Having designed a mobile survey, the steps in managing the project are:

- *Testing*

- *Launching*

- *Monitor and support*

- *Analysis.*

TESTING

Testing mobile surveys tends to take longer than testing surveys for most other modes, because there are usually more variations among mobile devices. Researchers should test the survey on the key types of devices they expect participants to use.

If the survey doesn't work correctly on some devices then some of the options to consider are:

- *If the problem is caused by just one or two questions, or just one type of question, consider amending the survey to make it work on the devices being used in the study. For example, if slider questions do not work on some devices, with the survey platform being used, consider using scales or open-ended numeric questions.*

- *The problem questions can be asked in a different way for non-compliant questions, for example converting sliders to open-ended numeric questions.*

- *If the questions that do not work are not core questions, consider skipping them for users with non-compliant devices, for example if they relate to photo or video uploads.*

- *If the non-compliant devices are a small part of the target population, identify those devices, avoid inviting them, and if some do start the survey, close the survey in a way that is respectful of the participant.*

It should be noted that asking questions in different ways to different participants, or screening out some devices, or skipping some questions for some participants can introduce biases.

Testing mobile surveys is broadly similar to testing online surveys, but with more variants. The better survey platforms have tools to indicate possible faults and to assess compatibility with different devices and operating systems. Many systems also have options to run thousands of test dummy interviews to check that all parts of the survey are being reached and that the questionnaire works at a superficial level.

One common approach to testing is to test the survey thoroughly on one platform and then test that it works and 'looks right' on the other platforms.

> **TIP:** *A good test is for the researcher to go through the survey as a respondent, checking that the survey does what was intended. The best way of doing this is with a printed copy of the questionnaire in one hand (or on a separate screen) and to repeatedly go through the questionnaire until every element of the questionnaire has been seen and checked.*

Mobile surveys can be tested by launching the survey on a range of devices and checking how they perform. However, many survey platforms have an emulator facility, which allows the survey to be tested on a PC. Different researchers have different views about how good emulators are, so the best advice is to try it and see, and check what your company's view is.

One key best practice in mobile surveys is to use a soft launch. In a soft launch the researcher releases a small number of survey invitations until 20 to 50 completed surveys have been achieved. These completed interviews (and any partial interviews) should be checked to ensure that the survey appears to be working correctly, for example that there is no missing data and that the routing is working as intended.

LAUNCHING

If the mobile project is being handled via a panel company or community, the details of the launch, including the precise time of day of the launch may be out of the individual researcher's control, but if client lists or other sources are being used then the researcher may have more input.

At the moment there is not a large amount of research-on-research about launching mobile online surveys, so most of the advice about using email invitation relates to online research in general. The advice tends to be to send emails at a time when people are likely to read them promptly, not at times of day when emails are going to get lost in inboxes. The research-on-research on mobiles does suggest that mobile users tend to respond faster than participants using a PC, which increases the desirability of sending emails at times of day that make it more likely they will be seen straight away.

Sending emails during the late morning, afternoon, and early evening are all good options, if the email is expected to be read on a mobile. The weekends can be a good time, but avoiding unsuitable times can be important. In a religious country, sending invitations at a time when people are likely to be worshipping is not great; if the research is targeting sports fans, the emails should not be sent when people are going to be involved in events.

If invitations are going to be sent via SMS, then the researcher needs to avoid sending invitations at times of day that are going annoy participants. In many cases this means sending the invitations between 9am and 8pm, during the week, and something like 11am to 8pm at the weekends. However, in countries where there are time differences, such as the USA and Australia, care needs to be taken to either narrow the time bands used, or to know where the participant is and factor this into the timing.

MONITOR AND SUPPORT

As well as testing a survey before it is launched, a survey needs to offer support to participants during fieldwork, particularly if the participants are not familiar with the type of survey being used, for example if a project has moved from online to mobile.

Good practice ideas for support include:

- *Telling participants what devices the survey supports at the invitation stage, telling the participant if they will need to download anything, whether the survey uses sound, and how long the survey is likely to take.*

- *Telling the participant how they can access support (ideally both an email address and a telephone number).*

- *Automatically detecting the hardware being used by the participant and letting them know if there is a problem.*

- *Providing support information and help from within the survey itself; many platforms support this on an individual question level.*

- *Providing an open-ended question at the end of the survey for participants to leave comments and ensuring that open-ended responses are monitored.*

The progress of the fieldwork should be monitored from the initial soft launch until the close of the study. Most survey platforms have a variety of monitoring reports and dashboards. Key items to monitor include:

- *How quickly are participants responding?*

- *Dropout rates?*

- *Are some devices causing more problems than others?*

- *If people are dropping out, what questions are they dropping out on?*

- *The contents of open-ends to see if participants are highlighting problems?*

- *Quotas and top line results.*

- *The use of 'Other', 'Don't Know', and 'None of these', and unanswered questions.*

ANALYSIS

Most aspects of analysing data from mobile are the same as data from other modes, but there are some important specific considerations, including:

- *Looking for differences between the data from one type of device and another, for example between tablets and smartphones, or smartphones and feature phones, or even between iPhone and Android.*

- *If passive data, such as GPS location, has been collected this needs to be combined with the survey data for the analysis.*

- *If multimedia has been collected (for example photos and videos) then this needs to analysed, which is often a much more time consuming process than analysing the survey responses.*

CONVERTING STUDIES TO MOBILE

Converting studies to mobile, as opposed to designing a new mobile study, tends to take two forms. The first case relates to ongoing projects, such as tracking studies. The second case is when a previously fielded survey is re-used, either in its entirety or as the basis of a new survey. Many product and concept tests fall into this second category.

This section of the chapter looks at the issues that confront researchers when converting a study from other modes to mobile. However, the first question that should be addressed is whether a conversion is the right approach, or whether a fresh start, maximizing the benefits of the new mode, is the best option. A change from one mode to another can often be a good opportunity to re-think a project, to trim out sections no longer necessary, and optimize for the new mode.

This section looks at three common conversions:

- *From face-to-face*

- *From CATI*

- *From online via PCs.*

SAMPLE AND MODE EFFECTS

When moving an existing survey from one mode to another (e.g. from face-to-face to mobile) there are two major factors that need to be taken into account:

1.   **Mode effects.** For example, a participant may answer the same question one way when asked by an interviewer but in a different way when the survey is self-administered, with no interviewer present.

2.   **Sample effects.** One mode may attract different types of participants than another, creating different results. For example, a central location, face-to-face study will often find it easy to recruit people whose lives are less busy and who shop in person, whilst a mobile study might increase the proportion of busy people, including online shoppers, but it may be less attractive to the over-sixties.

Mode effects and sample effects do not mean the information is necessarily better or worse, just that it is different. For example, two reasons to use mobile surveys are to broaden the range of people who can be reached (a sample effect), and to interview people 'in the moment', when the experience is fresh (a mode effect).

Differences between one mode and another do not imply one is better than the other, but they do mean that it can be harder to compare the results, and differences can cause problems for end-clients, for example if benchmarks or norms are in place.

Whenever a new mode is used, the researcher should check for mode and sample effects, and this is true when mobile surveys are being used as a replacement for another mode (or alongside another mode).

The process of testing and dealing with mode and sample effects is covered in market research methodology text books, so the description here is simply a quick note of the data that needs to be collected and the elements of looking for these effects:

1.   The individual data records need to have their mode attached. If some of the data was collected on feature phones and some on smartphones, this needs to be recorded.

2.   Look for sample effects first. In this example, the researcher might look to see if the demographics of the feature phone owners were different to the smartphone owners. If there are differences, then there are sample effects.

3.   Control for sample differences and see if there are differences by mode.

If sample and mode effects are found the researcher and research owner have to decide what the best strategy is. Common options include:

- *Changing the sampling process to re-balance the data.*

- *Weighting the data to change the sample balance.*

- *Modelling the data to make it comparable.*

- *Accepting and noting that there has been a change.*

CONVERTING FROM FACE-TO-FACE

Typical reasons to convert from face-to-face to mobile include:

- *Faster: face-to-face can be very slow.*

- *Cheaper: face-to-face is often an expensive option.*

- *Better: this can mean quality control, but in the case of mobile it often means: 'in the moment', including passive data, using multimedia, and reaching a wider range of people in a wider range of situations.*

Mode effects converting from face-to-face

The most likely mode effect when converting a study from face-to-face to mobile is the shift from interviewer administered surveys to self-administered surveys. Interviewers do more than just ask questions. They explain the survey, motivate the participant, spot confusion, and report problems back to the researcher or research agency. However, the interviewer can also make it more likely that respondents will offer socially acceptable responses, i.e. give answers that present themselves in a positive light. The research-on-research has shown this to be a genuine concern.

A second major mode effect can arise because questions often appear differently in a face-to-face survey than in a mobile survey. In a paper-based, face-to-face survey, a show card may contain a large number of items, for example several photos. On a mobile device the participant tends to look at items one at a time, which sometimes results in changes in the data. For example, in prompted recall, showing items one at a time or in small groupings tends to elicit higher levels of recall than showing long lists (Witt 2000).

Another potential mode effect is the environment where the survey is conducted. In a face-to-face survey the participant is not doing anything else, they are typically at home or at a central location. A participant taking part in a mobile survey might be in a retail outlet, at work, on a bus, in bed, watching TV, and so on. One of the perceived benefits of mobile studies is that they can catch people 'in the moment', for example when buying or using a product. However, a benefit is also a difference, and this difference is a potentially an important mode effect. Although this issue remains a concern, there is no research-on-research that suggests it is a major issue.

Sample effects converting from face-to-face

Sample effects refer to different sorts of people being researched. One of the perceived advantages of mobile market research is that it can reach people that more traditional market research modes do not reach. With face-to-face surveys, the interviews can only take place when the interviewer and participant can be brought together in the same place. This tends to be between 9am and 8pm, in participants' homes or in central locations, in relatively densely populated areas.

Mobile studies are not limited to just those people who are in certain locations or to those free at specific times of day. However, mobile studies are only going to reach people who have the right type of device and who are willing to take part in a survey via their mobile device.

The type of people who can be reached by a mobile survey will depend on the country, the target group, and the type of mobile study being run. If the study is online and only available to smartphone owners the sample will be different from one where web-enabled feature phones are included, which in turn will be different from one based on SMS, where any type of phone can be used.

CONVERTING FROM CATI

Computer Assisted Telephone Interviewing (CATI) combines interviewers and a centralized computer system for the questionnaire. Amongst the common reasons for moving from CATI to mobile surveys are: to reduce costs and to access the specific benefits of mobile, such as 'in the moment' and passive data.

Mode effects

As is the case when converting from face-to-face interviews to mobile self-completion, the main mode effect is the removal of the interviewer. This reduces interviewer-related bias, but it also removes the ability of the interviewer to help and motivate participants and to help identify problems with the survey.

In addition, participants may also interpret questions differently when they see them displayed on a screen as compared to hearing them read over the telephone.

Sample effects

In many markets CATI can reach a much wider range of the population than can be reached with a mobile survey, particularly a mobile survey relying on the internet. This is partly to do with the incidence of internet-enabled phones, but it also reflects differences in sampling. Mobile online surveys will often use panels, lists, and communities as their sample source, all of which are a subset of the population. CATI can use RDD that gives it a much wider sample source.

In these situations, a shift from CATI to mobile surveys can create differences in the composition of the sample which can create differences in the results.

CONVERTING FROM ONLINE SURVEYS DESIGNED FOR PCS

From a global perspective, clients spend more money on online surveys than any other data collection mode. However, in terms of the number of interviews, and in many countries, either CATI or face-to-face is the dominant method, with online dominating in the more developed of markets, such as Japan, the USA, Germany, and Australia.

The key reasons for converting an online survey to a mobile survey are:

1. To create device agnostic research that can be completed on both mobiles and PCs.

2. To widen the range of people who can be reached, especially in countries where online internet access via PCs is substantially less than via mobile devices.

3. To take advantage of the benefits of specifically mobile research, including 'in the moment' research, capturing multimedia, and utilizing passive data.

Mode effects

As noted earlier, a key consideration when moving from online surveys designed for PCs to mobile devices is the reduction in the size of the screen (sometimes referred to as 'screen real estate'), especially when the mobile device is a phone. When dealing with feature phones, the difference in how questions appear on a PC and a mobile device is larger.

Another potential mode effect may arise because of the change in context/location in where surveys are taken. For example, taking part in a survey in a coffee bar or on a crowded train might produce differences compared with sitting at a PC (which usually means at home or in the office).

The Research-on-Research chapter includes a number of projects that have specifically looked for mode effects when comparing online and mobile. In general, differences appear to be few, but some important effects have been shown. For example, multiselect grids appear to produce higher scores on mobile than on PC. More information is available in that chapter.

Sample effects

Most online surveys are conducted with people recruited from lists, for example, online access panels, client lists, or online communities. This tends to be the same for most mobile surveys, although at present most of the lists for mobile research are not as large or as well organized.

However, there are still likely to be sample effects when moving from online via PC to mobile. One of the reasons for using mobile surveys is to reach people on the move and to reach people who have been 'turned off' conventional research approaches – both of which imply sample differences.

In markets where more people are accessing the internet from mobile devices than from PCs, and more generally as mobile sample suppliers develop their business, it is likely the sample differences between PC online and mobile will grow, with mobile often being potentially more representative.

MIXED-MODE SURVEYS

Mixed-mode, or hybrid, surveys are surveys where the researcher intends for some participants to answer the survey using one mode, such as in a face-to-face interview, and for others to use another mode, such as a smartphone. Mixed-mode can mean as few as two modes, but it can also refer to studies utilizing many modes. The term 'mixed-mode' can also be used for studies where participants use one mode during one stage of the survey and another mode at another stage, for example a CATI interview could be followed by a mobile survey.

Mixed-mode is the subject of a whole chapter later in the book, so this section will focus on the core items that relate to designing and managing mobile surveys.

OPTIMIZING THE PLATFORMS OR MINIMIZING THE DIFFERENCES

One key choice that needs to be made when designing for mixed-mode is whether to optimize the survey for each mode or to minimize the differences across all modes. A similar decision was covered earlier in the chapter when looking at transitioning questionnaires from one mode to another. There is no right or wrong answer to the choice of optimizing for mobile or minimizing differences. The researcher must choose the best solution for the specific research being conducted, aware that both approaches have potential shortcomings.

Optimizing for specific platforms

If a mixed-mode study is to be optimized for specific platforms, the tablet version might utilize a larger screen. For example, the respondent might be shown a list of all the brands on one screen, perhaps with logos as well as names shown. The smartphone version might simplify the look, and show the brands (with or without logos) in groups of say five, over several screens. The feature phone version might show the brands one at a time, without a logo.

In this simple example, the use of logos and text on the tablet might increase the number of brands recalled, but showing them in a larger group might reduce the number recalled. The feature phone's lack of logos might reduce recall, but asking the brands one at a time might increase the recall.

In an extreme case of tailoring to the platform, some questions might be skipped altogether for some modes. For example, an online study designed to be conducted via a PC might take 30 minutes and include interactive graphics. The mobile version might comprise only the most critical questions, avoid interactive graphics, and take only eight minutes to complete.

When surveys are optimized for different devices, the researcher should analyse the data carefully to determine if there are differences that appear to be caused by mode effects (the impact of the way the questions are asked) or sample effects (different modes can attract different people). If there are differences, the researcher should attempt to remove them or report the data separately.

Minimizing the differences

If the researcher decides to minimize the differences between the modes then the first step is to find out which mode is the most limited. This approach is sometimes referred to as 'the lowest common denominator'. If smartphones are going to be used, then this will require the online survey to be simplified to ensure it looks and behaves in the same way across platforms. If feature phones are going to be used, then a PC survey will have to be considerably restrained, to make the experience broadly comparable.

The downside of minimizing the differences is that the simplified online survey may remove features that might produce better data. For example, in a choice task using four or more 'cards' on the screen may give the best results, but such a design is not possible if the research is designed for a smartphone. Choice tasks based on two options per task may work on all the devices, but it may produce data that is less accurate than the four choice option.

'UNINTENTIONAL' MOBILE RESEARCH

As reported elsewhere in this book, a growing number of participants in online surveys are choosing to complete surveys on mobile devices, which, in effect, turns many (perhaps most) online surveys into mixed-mode surveys.

Researchers conducting online surveys should either accommodate the mobile participant or seek to exclude them. The trend in most research is towards platform agnostic research, leaving the choice to the participants. However, for some mobile projects there are good reasons to exclude PCs, for example when using location-based 'in the moment' type approaches.

GOOD PRACTICES WITH RESTRICTING ACCESS TO AN ONLINE SURVEY

If the researcher determines that some devices are not suitable for a particular survey then the following advice should be followed:

1. Tell the participant at the invitation stage (and repeat at the start of the survey) the limitations in terms of what devices can be used. For example, whether it is smartphone only, or PC and tablet only, or suitable for any device capable of connecting to and browsing the internet.

2. Use software that detects the device being used for the survey and that checks it meets the minimum criteria for the study.

3. Do not describe the participant's device as unsuitable for the survey; describe the survey as unsuitable for their device.

4. Consider sending the invitations via SMS instead of email if the survey is intended for phones.

SURVEYS AND APPS

There are a variety of reasons to use an app for surveys, instead of an online/browser-based mobile study, including:

*   *Being able to trigger the survey in more ways, including geofencing, timed alerts, and signals from the researcher.*

*   *Being able to access and utilize passive data.*

*   *Not having to rely on the internet being available.*

The case for and against apps is considered more fully in the chapter entitled The Technology of Mobile Market Research, along with more material on working with apps.

Designing for Mobile

The agency, MMR, needed to research out of home breakfast habits in the UK, and wanted to conduct it in the moment, which meant mobile. Key items in their implementation were:

- *An online survey was used to profile the participants on key behavioural and attitudinal measures.*

- *An app was used for the 'in the moment' research, to ensure that the data collection would be always on and respond quickly.*

- *The participants kept a breakfast diary for seven days, using the app at meal time.*

- *By providing extensive support for participants, 53% of those eligible downloaded the app and 83% of these completed all seven tasks.*

- *Initiatives included phased incentives (making it worthwhile to do all seven tasks) and push notifications each morning to remind participants.*

The survey was kept very short, asking key details only, such as where they were, who they were with, and what they ate.

MMR utilized the benefits of mobile by asking participants to take a photo of their meal, ensuring they knew exactly what people had chosen and not what they claimed, and also the ability it gives for people to complete the survey in the moment, maximizing data quality and providing the ability for people to accurately convey how they actually felt at that specific point in time.

Working with their supplier, MobileMeasure, the data entry was modified to make it intuitive and fast for mobile users, for example using simple taps instead of the drag and drop used in their online version. The bullseye data entry shown in Figure 8.4, based on using phones in landscape mode, simply requires the participant to tap once on the screen, at which point the next statement is displayed.

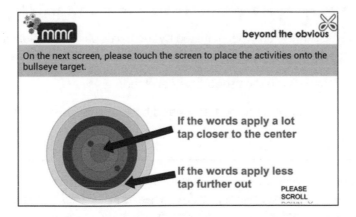

Figure 8.4   Bullseye data entry (note actual screen is in colour)

MMR's CEO Mat Lintern is clear that when creating a mobile solution the benefits of the new mode should be maximized and makes the following recommendation: 'When mobilising an existing system redesign it from a mobile user's perspective and then that becomes the new standard.'

A longer version of this material is available online, on the book's companion website, at http://www.handbookofmobilemarketresearch.com

Surveys conducted via apps tend to be organized in one of two ways:

1. Each survey uses a separate app.

2. Using a survey app that participants (often members of panels or communities) have already downloaded.

The second option, when available, is the easier and usually cheaper option. The first option typically requires more effort in recruitment and support, but if the research has special requirements, or in situations where no preloaded app is available, it may be the only option.

Most of the issues discussed in the earlier parts of this chapter, for example fitting the study to the screen and operating system, and the tension between optimizing and compatibility, are issues that need addressing for surveys delivered via apps. However, with apps there are often more choices, which means there are more things that need to be decided.

Researchers should consider the following points when deciding which survey app to use:

1. Should the survey be available when the internet is not available?

2. Should the survey run when initiated by the participant, or should it be triggered in other ways (e.g. signals from researcher, timer, or location)?

3. What, if any, passive data should be collected?

4. How is the data going to be transmitted back to the researcher?

TIP: *Replicating designs from online directly to mobile can affect survey completion times and user experience adversely. Redesigning existing question types to suit mobile reduces survey completion times and improves user experience.*

USING THIRD-PARTY APPS

Working with apps can be more complex than working with online browser-based surveys. Creating a survey via an app tends to mean being closer to the workings of devices and operating systems. Because of the potential complexity, some agencies prefer to work with mobile market research app specialists when conducting this sort of research, especially if they are producing customized or one off solutions.

Access panels that have their own app already installed on their members' mobile devices are another way of outsourcing some of the technical issues associated with using an app.

WHICH IS BEST, APP OR BROWSER?

There is no general right answer to this question. In many cases, if the research is possible with a browser-based approach, then that will be the cheapest, quickest, and most efficient way of conducting the study. However, that may change as more panels and communities build up collections of members who have already downloaded a survey app, who are already incentivized to use it, and are familiar with using it.

The most common reason to use an app at the moment is when it provides a better solution than a browser-based solution, or where there isn't a browser-based solution. Most mCAPI projects where interviewers use mobile devices to collect face-to-face interviews use apps. Most projects using location information, such as GPS or Bluetooth beacons, use apps. Most diary or ethnographic type projects where participants have to enter data repeatedly, irrespective of whether the internet is available, use apps.

SURVEYS AND FEATURE PHONES

Adding feature phones to the range of mobile devices a survey supports increases the complexity and the probability that the survey will look broadly similar across all devices is reduced. There are three ways of conducting surveys via feature phones:

1.   Surveys with web-enabled feature phones, using the internet.

2.   Surveys via programs downloaded onto feature phones.

3.   Survey using most types of phones, not just the web-enabled ones.

Downloading programs onto feature phones is a specialist area and beyond the scope of an introductory book like this. Researchers looking to undertake this sort of research should approach a specialist agency, one with both technical and market research experience.

Surveys with feature phones that are not connected to the web are again a specialist field, utilizing SMS, sometimes USSD, and possibly IVR (interactive voice response). This approach is also beyond the scope of this book, but some of the issues are discussed in the chapter on International Mobile Research. Many of the projects that use feature phone friendly approaches for their data collection also use innovative methods of incentivizing participants, such as paying them with airtime, automatically. Researchers wanting to utilize these approaches should seek experienced agencies to partner with.

In the less developed markets, online mobile surveys are often completed by participants using web-enabled feature phones (rather than smartphones), and this is expected to be the case for several more years. There are a number of companies who specialize in this sector and many of the survey platforms are capable of rendering some or all of their question types on web-enabled feature phones.

Researchers planning to use web-enabled feature phones to allow them to conduct mobile research in an international study should keep two key factors in mind:

1.   If some participants are completing the study on smartphones and some on a feature phones, the questionnaire can look quite different, which may introduce bias.

2.   Different countries have different rules and expectations about things like incentives, so working with partners who know each market is vital, where knowing a market includes understanding the technology and the research environment.

OTHER WAYS TO LAUNCH/INITIATE SURVEYS

Most of this chapter has focused on surveys running in conjunction with access panels, client lists, and insight communities; and in the context of a standard survey platform. However, there are a variety of other ways of sourcing sample and of initiating surveys, and these other routes require additional steps during the design and management of the survey.

Additional ways of launching/initiating surveys include:

1.   By publicizing the survey URL or QR code. This can be via a wide range of routes, such as: advertising, on products, on shopping or till receipts, in mailings, websites, and social media.

2.   Through popups on mobile sites, or simply invitations from mobile sites.

3.   As part of online river sampling such as RIWI.

4.   Via SMS invitations, in cases where mobile telephone numbers are known.

5.   From embedded apps, either embedded on the phone, or as part of another app (e.g. as part of a game).

6.   As part of a geofencing marketing campaign, where shoppers have downloaded an app to help them shop or to collect coupons, for example ShopKick.

7.   Via conventional market research recruitment channels, such as telephone, face-to-face, postal, and so on.

SURVEY DESIGN

When participants are not recruited from mainstream research channels, i.e. they are not from a panel or a research community, they are usually less familiar with the look and style of online surveys. This means the survey design should be welcoming, engaging, and intuitive. Most researchers believe that participants recruited from these non-standard routes are even more sensitive than regular participants to survey length, making the case for shorter surveys even stronger.

CUSTOM-BUILT SOLUTIONS

Most breakthroughs in mobile market research have come from custom-built solutions. The term 'custom-built' covers a wide range of situations. At one extreme it means adding some custom code to an existing product or platform, at the other end it means creating a solution from scratch. In general, custom-built solutions cost more, take longer, and may be 'riskier' (riskier than a platform solution that may have been used tens of thousands of times before your project uses it).

The benefits of custom-built solutions are that they can access more of the features of the mobile device and they do not constrain the research to fit what the platforms offer.

With custom-built solutions, many of the design principles discussed in this chapter still apply, keeping the survey short and intuitive, making a decision on the balance between mobile optimization and comparability with other modes, and thinking about the sorts of mobile devices that the participants are likely to use.

When working with designers and software engineers it is a good idea to agree three key conditions:

1.   The research tool should comply with market research guidelines. For example, any data collected must be in the context of informed consent. Software engineers not familiar with the research industry may find it natural to collect background information, perhaps to enable them to optimize their design.

2.   Check that the survey includes market research essentials. These essentials include: adding an 'other' or 'none of these' to response lists, the ability to randomize answer lists, and the ability to branch depending on the answers to earlier questions. Your app designer may not know about market research, so they may not factor these features in.

3.   Ensure that the data that is produced is in a standard market research format or can easily be exported in a standard format, for example something that can be read into a spreadsheet or statistical software package.

SUMMARY

Mobile market research is still a developing and evolving field, which means that there are few settled and agreed guidelines about how mobile surveys should be designed and managed. Whilst many organizations talk about 'best practices', these are typically a set of rules of thumb that appear to work at the moment – but they should not be taken as definitive guides. Indeed, even the notes in this chapter reflect a moment in time, and should be treated more as a set of suggestions and issues to consider, rather than as a prescription for how mobile surveys must be done.

The general themes that do appear to be broadly agreed, in the area of mobile surveys, when giving advice to people new to the area are:

- *Be clear about why mobile surveys are being used. Is it for speed, cost, being 'in the moment', to capture passive data, to reach a wider audience?*

- *Is the study going to be mobile only, or part of a platform agnostic, mixed-mode solution?*

- *Is the research going to be browser-based or app-based?*

- *Mobile surveys should be intuitive, engaging, and short.*

- *A conscious decision should be made about the balance between mobile optimization and maximizing comparability – comparability with other modes and comparability with historical benchmarks.*

- *Changing mode to mobile surveys is likely to make some difference to the results; this should be flagged as a possibility at the proposal stage and looked for at the analysis stage.*

- *Working with a standard survey platform is likely to be quicker, easier, and more reliable than a custom-built solution. Working with custom-built solutions allows more access to the functions of a mobile phone and avoids the need to fit the research to the constraints of the software solution.*

PART III

The Methods and Applications of Mobile Market Research

This part of the book looks at the different methods that are used to implement mobile market research projects and finishes with a review of international mobile market research.

Part III covers:

PART II

The Methods and Applications of Niche Market Research

9 mCAPI – Mobile Computer Assisted Personal Interviewing

INTRODUCTION

Mobile CAPI is a form of face-to-face interviewing where the interviewer uses a mobile device as part of the interviewing process, and is a form of CAPI. CAPI stands for 'Computer Assisted Personal Interviewing', a term that arose in the 1980s, along with growth in the use of PCs for market research. Mobile CAPI, or just mCAPI, refers to the extension of this method to mobile devices.

Although PC-based CAPIs share of data collection spend is in decline (especially in the developed research markets), mobile CAPI, or mCAPI, has been growing, as a niche in the more developed markets and as a replacement for paper questionnaires in the less developed markets. Research that is defined as mCAPI is typically conducted using smartphones, tablets, or a combination of the two. However, feature phones are also used for mCAPI, and some researchers describe laptop or netbook research as mCAPI, especially if they want to stress the mobile element.

The definition of mCAPI adopted in this book covers interviews where a survey is conducted on mobile devices that are not already owned by the respondent. mCAPI can be conducted with the interviewer holding the device, the participant holding the device, or a combination of the two.

THE BENEFITS OF mCAPI

The core strengths of mCAPI are:

- *Not depending on respondents having suitable devices of their own.*

- *Being more secure than transferring material to participants' devices.*

- *Being consistent, in terms of what each participant sees and hears.*

Compared with online, PC-based CAPI, and CATI modes, mCAPI has (like other forms of mobile research) the advantage of being more 'in the moment'. For example, interviewers can interview participants in retail outlets, at events, in planes, on trains, and so on.

In less developed markets, the key driver of the growth of mCAPI is the desire to replace paper questionnaires in face-to-face interviews. The desire to move from paper questionnaires is driven by the same reasons that CAPI made inroads in the 1980s and 1990s, in particular:

- *Eliminating paper, printing, transportation, and data punching.*

- *Improving data quality, data validation, and the removal of data punching errors.*

- *Improving turnaround times, project management, and quality control procedures.*

HISTORICAL NOTE

CAPI was a major mode of data collection in the 1980s and 1990s, and was associated with several advances in data collection, for example Adaptive Conjoint Analysis (developed by Sawtooth Software). PC-based CAPI was sometimes administered by the interviewer, but it was often conducted so that the respondent entered their own responses into the computer.

From about 2000, CAPI was in decline as a data collection mode in developed markets, because of the growth of online data collection, but saw growth in developing markets.

Currently, the term 'mCAPI' refers to the use of phones and tablets. However, the term has been around for a number of years. In 2003 Quirks had a two-part series looking at mCAPI, based on handheld computers. In the article, the author claimed that the term 'mCAPI' dated back to the 1980s, but stated that mCAPI was held back by the lack of success of handheld computers, until the launch of the Palm Pilot in 1996 (Weisberg 2003).

CASE STUDIES

In this part of the chapter, two case studies are used to highlight the sorts of research needs and opportunities that market researchers are tackling with mCAPI. The first case study looks at the UK, one of the more developed markets. The second looks at using mCAPI in India, one of the economically and technically less developed markets.

Using Mobile Research to Implement One of the UK's Largest Voices of the Customer Programmes

Tesco is the UK's largest retailer and one of the largest in the world. Its history is in grocery retailing but in recent years it has expanded into general retailing, and internationally. In 2012, Tesco announced it was going to invest £1 billion (about US $1.5 billion) in improving its UK shopper experience. To support this expenditure, Tesco needed a customer experience programme to monitor customer satisfaction, at store level, in ways that facilitated action.

Previously Tesco had used a mystery shopping programme, but it was felt the focus should not be on specific standards, but that it should be on customers. And the best way to get customer feedback about the shopping experience was face-to-face, at the stores themselves.

The scale of the project that UK agency Marketing Sciences was commissioned to deliver was enormous:

- *100 interviews per store at over 950 Tesco stores, over a two-week period each month including a number in rural and hard to reach locations.*

- *The store level reports were needed two weeks after fieldwork, available to store managers.*

The solution was to use tablets loaded with research apps from Confirmit, meeting the following criteria:

- *Battery life that lasted a full interviewer shift.*

- *Light enough for an interviewer to hold for about six hours.*

- *Cost effective.*

- *The screen needed to be as big and bright as possible (consistent with being as lightweight as needed and with a good battery life).*

- *Not too attractive to potential thieves!*

- *Able to run offline (when no internet available).*

- *Capable of handling questionnaire updates and live messaging.*

To get the project up and running, over 300 interviewers were trained, across different locations around the country. Once the system was live, 1900 shifts needed to be logged each month. If the weather was bad, or interviewers were ill, alternatives needed to be put in place immediately.

The quality control procedures included the following:

- *Were the interviews done on the right day, at the right time, and across the full shift?*

- *Did interviewers take any strange or long breaks during a shift?*

- *How did the patterns of interviews compare with those of other interviewers?*

- *GPS could be switched on to show where interviews were conducted, but battery drain was a concern in these cases.*

The dashboards and reports provide information that is local, regional, and national, and provide a common language between store managers and those further up the chain of command.

By November 2013 the project had collected over 1.5 million interviews and saved 581 trees, by not using 24 tons of paper. For the client it meant getting very close to customers, at every store, with a rapid delivery of meaningful results. For Marketing Sciences it meant delivering one of the UK's largest voices of the customer programmes.

Thanks are extended to Tesco and Marketing Sciences for providing this case study.

---

mCAPI in India – Improving the Efficiency of Data Collection

This case study looks at how Indian market research agency Market Xcel are using German mCAPI supplier cluetec GmbH's mCAPI product, mQuest, to convert research from paper-based face-to-face surveys to mCAPI. In 2013 Market Xcel estimated that 90% of interviews in India (a country of over 1 billion people) were being conducted via paper-based surveys.

Market Xcel's initial move was to buy 450 internet-enabled tablets, and to equip them with cluetec's mQuest. The benefits of mCAPI included the following:

- *It provided a focal point for their training programme.*

- *It removed the need to post questionnaires to interviewers at regional centres.*

- *The problem of gathering and punching the completed surveys was eliminated.*

- *GPS and time/date stamps to track and validate the interviewing process.*

- *Real-time reporting via a web interface – something not possible with paper questionnaires.*

- *Photographs were uploaded, not only as part of the research, but also as a part of the quality control process.*

- *Centralized translation of questionnaires (Market Xcel are using 22 languages within India).*

- *The use of more sophisticated surveys, for example, routing, piping, and adaptive processes.*

The net effect has been faster turnarounds and better quality control processes. The processes outlined here deliver to face-to-face research in India benefits that technology has brought to more developed markets.

Thanks are extended to both cluetec GmbH and Market Xcel Data Matrix Pvt. Ltd. for sharing this case study. A fuller version of the case study is available from the book's companion website: http://www.handbookofmobilemarketresearch.com.

mCAPI CONSIDERATIONS

If a research project is going to use mCAPI then there are a number of considerations to review, in order to be able to select the right solution. In this context, the considerations include issues such as: smartphones or tablets, whether to use apps, what software to use, and the specific devices to choose.

This section reviews the key considerations and provides help and advice. Although this section lays out the considerations in a linear pattern, the considerations are all integrated, the choice of device will influence the software, and the choice of software will influence the choice of device.

HOW WILL THE INTERVIEWS CONNECT TO THE INTERNET?

There are three basic models of how mobile CAPI operates, in terms of connection to the internet and to the researcher's data files:

1. The device is connected throughout the interview to the internet, usually via the telephone network, Wi-Fi, or some combination of the two.

2. The device is connected periodically to the internet, to upload completed interviews and download project information and updates to questionnaires or quotas.

3. The device is not connected to the internet during the project. The collected data is stored on the mobile device and transferred periodically, for example to a PC via a cable.

The issues connected with each of these three choices are outlined next.

Connected to the internet, throughout the interview

If the device is connected to the internet throughout the interviewing process (with sufficient reliability and bandwidth), then the researcher has the option to use web-based software, as opposed to app-based software. Being connected to the internet throughout the process makes it easier to control quotas and to update the survey and/or instructions. However, assuming that the internet will remain available and reliable can be a problem in many cases, and it can run down the device's battery more quickly than running in standalone mode.

If the research plans to utilize Wi-Fi, the researcher needs to ensure that this will be possible. Wi-Fi connections are not always reliable, even in developed economies. For example, many conference organizers have found that the Wi-Fi connectivity they have purchased lets them down when all the delegates try to access it at the same time. If the connection to the internet is via the mobile telephone network then the researcher's choice of device will be narrower, and the costs may be higher for both the device and the data transfer. Note that the cheapest devices are often tablets that do not have a SIM, and which connect to the internet via Wi-Fi.

Connecting to the internet periodically

If the connection to the internet is periodic, then the survey software will need to reside on the mobile device, and the device will normally need to be able to store more than one interview. The survey data will be transferred when there is an internet connection, and updates can be downloaded at the same time. The researcher should keep in mind that until the data has been transferred it is at risk from loss, theft, and/or corruption. In some cases the devices are only connected to the internet twice, once at the start and once at the end of the project. However, this maximizes the risks of losing data and minimizes the opportunities for centralized oversight.

Not connecting the mobile devices to the internet

If the device is not going to be connected to the internet, then it is even more important to get everything right first time, and to think about how issues like quota control are going to be achieved. As with periodic connection to the internet, the researcher should take into account the risk of losing data through the loss, theft, and/or corruption of devices.

WHETHER TO USE AN APP?

A large proportion of mCAPI is app-based because of concerns about whether an internet connection is going to be reliably available. The benefits of using an app are that the internet is not required to be available all the time, the system can access more features of the mobile device, battery life can be better, and the system can be more responsive (e.g. no delays whilst questions and media are downloaded).

The main negatives associated with an app are the need to install it on the devices (but this is less of an issue with interviewers than with consumers), the loss of control (e.g. ability to change the questionnaire and quotas), and the reduced security of not having the data transferred to the researcher in real time.

SMARTPHONE OR TABLET?

Although it is possible to use feature phones for mCAPI, it is increasingly unnecessary to do this, due to the falling cost of Android-based phones. The question facing researchers tends to be 'tablet or smartphone?'

The question of smartphone or tablet is being made even more complex by the arrival of 'phablets' (larger than a traditional smartphone, smaller than a traditional tablet). Key questions that researchers should consider are shown in Table 9.1.

Table 9.1 Key questions that researchers should consider

Question	Consideration
Does it need to be a phone?	Phones tend to cost more than tablets and can be more tempting to thieves. A tablet can seem more 'work like' to both interviewers and participants.
Is a larger screen needed?	If the research involves showing several items together, as in some discrete choice modelling projects, or if advertisements or videos need to be shown, then the larger screen of a tablet may be desirable or even essential.
	If both interviewer and participant need to be able to read the screen, then a tablet will often be the better option.
How portable does the device need to be?	A short interview on a table or at a desk is equally convenient on a tablet or phone. But if the interviewer is using the device whilst moving, perhaps by interviewing shoppers, a larger tablet can become a burden, favouring phones or smaller tablets.
	When the larger screen of the tablet is felt to be a necessity, some researchers have utilized shoulder straps or similar devices to help carry the tablet in a convenient way.
What functions do you need?	Many phones have a range of services that are not present on most tablets, including SMS. If the research would benefit from using these, then a suitable phone or phablet would be the best option.
Will a specific device increase cooperation rates more than others?	Some researchers have found that the prestige or status of asking people to use, for example, an iPad has helped increase the willingness of people to take part in research projects.

CHOICE OF SOFTWARE

There are a wide range of issues that will influence the choice of software, including the ones shown in Table 9.2.

Table 9.2   Issues that influence software choice

Topic	Issues to consider
Functionality:	A list of functions required should be created, including items such as: scripting, testing, project management, and question types supported.
Languages:	Does the software support the interview languages needed, including character sets? In locations with multiple languages, can the survey readily switch between languages?
	Also, what languages does the software support for administration? Many systems that can interview in a large number of languages may only support English at the administration and project management level.
Cost:	The key issue with cost is the total cost, either the total cost of a specific project, or the likely cost over a period of time, for example a year.
	The total cost is likely to be some combination of licence, cost per interview, cost of support and training, and possibly the cost for transferring and consolidating the results onto a central server.
Training and support:	There are two key training and support issues to consider:
	1. The training and support for the research team, i.e. learning how to use the system. For example, how to script surveys, how to deploy them, and how to gather the completed information.
	2. The training and support needed for the interviewers using the system.
Security:	Client and respondent data needs to be kept secure. With mobile devices, data security can be under threat if devices are lost or stolen, or if data transmission is compromised. Software solutions differ in the extent to which they protect the data, for example through encryption.
Customizing:	Can the software be customized to add extra features that might be required?
Scalability and deployment speed:	Software solutions differ in how quickly they can be deployed in new situations, and they differ in their ability to be scaled up to larger projects, or projects in multiple countries.

CHOOSING A SPECIFIC DEVICE

Whilst it is possible to run mCAPI projects with a variety of devices, most researchers prefer to have all the interviewers using the same device, to make the project easier to manage. This raises the question of which device to use. The section looks at key questions related to the selection of suitable mobile devices.

Will you have to buy the devices?

If the field partner already has mobile devices, then usually the best choice is to use those. If the project will require devices to be bought or rented, then the cost, portability, risk of loss or theft, and the ability to insure the devices will all have an impact on the selection of the best option.

Choice of brand and model

The best option is to adopt a single device (form, brand, and model) for all of the interviewers. A single device makes training, support, and project design easier. The first elements in the choice process are the form (tablet, phablet, or phone), the software, and the operating system.

The next considerations should be ease of use, ease of replacement (some will go missing), lifespan (tablets and phones can be prone to damage), and battery life. The cost of the devices is a major consideration, irrespective of who will be buying/owning the devices.

Which operating system?

The operating system should normally be determined after deciding on research software, not before. The only common situation where this is done the other way round is when devices are already available, and the operating system on them is taken as a given.

When thinking about operating systems the version can be as much of an issue as the type of operating system. A software option might run on current versions of Windows Phone, Apple iOS, and Google Android, but it might not run on older versions of the operating system.

> **TIP:** *Even newly purchased mobile devices can have relatively old versions of Android on them, which can create either compatibility problems or a lengthy updating process. Researchers should check that the software will run on the installed operating system.*

Battery and charging considerations

In choosing mobile devices and when designing a project, the researcher needs to consider the likely battery life of the mobile devices being used and plan for how they are to be recharged – something that is typically the responsibility of the field company. If each interviewer has a single device, then they can probably be left to organize its regular charging. If one person is looking after numerous devices, it might make sense to acquire a device that will charge several mobile devices at once – some of these come in the form of a case or chest that will also provide some security against theft. Providing extra batteries for mobile devices can help prevent running out of power during fieldwork.

PROJECT CONSIDERATIONS

Successful face-to-face research projects require good coordination between the researcher and the interviewers, typically through the medium of the fieldwork provider. This is just as true of mCAPI as it is for more traditional forms of face-to-face research. Additionally, with mCAPI there are some specifically mobile issues to consider.

Study design

Most of the design issues for mCAPI projects are the same as for other forms of mobile quantitative research. For example, the questions need to fit on the screen, be intuitive, and load quickly. If the study requires the participants to enter their own data, it needs to be even more intuitive than a typical mobile study since the person entering the data may never have used a tablet or a smartphone before.

In terms of study length, mCAPI behaves like other forms of face-to-face interviewing. Intercept interviews, for example as people leave a retail outlet, are likely to need to be short; scheduled in-home interviews can often be longer.

Since mCAPI is using an interviewer the researcher should seek to maximize the benefits of the mode, for example asking the interviewer to provide feedback on the study and on participants.

Training

Unless a research project is using a field company that has already been trained in the specific mCAPI solution being used, it will be necessary to train the interviewers. In a central location test, this can often be achieved via a central briefing and training session. However, if a project is being administered nationally, or internationally, some form of devolved or remote training will be necessary. One aid to distance training is the use of video or webinars.

> **TIP:** *During training, remind interviewers that the device is likely to record when they have conducted an interview, where they conducted the interview, and may collect other data about the interview.*

Logistical support

A mobile device can do much more than just capture participant data. Depending on the type of device being used support can be provided in the following sorts of ways:

- *Phone calls, providing help, instructions, and feedback*

- *Helping with navigation*

- *Updating questionnaires, discussion guides, or quotas*

- *Playing training videos*

- *Sending or receiving messages, for example via email, IM, or SMS.*

SUMMARY

CAPI has been in relative decline for a decade or more, having been largely superseded by online (just as face-to-face and CATI have been impacted by online). However, the introduction of mobile devices into the world of CAPI has re-invigorated the method.

mCAPI is proving attractive in situations where face-to-face interviewing is preferred, either because it is the best option (as in interviewing people as they leave retail outlets) or because the alternative is paper-based questionnaires, as is the case in some of the less economically and technologically advanced markets.

The future potential of mCAPI is underlined by the fact that many of the leading survey platform providers have mCAPI options, typically app-based products, allowing a wide range of organizations to utilize these developments.

The following are the key mCAPI considerations:

- *In a mCAPI project the most critical element is the interviewer.*

- *mCAPI is more likely to be app-based than browser-based.*

- *Most of the leading market research software platforms have a mCAPI solution.*

- *As the market matures it will be increasingly rare for researchers to focus on hardware choices; they will look for fieldwork suppliers who can work with their existing platform choices.*

- *In challenging markets researchers will tend to look for fieldwork suppliers who can provide a complete solution.*

- *When choosing a device for mCAPI, the five key issues to consider are: size, browser or app, battery life, training and security, and choice of software.*

10

mCATI – Mobile Computer Assisted Telephone Interviewing

INTRODUCTION

As a data collection mode, CATI (computer assisted telephone interviewing) is currently far larger than modes typically described as mobile. In 2012, ESOMAR estimated that CATI accounted for about 17% of quantitative projects by spend (ESOMAR 2013). Until recently, in the more developed economies, CATI was perceived as relating only to landlines, but increasingly CATI has started to include mobile phones (hence mCATI). One of the key drivers of this growth in interest in CATI and mobile devices has been the rise of mobile only households in the developed markets. For example, by January 2013, the US CDC (Centers for Disease Control and Prevention) National Health Interview Survey was quoting that 37% of US adults lived in a home without a landline (up from about 4% a decade earlier).

In the less economically developed markets, mobile phones have been a core part of CATI for much longer.

In 2013 the ITU (the UN agency focused on information and communication technologies) estimated that in the developed world there were about three times as many mobile phones as landlines (which they refer to as fixed lines), as shown in Figure 10.1. The gap was even wider in the developing world where the ITU estimated that there are more than seven times as many mobile subscriptions as landlines.

The chapter starts by reviewing CATI in general and looking at why the introduction of mobile phones has made a difference. The chapter then looks at CATI and mobile devices from two perspectives. Firstly, the modifications that are required to existing CATI practice to deal with issues created by mobile phones. Secondly, to draw some wider implications about interviewing people via mobile devices, as opposed to other modes.

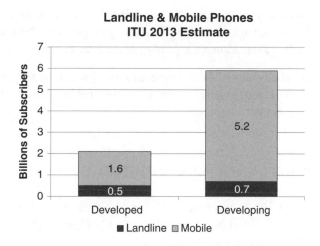

Figure 10.1   Landline and mobile subscriptions

UNDERSTANDING CATI

Before exploring the role of mobile in the context of CATI, it is useful to review CATI (as applied to landlines) and its perceived strengths and characteristics. This section covers how CATI is used with RDD for random probability sampling and why landline only research has, in the past, been preferred to telephone interviews with mobile phones.

RANDOM SAMPLING AND RDD

CATI has been used by researchers as one of the two leading ways of delivering a reasonable approximation of a random probability sample (along with door-to-door interviewing) – in countries where most people have a telephone. These random probability samples are delivered via a method known as RDD, where RDD stands for random digit dialling. RDD refers to a method of creating random probability samples from the characteristics of telephone numbers, by generating random numbers in patterns that match the use of telephone numbers (rather than by looking them up from directories).

Whilst RDD has been a mainstay of market research sampling, in many of the developed markets for many years, it does have some important limitations in terms of being a true random probability sample:

- *Not everybody has a landline. The penetration of phones varies from country to country, and within a country by issues such as income and age. In the less developed markets landlines never reached very high levels in most cases, and in the developed markets there has been a rise in the number of mobile only households.*

- *Not everybody with access to a landline is equally likely to answer it. Busy people are out more than others, and younger members of the household may be less likely to use the family phone than others.*

- *Not everybody who is phoned agrees to take part in the research, which means that the contacts may represent a random probability sample, but response bias may impact the outcome.*

UNDERSTANDING LANDLINES AND CATI

The history of CATI has been the history of using landlines to contact research partici-pants. This section looks at the key issues relating to CATI via landlines, the next section does the same for CATI via mobile phones.

The benefits of landlines

When mobile phones first appeared, many researchers preferred to confine their CATI studies to landlines. The key reasons for preferring a traditional landline sample were:

1. Landline methodologies were better established, so there were efficiencies in staying with this approach, and a degree of comfort. The methods included the mathematic modelling of how to create a random sample and technical devices for handling calls, for example predictively pre-dialling numbers, to enable the efficient use of interviewers.

2. A belief that mobile phone interviews needed to be shorter than landline surveys. (A point of view that echoes the discussion between online surveys via a PC and mobile device.)

3. In many countries, landline numbers can be mapped to geographic locations, making it easier to set regional quotas. By contrast, mobile phone numbers are often mapped to things like telephone service providers.

4. The sound quality of mobile calls might be lower, because of poor connections, distractions, and lost calls.

5. Mobile research can be more expensive than landlines. AAPOR (2010) reported that in the US, the cost of a cell phone complete is often twice as expensive as a landline complete, and can be three or four times as high. Pennay et al. (2013) estimated that in Australia the cost of a nationally representative sample is 30% higher if conducted from a mobile sampling frame, compared with using landlines.

6. Mobile research may require more phone calls to be made to achieve the same number of completed interviews, due to factors such as call screening, refusals, and higher dropout rates.

7.	Restrictions on the technology that can be used for mobile studies. For example, in the US auto-diallers (including predictive diallers) cannot be used to ring mobile phones without the owner's prior permission. If the interviewer has to enter the number manually then it takes longer.

GENERATING A SAMPLE FRAME

When a researcher wants to generate a sample that approximates to a random probability sample, the first step is to create a suitable sample frame. A sample frame is typically a list or definition of every member of a target population. In terms of telephone interviewing the sample frame is normally approximated by estimating the phone numbers in use.

Generating landline samples

There are variations in how landline samples are generated, but the basics are broadly similar, as shown here:

1.	Ascertain the range of numbers allocated for the target locations from the telephone companies. In many cases, the numbers relate to geographic regions, allowing the numbers generated to be related to census estimates of population.

2.	Generate random numbers from the valid ranges.

3.	Test the numbers to establish that they are in use, usually via pinging them with a test signal.

4.	Create a collection of numbers from those that appear to be in use.

This collection of numbers is then used as a source for random selection. The random selection of numbers is then based on how many numbers are required to achieve a completed interview. For example, if 1000 completes are needed, and if it is assumed that eight numbers will be required for each complete, on average, then 8000 numbers will be selected.

In many cases the process of generating collections of suitable numbers and of drawing random selections is taken care of by third-party sample providers. These companies will typically create a collection every so often, for example yearly, and then draw from the collection.

UNDERSTANDING CATI VIA MOBILE PHONES

The world of landlines and CATI has evolved over 40 years. By comparison the learnings about mobile and CATI are much newer and less thoroughly researched and evaluated.

Why add mobile phones to CATI?

Given that landline-based research was well established and likely to be cheaper than including mobile phones, why have mobile phones appeared in CATI projects? The main reason to add mobile only households to CATI projects was because of the rise in mobile only households. As mobile only households became a larger and larger percentage, researchers felt they could not risk excluding them.

Mobile only people are different

There is now a substantial amount of evidence that there are important differences between people who can be accessed via landlines and those who can only be accessed via mobile phones. For example, Hu et al. (2011) reported that a cell phone only sample differed from a landline sample and had higher proportions of males, people aged 18 to 34 years, people who had never married, and those with annual household incomes of less than $35,000. Similarly, UK regulator Ofcom reported in 2013 that the proportion of mobile only households was 'significantly higher among younger and less affluent households' (Ofcom 2013). While in studies looking at Australians, Pennay et al. (2013) reported that the mobile only sample are more likely to be: male, younger, to have been born overseas, and to be living in rented accommodation.

These differences echo the findings of online research, where the demographics of people choosing to answer online surveys via a mobile device are different from those choosing to answer via a PC. The research implication in both cases is that adding a mobile option excludes fewer people, and can help make the sample more representative of the target population.

Why not use mobile only samples?

In many markets, both developed and less developed, there are more people with access to a mobile phone than have access to a landline. For example, according to the CDC, in the US in 2013 about 90% of households had access to a mobile phone, but only 60% had access to a landline (about 50% of US households had access to both) (Blumberg and Luke 2012).

So, given that there are so many mobiles, why don't researchers switch to using mobile only samples? The main reasons are those set out earlier as the benefits of landlines, in particular it is typically cheaper to use landlines than mobiles. There is also the issue that it is easier to sample landlines and the methods of sampling are better established.

However, the trend is towards samples that are increasingly mobile and it should be noted that in some of the newer economies samples tend to already be mobile only, because landlines are very rare and mobiles relatively common.

Benefits of mobile only samples

One of the benefits of mobile sample frames is that the person answering the phone is the relevant person. In a landline survey the interviewer's first task is usually to determine how many people live in the household and then go through a procedure to select the correct person to interview.

Another benefit is that mobile phones are with people all the time, but landlines are only available when people are at home (or at the office for B2B research). There can be important differences in demographics, behaviour, or attitudes between people who are often at home and those who are only occasionally at home.

Mobile response rates

The general consensus seems to be that response rates for mobile CATI are lower than for landlines, which means the non-response rates are higher. For example, on page 6 of the 2010 AAPOR Cell Phone Task Force Report (AAPOR 2010), it suggests that '[n]onresponse in RDD cell phone surveys is somewhat greater than in comparable RDD landline surveys in the US'. However, the AAPOR report suggests that rates may become more similar over time, because of falling response rates for calls to landlines. Similar evidence is provided by Pennay et al. (2013), who found that they needed six landline telephone numbers (referred to as records) per complete, while for their mobile data collection they required eight numbers per complete. The mobile study required just over 28 calls per interview, whereas the landline study required just under 27 calls per interview.

Quality concerns about mobile surveys

Researchers have raised a number of concerns about the quality of CATI interviews conducted via mobile phones. For example, AAPOR (2010) raised a number of possible concerns about the quality of the data collected via mobile phone, including 'audio quality, asking about sensitive topics while a respondent is in a public place, and asking about cognitively complex topics while a respondent is multitasking'.

However, there appears to be no evidence to date that survey data collected via mobile phones is less good than data collected via landlines (AAPOR 2010, Pennay et al. 2013). Nevertheless, the advice from the relevant bodies is that researchers should be vigilant for potential differences caused by the data collection mode.

Generating a mobile phone sampling frame

Although there are variations from country to country (and to a lesser extent from company to company) in how mobile sample frames are created, the broad approach is similar to landlines. From the number ranges allocated to the mobile phone operators, randomly generated extensions are produced and the resultant numbers tested to see that they are valid and in use.

One of the weaknesses of RDD with mobile phones is that in many cases the mobile phone numbers used in a country are not related to geographic regions, making it harder to map numbers to areas or regions.

COMBINING LANDLINES AND MOBILE PHONES, FOR CATI

This section looks at the logistical implications of conducting CATI studies where some participants will be interviewed via their landline and some via their mobile phone.

DUAL FRAME SAMPLES

If a researcher wants to include both landlines and mobile phones in an RDD study it is necessary to use a dual frame approach to define the sample. A dual frame is needed because there is no single method of selecting phone numbers that will deal adequately with both landlines and mobile phones.

Overlapping and non-overlapping frames

There are two approaches to dual frame sampling, overlapping and non-overlapping (AAPOR 2010):

- *In the non-overlapping approach, the landline frame is used as the main frame, and the mobile frame is used solely to add mobile only households. In the non-overlapping frame model, anybody contacted from the mobile frame who lives in a household with a landline is rejected.*

- *In an overlapping frame, mobile phone users who also have access to a landline can be recruited from either the landline frame or the mobile frame. In this case, the researcher needs to determine what proportion of the total sample should come from the mobile frame and what proportion from the landline frame.*

Mobile users contacted via landline can be different from those contacted by mobile

One reason for using overlapping samples, i.e. samples where the mobile users are sourced from both the landline frame and mobile frame, is that there is evidence that mobile samples sourced from a landline frame show relevant and measurable differences from a mobile sample sourced from a mobile frame (Pennay et al. 2013). What this means is that mobile phone owners contacted via a landline are different, to an extent, from mobile phone owners contacted via their mobile phone, even when both groups of people have both a mobile phone and a landline.

Weighting/blending landline and mobile phone samples

If data is collected from two sources, it needs to be combined or blended, which means determining the proportions, or weights, that should be used. Amongst the problems are:

- *The complexity of the link between an individual and the mobile device they have been contacted on. Some devices are shared by several people, such as the household landline, whereas some individuals have access to several devices, for example somebody might have two mobile phones and a landline.*

- *The absence of good, regional data on the characteristics of people in: landline only households, mobile only households, and dual use households.*

- *Taking differential non-response into account. For example, the data suggests that non-response is higher amongst mobile phone users.*

Researchers looking to blend landline RDD and mobile RDD are recommended to check the recent literature and their industry bodies. A summary of approaches and some links to further resources can be found in the AAPOR 2010 report.

Mobile CATI in non-RDD situations

RDD is a major part of telephone surveying, because it is felt by many researchers to approximate to a random probability sample, but RDD is not the only form of telephone/CATI research. Examples of other uses include telephone interviews with participants sourced from:

- *Customer lists*

- *Members of panels*

- *Members of research communities*

- *Inbound calls, for example when people phone a call centre.*

In non-RDD cases, the researcher typically treats mobile phones and landlines as being interchangeable. The only exceptions to this rule are where the research is related to a specific type of phone service, for example about landlines, or about mobile services.

CATI WITH MOBILE PHONES

This section looks at the implications of using telephone interviewing with mobile phones, both in the context of mobile only samples and combining mobile phones and landlines.

SPECIAL CONSIDERATIONS WHEN DIALLING MOBILE PHONES

In addition to all the normal conventions that apply to phoning landlines, such as not causing a nuisance, not ringing at anti-social hours, and not contacting people who have requested no contact,[1] there are special considerations that apply when seeking to ring mobile phones (or where it is possible the number is a mobile phone).[2]

Special considerations for ringing mobile phones can include:

1. If the country where the research is taking place has time zones, these will have to be taken into account when avoiding anti-social hours.

2. Check with the person answering the phone that it is safe for them to speak. For example, check they are not driving a car or operating machinery.

3. Wherever possible, check whether the participant would like to do the survey now, or later. If they'd like to do it later, the best practice is to make a definite appointment.

4. Offer to call back on a landline, particularly if the voice connection is poor, or to call back at another time.

MOBILE CATI ETHICS

As with all market research ethics, there are broadly four categories to consider:

1. The laws and regulations that operate within the country or countries where the research is taking place.

2. The rules and guidance from the market research organizations in the country or countries where the research is being conducted.

---

[1] In many markets 'do not call' lists do not restrict market research calls, but even in these cases many market researchers choose to exclude these numbers.
[2] In most markets, mobile phones can be identified by the leading digits, so even in a project where the research is using mobile and landline phone numbers interchangeably, specific procedures can be put in place for mobile phones. However, some authorities have raised concerns about phoning mobile devices where the initial number is a landline that has been forwarded to a mobile device.

3.   International guidance, for example from ESOMAR and the Mobile Marketing Research Association.

4.   The researcher's own moral compass, supported by a sense of what is likely to offend the public.

One of the challenges for market researchers is that the laws, rules, regulations, and guidelines can vary from country to country. For example, in some countries all of the following are illegal:

1.   Using auto-diallers to call mobile phones. When auto-diallers are illegal the interviewers have to dial numbers manually.

2.   Ringing people at anti-social times of day.

3.   Ringing people who are on a 'do not call' list.

4.   Ringing people and dropping the call if an interviewer is not ready.

Researchers should check the rules that pertain to telephone research via mobile phones in target markets, ideally via a local research organization.

GENERAL PRINCIPLES

The following points are likely to be good practice in most markets:

- *Explain the purpose of the call and how you obtained the number.*

- *Tell them how long the call will take, and ask if that is OK.*

- *If you are going to be asking personal questions, ask them whether they are likely to be overheard.*

THE BROADER IMPLICATIONS FOR MOBILE MARKET RESEARCH

The lessons being learned by researchers seeking to integrate mobile phones into the well-developed field of landline-based CATI research have interesting implications for other researchers. The key implications are:

- *People who can be reached via mobile devices are sometimes different, in important ways, from people who can be reached via more traditional means. The implication of this finding is that by including mobile devices the research represents more of the target population.*

- *Although there are fears that interviewing people via mobile, rather than land-line, might produce different responses (from the same respondent), there is little evidence to support this concern – and the same is broadly true with other mobile versus traditional route comparisons.*

- *Combining data drawn from two samples sources is complex and typically requires modelling and/or weighting.*

SUMMARY

The key points that the chapter has highlighted are:

- *CATI based on landlines only is largely a thing of the past, the present is a combination of landlines and mobile, and the future (in many markets) is likely to be mobile only.*

- *The processes for combining landline RDD and mobile RDD are not settled or fully agreed – researchers working in this area should consult the leading texts and reports in the area.*

- *Mobile CATI often introduces more constraints than is the case for landlines. For example, more restrictions on how calls can be managed/organized and less information about the link between numbers and geographic areas.*

- *People who have mobile devices are demographically different from those who do not, and those with a landline are demographically different from those who do not. These differences mean that offering the widest range of options will result in the widest range of research participants.*

- *At present, mobile CATI tends to cost more than landline-based CATI.*

- *The lessons from CATI, when comparing mobile with traditional modes, are broadly similar to those obtained by comparing mobile surveys with online surveys.*

11 | Mixed-Mode Research

INTRODUCTION

This chapter looks at a variety of approaches that can be described as mixed-mode, where mobile is one of the modes in the mix. This chapter includes projects that are quantitative, qualitative, and those that utilize both active and passive research. The chapter covers projects where mixed-mode means that different modes are used at different stages of the project and those where different modes are used by different participants at the same stage.

In the area of mobile research, the term 'mixed-mode' often refers to combining online research with mobile research, typically offering a mobile participant the chance to connect to online research projects from a mobile device, rather than from a PC. Offering participants the choice of connecting via a PC or via a mobile device is often termed 'platform agnostic'.

Other terms are sometimes used for mixed-mode, for example 'multi-mode' or 'hybrid' research. Some researchers draw a distinction between, say, mixed-mode and multi-mode, but these differences are not consistent across the market research profession, and this book will restrict itself to using the term 'mixed-mode'.

The chapter starts by looking at how mobile only studies differ from mixed-mode studies, in the context of phones, smartphones, and tablets. The next section looks at studies that are mixed-mode in the sense of using different modes at different stages. The final section looks at designing and implementing a mixed-mode study.

'MOBILE ONLY' VERSUS MIXED-MODE

Although this is a book about mobile market research, many research projects are mixed-mode, rather than mobile only (i.e. one that only uses mobile devices). Indeed, one of the first decisions a researcher needs to make when conducting a mobile market research project is to determine whether the project should be mobile only or mixed-mode.

The general trend within the research world is towards device or platform agnostic research, where the participants are given as much choice as possible in how they take part in research projects; for example, giving participants choices in terms of time, place, and device. Adopting this approach means that projects should only be created as 'mobile only' if there are tangible benefits to the study of it being mobile only.

The key question to ask is 'Why should participants wanting to use a PC be excluded?' If there is no good reason to exclude people using PCs, then the research should be mixed-mode, at least to the extent of allowing PCs.

Four situations that might create a preference for mobile only are:

1.   If the research needs to be so mobile that a PC is unlikely to be suitable. For example, if we want people to enter data during the day, perhaps every time they engage in a specific activity or whenever they encounter a specific stimulus. Researchers looking into drinks consumed during the day or public transport experiences would fall into this category.

2.   If the research uses features that are on mobile devices, but not on PCs, such as app-based research. Examples of this category include: passive data collection, research that incorporates SMS, geofencing technology, taking photos, or recording videos.

3.   If the research relates to a mobile feature, such as game usability, mobile advertising, or app functionality.

4.   Where very fast or time specific responses are required, for example if a researcher wanted to send a message to participants at various points throughout the day and ask them what they were doing at that moment, or whether they had heard about a breaking news story or ad campaign.

PHONE ONLY STUDIES

The term 'mobile only' implies that participants can use both phones and tablets. However, some studies are restricted to phones only. The definition of a phone is variable, but for the purpose of this section, a phone is defined as a device small enough to be carried all day, with a SIM (i.e. a mobile carrier connection), and capable of making voice calls (i.e. it has a speaker and a microphone). This definition would include feature phones, smartphones, and phablets.

Key reasons for a phone only study include:

1.   Where the participants need to have their device with them throughout the day, whilst they are out and about.

2.   Where the project uses features that exist on phones, but not tablets (or not on most tablets). These features can be as basic as SMS or as complex as using the phone's inbuilt GPS. (It should be noted, however, that the range of tablets with these features is growing.)

SMARTPHONE ONLY STUDIES

Smartphone only studies tend to be used when the research software or approach being used only runs on devices with operating systems such as Google's Android and Apple's iOS and where the research is not suitable for a tablet. This tends to mean the device needs to be with people all day and/or is using features found on smartphones and phablets, but not on most tablets.

TABLET ONLY STUDIES

Tablet only studies are rarer than PC only and phone only studies, at the moment. The main reason for defining a study as tablet only would be that it needs the mobility of a mobile device, and the screen size of a tablet.

The most common type of tablet only studies are found in mCAPI, where tablets are used by interviewers to conduct interviews, and tend to be owned by the company conducting the research or a fieldwork company. This is covered in more depth in the mCAPI chapter.

DIFFERENT MODES AT DIFFERENT STAGES

Some projects benefit from using different modes at different stages, and potentially using different research approaches at different stages, for example using a qualitative discussion to follow a quantitative survey. In a multi-stage project, the question of mode arises for each of the stages.

As mentioned earlier, the general preference, these days, is to use a platform agnostic approach towards the modes employed, aiming to provide participants with a choice in how they take part in research projects. In a multi-stage project this process is repeated for each stage. This is shown in the hypothetical example outlined next.

APPLYING MIXED-MODE THINKING TO A HYPOTHETICAL RESEARCH PROJECT

The project looks at the consumption of food over a single day, in a developed market, i.e. one where smartphones are common and data charges are low. During the day the participants are asked to complete a very short (2 minute survey) every time they eat something, for example what they are eating, the situation, the preparation, and the calorific value of the item being eaten.

The three stages of the project are:

1.   A pre-project survey to capture background information

2.   One day of recording food consumption

3.   A post-event discussion forum to probe the reasons and motivations behind the observed behaviour.

Table 11.1 illustrates how a mixed-mode approach could be applied to this project.

Table 11.1   Application of a mixed-mode approach

Stage	Description	Mode Description
1	Pre-project background and profiling survey	An online survey, configured to run on PCs, smartphones, and tablets. Ownership of the correct device for stage 2 will be checked at this stage.
2	Collecting one day of food data	This stage is smartphone/phablet only,* partly because the device needs to be carried all day, partly because we want participants to use an app to estimate the calories in their food at the time that they eat their food, and the camera to take pictures.
3	Post-event discussion, lasting three days	An online discussion forum, configured to be suitable for PCs, smartphones, and tablets.

*For some people a tablet would also be an option, if they are likely to have it with them all day, for example if they are likely to be at home all day.

In this project, it would have been possible to insist that the participants use their phone for all three stages. However, researchers have found that some participants prefer to use their PC for online surveys and to take part in online discussions, so offering them the choice for the first and third stages is a good option.

DESIGNING A MIXED-MODE PROJECT

This section looks at how to design a mixed-mode project; one that combines mobile options with PC-based options. The basic elements of designing a mixed-mode project are the same for quantitative and qualitative projects, but the details are different, so this section will review both.

THE CORE ELEMENTS OF MIXED-MODE DESIGN

There are two guiding principles in designing mixed-mode research:

1.   Select techniques that will best meet the research needs.

2.   Select techniques that are equally suitable for all of the modes being used.

Although these two guidelines seem straightforward, problems can occur when they conflict with each other. For example, if the best research approach is to conduct webcam-enabled focus groups, participants using a smartphone might not have the bandwidth to take part if they are relying on a 3G connection, and if the intention is for participants to see all of the other attendees, then a smartphone's screen may not be large enough. Similarly, if the research design is for a discrete choice exercise, with sets of eight cards to be shown together, then the reduced screen size of a smartphone may make the exercise too different from the PC or tablet-based interview.

There are four approaches that researchers can take when trying to reconcile conflicts between these two guidelines:

1.   Amend the research method to make it suitable for all modes. For example, in a choice exercise, reduce the number of choices being offered, or accept that they won't all be visible at the same time.

2.   Modify the way a question works in one or more of the modes. For example, a grid question might be asked in a traditional way on PC interviews, but as a sequence of questions on a smartphone, or via dropdowns. This requires the researcher to know or assume that the different styles of asking the question will produce similar results. Sometimes these modifications can be quite subtle, for example if the participant needs to view a video, it might be delivered via streaming to PCs connected to broadband, but a more compressed file might be transferred prior to viewing, for participants using a phone in locations where their mobile internet might be slower.

3.   Exclude the elements that are not compatible with the research design. This is only possible if the research needs can still be met. For example, can a video be replaced with a series of still images?

4.   Exclude elements that are not compatible with a mode from those participants who are connecting via that mode. For example, if a project is designed to capture video interviews, those participants using PCs without a webcam would not be asked to record an interview. As with option 2, this option requires the researcher to know or assume that the differences created by dropping some elements from some participants will not have an unacceptable impact on the results.

QUALITATIVE MIXED-MODE RESEARCH

The key issues that confront researchers using mixed-mode qualitative research are:

- *Participants using mobile devices may find it harder to view multimedia, especially if using a slower internet connection.*

- *Participants using PCs may find it harder to upload photos and video than users of mobile devices. For example, they may need to use a camera or phone to capture the media and then transfer it to the PC before uploading it.*

- *There may be differences in entering open-ended comments into different devices. The existing research-on-research has provided a mixed picture, some studies showing that open-ended responses on mobile are as good as or better than text entered on a PC, but others showing the mobile text to be more limited. The differences may relate to who is taking part in the research – people who use mobiles heavily may be happier or find it easier to type text answers into their phones and tablets than occasional users.*

As with any feature of a qualitative research project, the different modes used by participants should be one of the many characteristics examined and considered when analysing and writing up the research. Differences can be a source of additional insight, if recognized and addressed.

QUANTITATIVE MIXED-MODE RESEARCH

Quantitative research, typically, seeks to measure samples of people that represent a specific group, and to use techniques that are consistent from one participant to another. Both of these criteria can be problematic for mixed-mode research.

Two important issues to address in mixed-mode quantitative studies are:

1. Sample frame effects (i.e. if the different modes attract different people).
2. Mode effects (i.e. if the way the question is asked or answered is changed by the mode).

SAMPLE FRAME ISSUES WITH MIXED-MODE RESEARCH

Much of the work looking at the impact of mobile devices on sample frames has been done in the area of telephone (CATI) surveys. This is particularly useful since there should be relatively few mode effects when comparing mobile samples with landline samples. Both modes are interviewer administered, using the same software from the interviewer perspective, with the same questionnaire, many landlines are cordless, and most mobile interviews are conducted in the home (Pennay et al. 2013).

The first difference between mobile frames and other frames relates to demographics. For example, mobile samples tend to be younger. This difference is fairly easy to spot and to manage (e.g. by weighting).

The second difference is psychographic. Researchers have reported (Hu et al. 2011; Pennay et al. 2013) that mobile samples, even after allowing for demographic differences, can display some behavioural and attitudinal differences. For example, the mobile sample reported more risk taking behaviours, including being more likely to take drugs.

In one sense, both of these differences are good things. They both indicate that the addition of mobile participants has found people who were previously being missed. The problem is determining how to combine the different sample frames and how to deal with changes over time. The 'over time' issue arises as there is an expectation that the proportion of mobile participants will increase over time, changing the balance of mobile participants within ongoing research projects and potentially causing benchmarks and norms to become out of date.

MODE EFFECTS WITH MIXED-MODE RESEARCH

Mode effects are situations where the data changes because of the way the questions are asked. Generally, the mode effects of mobile versus PC appear to have been smaller than was initially feared. This topic is covered more fully elsewhere in the book and in the Research-on-Research chapter. However, it should be noted that research-on-research shows that there are some differences in the data collected from PC and mobile surveys caused by mode effects, and this should be kept in mind.

There are broadly three strategies for dealing with mode effects in mixed-mode quantitative research:

1. Avoid those questions most associated with mode effects, such as multi-select grids.

2. Standardize the data from each participant before aggregating it.

3. If the project has multiple waves, control for mode, typically by ensuring that the proportion of the sample using mobile devices is constant across waves.

There is a widespread concern that many users of mixed-mode research, especially those conducting unintentional mobile research, are not checking for mode effects and therefore not dealing with issues that may be in their data.

CHECKING FOR MODE EFFECTS IN MIXED-MODE DATA

Although there have been a number of research-on-research studies looking at the mode effects of mobile versus PC-based online research, the picture is not fully resolved.

(Several of these studies are reported in this book in the Research-on-Research chapter.) However, some findings about mode differences are summarized next:

1.   Most standard question types appear to give broadly similar answers when answered via mobile and PC.

2.   Some question types appear to generate different answers, for example multi-select grids and large complex conjoint questions. For example, when using grids it would appear that on mobile devices more items are selected, and large conjoint analysis choice sets appear to generate more confusion.

3.   There is a widely held view that a 20–30 minute online survey is acceptable, but the same researchers tend to assert that a 20–30 minute mobile survey is not acceptable. This would suggest mode effects (or sample frame effects) if long surveys were conducted as mixed-mode studies. However, there are also many researchers who doubt the quality of a 25 minute PC/online survey, and some who claim long mobile surveys are acceptable.

Because research-on-research into mode effects is still being conducted, and is likely to be researched for the next few years, researchers should take responsibility for checking their results for mode effects.

The key steps in checking for mode effects include the following actions:

1.   Ensure that the type of device used by the participant is captured. At the very least, the data should be identified as mobile or PC, but ideally the data should be more detailed, such as phone, phablet, small tablet, and larger tablet.

2.   Compare the aggregate data, looking at mobile versus PC. If there are no important differences then there are probably no major problems. However, it is likely there will be differences because the demographic profile of the mobile participants is likely to be different from the PC sample.

3.   Create cells based on demographic or other groups and compare mobile versus PC within these groups. For example, the data could be divided into four groups, Young Males, Young Females, Older Males, Older Females, and for each of these four, compare mobile versus PC. If any of the cells are too small, they can normally be ignored as they are unlikely to change the answers of a quantitative project. If there are no differences within these groups (between mobile and PC) there are unlikely to be mode effects big enough to distort the findings.

4.   If, after all these steps, there are still differences, then it is likely that there are mode effects. The options that are available to the researcher include: standardizing those responses with differences; using weighting; analysing the data separately; or simply highlighting/annotating the effect in the results.

These checks are less relevant for a single project comparing cells (e.g. a four-cell concept test), where the mode effects are more likely to be evenly distributed across the cells. However, these steps are likely to be more important when conducting studies over time (such as a tracking study) or a study where people are going to be divided into groups depending on their responses, such as in a segmentation study.

SUMMARY

The trend in market research is towards a device agnostic position, where participants are free to choose how they want to take part in research. The only way a researcher can avoid mixed-mode studies is by taking specific measures to exclude participants who seek to use other platforms and devices.

Given that mixed-mode research is likely to be the norm, more work needs to be done by the market research industry to evaluate the sampling frame and mode effect impacts of combining mobile research with PC-based online research. This research should not be seen as a reason to avoid using mixed-mode, but as a method of improving mixed-mode research.

There are a number of key issues that researchers should consider in the context of mixed-mode research:

- *Offering participants a choice of modes is likely to widen the range of people represented by the study.*

- *Mixed-mode research can introduce mode effects, where the answers that participants give are impacted by the choice of modes offered.*

- *Unintentional mobile (an online study intended for PCs, but where some participants use mobile devices) is a mixed-mode study.*

- *Researchers should consider mixed-mode at the design stage, determining what modes will work for which stages of the research, and how best to design the research for the modes they are using.*

- *Researchers should inspect the data to see if there are mode effects.*

- *The most basic requirement in looking for mode effects is to capture the type of device being used, so the data can be analysed by device differences.*

- *Whilst most question types appear to give similar answers when asked on, say, mobile devices and PCs, a few do seem to give different responses.*

- *There is likely to be ongoing research-on-research into multi-mode research; researchers are advised to monitor learnings and developments in the area.*

12 Utilizing Passive Data

INTRODUCTION

Passive data collection refers to the process of collecting data without participants having to enter their data. For example, the GPS location facility of a mobile phone can record where a participant travels without the participant having to do anything other than: agree to the process; download or utilize an app; and ensure that GPS tracking is turned on. There is a short summary of some of the key features and sensors found on modern mobile devices, near the end of the chapter.

In essence there are three things that passive data collection can achieve in conjunction with mobile devices:

1.   Track where the device goes.

2.   Track what the device is used for.

3.   Gathering background information.

The chapter starts by giving a brief overview of the current situation for passive data collection and market research and then reviews each of the three points above.

THE CURRENT STATUS OF PASSIVE MEASUREMENT IN MARKET RESEARCH

In general, the use of passive data collection for market research requires the use of apps, which tends to mean persuading participants to download an app to their device in order to take part in the research project. For providers of apps and providers of handsets there is also the option to embed passive data collection code.

Although the idea of passive data is very attractive to marketers, market researchers, and data scientists, there are relatively few cases in mainstream market research, to date, where passive data collection has been shown to be particularly useful in market research. Most of the good examples of passive data delivering value come from specialist parts of the market research world (such as media measurement) and from outside market research.

The relative absence of a body of market research knowledge about how to turn passive data into actionable market research insight is partly a reflection the newness of the approach and also the complexity of combining the sort of information produced by passive tracking with the sorts of questions asked by market research.

The future of passive data collection is likely to be a combination of richer measurements (as devices develop an enhanced range of features and sensors), better analysis approaches and tools, and integration with active information (e.g. using passive information to trigger a survey, discussion, or some other activity).

USING PASSIVE INFORMATION TO TRIGGER AN ACTION

One use of passive data collection is to trigger an action. For example, if the location system says a research participant is at a specific restaurant an app can trigger a survey or an open-ended question about the visit, or a request to take a picture. At this stage the data collection ceases to be entirely passive, but things like time of day, location, and so on are still captured passively and combined with the user entered information.

PASSIVE DATA AND ETHICS

Just like any other form of market research, market research based on passive data collection requires informed consent. However, non-market research use of passive data collection, such as embedded apps, is often not based on informed consent.

Passive data can be personally identifiable, and it can be sensitive, so researchers need to ensure they protect the data privacy and data security of participants and clients when conducting passive data collection.

TRACKING LOCATION

Although the technology of tracking relates to mobile devices, in most research cases the intention of tracking is to determine where research participants are. For this reason, tracking-based research is usually focused on phones rather than tablets. There are three key approaches that market research utilizes, in terms of location:

1.   Geographical location, i.e. where the device/participant is on a macro scale. For example, what route did participants take when travelling to work, including what media they came in contact with, for example billboards, public screens, broadcasts, and so on?

2.   Location within a site. For example, which shopping aisles did a participant visit?

3.   Location within a system. For example, using a mobile device to swipe in or out of a specific service?

These three types of location research tend to utilize different technologies, are often used for different purposes, and sometimes require different levels of cooperation from the participant.

1. TRACKING GEOGRAPHIC LOCATION

There are a variety of reasons why somebody might want to record the location of participants, with many of those reasons extending well beyond the normal area of interest for market researchers. These reasons include:

●   ***Traffic planning and management.*** *Knowing where pedestrians and even cars are, can allow traffic controllers to manage day-to-day affairs and to plan for changes and developments. Similarly, marketers can use this information to identify routes with high traffic levels, in order to prioritize them for marketing materials and activities.*

●   ***Tracking specific activities.*** *At the simplest level, RFIDs are used to record the progress of runners in events such as marathons, at the more complex end phones and smart watches can track routes, speeds, calories used, and can even be linked to biometric measures such as heart rate. At events such as trade shows and conferences, Near Field Communication (NFC – see glossary for more information) can be used to identify who enters specific rooms, visits booths, or asks for information.*

●   ***Opportunity to see.*** *Tracking where a participant is, allows researchers/ advertisers to assess whether the participant has had an opportunity to see something, for example outdoor advertising.*

●   ***Tracking life events.*** *For example, by tracking location, the researcher can understand how much time the participant spends at home, at work, and how long they spend travelling. This information can be used on its own or in conjunction with the answers to questions.*

The technology of geographic tracking

Geographic tracking tends to use one of the following three technologies:

1.   **GPS.** This requires: the device to have a GPS receiver, the receiver has to be turned on, and the device has to be able to contact at least three satellites (which tends to mean the participant cannot be in a building or underground). To utilize GPS tracking the participant typically has to download an app, which will interface with the GPS receiver and supply the researcher with the location coordinates.

2.   **Tower location.** The mobile phone service providers can locate phones (and any device using a SIM) via the broadcast towers they use to provide their services. Third parties can only access this information via the telecommunication companies. Wired.com reported (9/12/13 www.wired.com/ threatlevel/2013/12/massive-domestic-monitoring/) that in the USA there were about 1.1 million requests for cellular data, including more than 9000 cell tower dumps from the police and relevant authorities – which identifies every mobile phone at a particular location and time (Kravets 2013).

3.   **Partial tracking.** Systems such as RFIDs (like those used by runners in marathons), Wi-Fi, NFC, and CCTV can be used to build up a picture of a participant's journey. For example, with CCTV a participant can be tracked as they move through a shopping mall.

Turning tracking data into information

Raw tracking data can initially be relatively unhelpful to market researchers. For example, the GPS data from a phone can supply location information in a near continuous stream, which can produce enormous amounts of data very quickly.

One key difference in how tracking data is analysed is whether the study is based on a small number of participants, for example ten people, or a larger number such as 1000, or a very large number such as tens or hundreds of thousands.

Dealing with small sample sizes

With a small number of participants the data gathered is essentially qualitative (even if there is a large amount of data per person). The analysis of individual data can often be dealt with graphically, for example by plotting the journey on a map and looking at it in connection with additional feedback from the participant (including photos, comments, or even reviewing the maps with the participants). There are a wide range of tools available that will take GPS data and produce maps.

Dealing with larger sample sizes

In most cases, with larger sample sizes, the data needs simplifying before being used as an input into a market research insight process. Strategies for simplifying/utilizing tracking data include:

1.   Turning the data into aggregate units, such as length of journey (time), journey distance, speed (e.g. maximum, minimum, and average), time of journey (morning, daytime, evening, and night time), and number of journeys.

2.   Using software to produce 'typical' journeys. For example, around the ring road, through the centre of the town, or A to B versus A to B to A.

3.   Turning the data into sectors. For example, a city centre could be configured as an 8 × 8 grid of 64 squares and the location data used to record which squares the participant visited. If the researcher knows what is in each square they can estimate participants' opportunity to see specific features (such as outdoor advertising).

2. TRACKING LOCATION WITHIN A SITE

Tracking a participant within a location might be on a scale as large as a festival site or shopping mall, or in an area as small as a shopping aisle. The type of data used will vary on the setting and technology. For example, journeys around a large festival might utilize GPS, journeys through a building might use RFIDs or Bluetooth LE.

Tracking location within a site can be used for the same sorts of reasons that geographic location can be used, for example measuring traffic flows, opportunity to see, or activities. In addition, within site tracking can be used for a wide range of site specific, typically tactical research, projects such as:

● *Optimizing layouts, shelves, signage, and promotions.*

● *Evaluating stimuli as varied as alternative packaging, point of sale wording, and announcements.*

● *Understanding visitor or shopping dynamics. In a museum or theme park this might involve studying how people assemble and create a trip. In retail environments, within site tracking can identify shopping patterns. For example, how many people go back for something, how many buy their cold items last, how many go up and down all the aisles, and how many go to a set number of specific destinations?*

As with geographic location, quantitative tracking analysis tends to require substantial aggregation or simplification before it can be analysed, producing patterns of routes, length of journeys, location of delays, hot spots within the site, and so on. Qualitative data is often viewed as a map, or as a video or image sequence.

The technology of within site tracking

The main outdoor option, GPS, tends not to work within a site, for example within a shopping mall, because there is no link to GPS satellites. Cell tower location can work within a site, but it requires a third party (a mobile telephone service provider) and may not be sufficiently accurate for the very specific requirements of issues such as browsing a shopping fixture.

Several technologies can be used for within site tracking:

- *Wi-Fi can be used to locate Wi-Fi-enabled devices. Standard Wi-Fi only locates a device to an area the size of a shop or large room, but some of the newer low power Wi-Fi devices, with portable transmitters, can locate a device to a much smaller area.*

- *Wearable technologies, such as cameras, phones used as cameras, eye tracking devices such as Tobii Glasses, and Google Glass, can be used to create a visual record of a journey, allowing routes and items viewed to be assessed. A large proportion of visual tracking is qualitative, as there are relatively few options to automate the translation of photos and video into quantitative information.*

- *RFIDs have been used for many years to track people around buildings and items such as shopping trolleys/carts around stores. RFIDs tend to be used for route mapping and the assessment of issues such as visit length and dwell time at specific fixtures. Tracking via RFID requires participants to carry an RFID (e.g. in a shopping basket or identity badge) and the location needs to be equipped with sensors to track the RFID.*

- *Beacon and app technologies, based on sound or radio (especially Bluetooth LE) beacons, are being used to locate people to specific locations, such as when they enter a store, or when they approach a shelf. One of the high profile products in this area is Apple's iBeacon.*

Market research use of within site location

It is too early define all of the uses that within site location is going to utilize, but two current uses are:

- *To identify when somebody enters a location, for example when they enter a specific branch of a coffee chain. This information can be used to record visits, but it is more typically used by marketers to offer coupons or marketing offers, and by researchers to initiate a research activity, such as a survey.*

- *To research participant interaction with specific store fixtures and features, such as shelves or point of sale promotions.*

3. TRACKING LOCATION WITHIN A SYSTEM

Tracking within a system refers to recording the points where a participant interacts with a system. One example of this sort of tracking is to follow passengers through a public transport system as they swipe in and out of different stations, buses, trams, and ferries. Other forms of tracking look at the usage of ATMs, digital payment systems, and mobile phone calls.

The tracking of location within a system does not produce a continuous record, it produces a series of points, in the form of a place and time.

The concept of passive tracking (i.e. that it is accurate because it does not require the participant to do anything) can be compromised or altered by engaging the participant in the process. For example, marketers have experimented with using NFC to collect information. In one case, participants in a project were encouraged to use their smart-phones to collect information from a series of data collection points within a site, in order to win a game and potentially gain a discount. This sort of process can provide information about the movement of the participant through the site, but the process is not entirely passive. However, the participants have been encouraged to change their behaviour and it is this changed behaviour (and the participants' ability/inclination to follow instructions) that is being recorded.

Utilizing existing apps

As well as recruiting participants to load their mobile devices with apps that track their actions and movements, a growing number of people are using apps and gadgets to collect data about their own lives. Generically this practice is referred to as the quantified self. Examples of the quantified self, are apps such as RunKeeper and Endomondo and gadgets such as Garmin Vivofit and FitBit Flex.

The quantified self represents millions of consumers and citizens collecting data about their own lives, routes, journeys, activities, and calorific usage. This pool of information is beginning to be recognized as a resource for market research and insight.

Location summary

Over the last ten years there has been a shift, in market research, from relying on people's memories and stated beliefs towards observational data. This is because people are often very bad at remembering what they have seen and unaware of many of the things they do. For example, asking people what outdoor advertising they have seen produces a very poor record of the material they have actually encountered.

Location data produces, potentially, accurate data about journeys, timings, and activities. The two key challenges in using location data are:

1.   The shortage of good market research tools for transforming quantitative scale location data into suitable forms for analysis and insight.

2.   The difficulty in linking observable behaviour to underlying motivations and meaning.

The Power and Perils of Tracking Device Usage

Marcelo Ballve (2013) provides an example of the power and the perils of using device usage tracking devices. He compared the data from Flurry and Experian in terms of the number of hours a day spent using apps and found an interesting difference. Flurry produced an estimate of 2 hours' app usage a day amongst US smartphone owners, but Experian produced an estimate of just under 1 hour.

Ballve (2013) explored the differences and at the same time provided some insight into the need to contextualize passive data.

Flurry were measuring apps on tablets and phones, but Experian were just measuring them on phones – so that could create some differences. However, the main point Ballve was making related to the context for the passive measurement.

Flurry provide app developers with a service. App developers can embed code from Flurry in their apps and every time the app is run it sends a signal to Flurry, who collect aggregated market information and provide the app developer with detailed and comparative information. From the app user's point of view this is truly passive, in the sense that most app users do not know it is happening.

Experian have a panel of people who have downloaded a monitor app onto their device that records what they do; panel members have given their consent for this to happen. Experian monitor things like calls, games, internet usage and then average it across the sample to get an overall picture.

So, the Flurry figure is based on a much bigger sample size, but a sample of people who are using apps. The Experian figure is based on a more representative but smaller sample, and includes people who don't use apps, and people who hardly use apps.

The lesson is that usage monitoring can measure something accurately, but a researcher has to make sure they know what the something is, and how it relates to their business question, before using it.

TRACKING DEVICE USAGE

With suitable applications, every aspect of a mobile device can potentially be used to track device usage. The list of uses that can be tracked is large and is constantly changing. Uses that are of interest to market researchers include internet usage, social media, email, phone calls, and apps used.

However, in practice some of these options are not available. The writers of apps do not have unrestricted access to all of the internal services of the phone, especially on iPhones. Some developers have found ways around the limitations, but these alternatives tend to break operating systems rules and a number of service providers, including Google, are seeking to make it harder/impossible to gather some sorts of usage behaviour, for example to monitor browsing activity.

A key research application of monitoring device usage is to understand the devices themselves. For example, tracking mobile internet usage can be used to optimize website and service design. Similarly, usage information about phones helps the design of phones and services.

Social researchers utilize phone usage, including the network of calls, IMs, apps, cameras, and so on, to research social characteristics of modern life. Research that reveals, for example, how often people look at their phone is based on passive data collection.

GATHERING BACKGROUND INFORMATION

As well as location and device usage, mobile devices can be used to collect background information. In this context this means background information about the device and background information about the world around the participant.

BACKGROUND INFORMATION ABOUT THE DEVICE

When a mobile device is used to take part in a research exercise, it can be queried to determine various pieces of information, such as the operating system, the screen size, and the type of connection. These sorts of information are very similar to the background information that can be collected when a participant uses a PC to take part in an online research exercise.

Permission to collect the more basic types of background data is normally obtained before making use of this processing. The options presented to the participant are typically to agree to the processing or to withdraw from the project (i.e. to take the survey or not take the survey).

INFORMATION ABOUT THE WORLD AROUND THE PARTICIPANT

One of the most exciting prospects about passive data collection is the move to collect a detailed picture of what is going on around the research participant. Cameras and video (e.g. Memoto and GoPro) can be used to collect images of the world around the participant. Audio recognition can identify the programmes and ads that a participant is exposed to.

Some mobile phones can collect information about the temperature, humidity, air pressure, noise, and a growing range of background factors – the list of features and sensors varies by phone. The phones can collect (through Bluetooth and similar) the presence of other devices and by implication other people. It is envisaged that smartphones will, at some point in the future, replace many of the specialist devices used by researchers, such as the people meters used in the auditing of media usage.

MEDIA MEASUREMENT

One of the longest standing uses of passive tracking has been media measurement. Devices such as Arbitron's Portable People Meter (PPM) is worn like a pager and identifies when audible radio signatures are heard. In late 2012 Nielsen bought Arbitron Radio Ratings Service and it is now Nielsen Radio. As well as PPM, Nielsen has added smartphone and tablet apps to its passive monitoring portfolio.

Three key reasons that media measurement is one of the relatively few market research areas that has so far dealt well with the quantitative use of passive data include:

1.   A long background in quantifying behaviour, dating back decades in the case of diaries.

2.   Having a large market, which means an investment can earn its ROI across multiple clients and projects.

3.   Being prepared to make large scale investments in new technologies.

Perhaps a fourth reason is being aware that if the current players do not use the new technologies, new entrants could enter the market utilizing new approaches, and offer a better, faster, cheaper service.

OVERVIEW OF PASSIVE MONITORING FEATURES

Table 12.1 shows several of the features and sensors of phones and tablets that can be used for passive data collection.

Table 12.1   Some features and sensors of mobile devices that can be used for passive data collection

Feature/Sensor	Measure	Comments
GPS	Collects GPS coordinates measured by longitude and latitude	Can identify the current location of the phone and can track the points travelled through, producing a record of a journey.
Cell Tower	Cell tower-based location detection	Cell towers are used to transmit voice and data to mobile phones and can be used by the service provider to locate users remotely and record their movement.
Gyroscope	Measures movement of a phone especially its 360 degree rotation of the mobile device	The phone's gyroscope has the potential to inform the researcher about the nature of the participant's journey, e.g. smooth or full of turns, as well as helping understand thing like the position of the phone during tasks like videoing and taking photographs.
Accelerometer	Movement of the phone	The potential uses for the accelerometer are similar to the gyroscope. While the gyroscope measures the tilting and the up down movement of the device; the accelerometer measures the lateral and speed of movement of the mobile device
Cookies	Browser history	Cookies allow passive monitoring of mobile sites visited.
Native OS activity monitoring	Programs (apps) can be embedded and read activity at the native level of the phone's operating system.	Potentially measures device usage, including turning features on and off, battery usage, calls, internet usage. However, this is not always permitted by the operating system.
Microphone	Sound recording	The microphone can be used, in addition to its normal uses, to listen for signals from audio beacons and signatures embedded in radio and TV ads.
Camera	Images, including static, repeated, and video.	Cameras can be programmed to run continuously, or to take a picture every few seconds or minutes, and this information can be linked with date, time, location, as well as information from the gyroscope and accelerometer.

SUMMARY

The key points about passive data collection, for market researchers are:

- *If it is market research it requires informed consent.*

- *It potentially offers a better way of measuring what people do and the things they interact with, compared to asking people questions and asking them to recall what they saw, did, or felt.*

- *Passive data collection can replace the inaccuracies of memory and estimation with the accuracy of tracked, automatically recorded, digitized behaviour.*

- *Passive data collection can require less effort from participants than other forms of conventional market research.*

- *Passive data collection is currently in its early stages, most forecasters expect it to develop and grow considerably.*

- *It tends to be app-based, which means asking participants to download the app.*

- *The areas that have made the best use of passive data so far are: media measurement companies, companies from outside of market research, and qualitative research.*

- *Mainstream quantitative researchers have struggled, so far, to combine the sorts of data produced by passive tracking with the sorts of business questions they are faced with.*

13 Panels, Lists, and Communities

INTRODUCTION

This chapter looks at three key ways that researchers connect with research participants, particularly when seeking to conduct quantitative research. These three routes are:

1. Access panels, i.e. a database of people who have signed up to take part in market research

2. Customer lists, i.e. the customers of the research client

3. Research communities, for example, MROCs, community panels, and insight communities.

All of these three routes are used to recruit participants for quantitative and qualitative research. However, traditional recruitment methods are also important for qualitative research, including mobile qualitative market research.

In addition to reviewing the key characteristics of these three approaches, the chapter includes a brief overview of alternative approaches.

ACCESS PANELS

Access panels are typically run by companies (or divisions of larger companies) specializing in making research participants available to other market research companies, independent market researchers, and organizations using research. In the language of the online access panel business, they are suppliers of sample. For example, companies like Research Now and Survey Sampling International specialize in providing sample, as does LightSpeed, which is part of the Kantar Group.

Access panels create databases of large numbers of people who have agreed to take part in market research, usually in return for incentives. The core business of an access panel is to make their members available for market research, usually for market research surveys. The panel companies make their money by charging the researcher a fee, typically for each completed interview.

Currently, most mobile access panels are derived from online access panels, but this is likely to change over the next few years, and there are already some panels whose focus is mobile. All of the considerations that apply when using an access panel for online research also apply when using access panels for mobile research.

THE ROLE OF THE MARKET RESEARCHER WHEN WORKING WITH PANELS

Access panels are constructed in many different ways and tend to have different nuances, with one of the key determinants being how they were recruited. For example, if one panel was originally a customer list and another was originally recruited via online advertising the resultant panels will tend to differ, even after several years.

Online access panels are rarely a good representation of the researcher's target population. They represent people who use the internet more than average and over represent people who want to take part in research to gain rewards. It is necessary for the researcher to use a sampling strategy, and/or a processing/modelling strategy, that takes this into account. Quota sampling based on demographic characteristics (age, sex, education, etc.) is one popular way of specifying an online sample. Quotas may also relate to behaviour, such as having recently purchased a specific type of product. Random sampling of the target population cannot be achieved via an access panel, except in the most unusual of cases, for example where people have been selected for membership through some random selection process and where devices and internet access are provided to people who don't already have it.

In most cases, the panel company takes care of all the communications with the research participants: sending survey invitations to them; sending them any required links; and dealing with incentives. The panel company is responsible for selecting a sample that meets the requirements of the research, although the researcher normally defines the sample.

Typically, in quantitative projects, the panel company will deal with any queries from the research participants. One of the key reasons for this is that the identity of the panel members is commercially sensitive and most panel companies are reluctant to share this with others.

However, when dealing with a qualitative project it is often necessary to put the participants in direct contact with the researcher, particularly if the research takes place over a number of days or weeks.

ONLINE ACCESS PANELS

At the moment, most access panels are organized around online surveys, rather than mobile surveys, qualitative research, or ongoing projects such as passive tracking.

When supplying people for a project that requires participants to use a mobile device (e.g. a smartphone or tablet), the panel company will typically adopt one of two options:

1.   They may have profiled their members in terms of what devices they own. In which case they can target invitations to the appropriate members.

2.   They may send invitations to panel members who meet the broad criteria (such as demographics) and screen for ownership of the correct device or devices.

The potential problem with using an online access panel to recruit mobile participants is that it assumes that mobile users are a subset of internet users. In many markets such as Finland, South Korea, the USA, and Australia, this is broadly true. However, in markets where mobile phone use is much more widespread than internet use (such as India, and indeed the whole of Africa) a mobile sample collected from an online access panel may be seriously skewed because many more people in these countries have access to the internet via a mobile device, than via fixed connections. In these parts of the world traditional online research is being skipped, with the trend being to go from face-to-face directly to mobile research.

As the penetration of mobile devices moves towards 100% in many markets, the possibility of mobile panels that are more representative than online panels arises. The self-selection and sensitizing issues will still be there, but the access issue will diminish. However, even when close to 100% of target groups have mobile phones, the proportion accessing the internet from their mobile device may still be well under 100%.

MOBILE SPECIFIC PANELS

Mobile specific panels are panels where the members have been recruited and profiled because they own a mobile device and have said they are prepared to take part in market research via their mobile device.

At the moment, most mobile panels are focused on phones, rather than specifically on tablets or other non-phone devices, but this is likely to change over time. Mobile panel companies will typically have more than one way that they can contact their members, for example email, SMS, and voice.

Some of the mobile panels are focused on smartphones, but others have feature phone options. Feature phones are a necessary element if the panel is intended to be broadly representative of any market, even a developed market.

UNINTENTIONAL MOBILE

As mentioned in earlier chapters, a large proportion of quantitative mobile market research is 'unintentional' mobile. For example, a project might be commissioned and specified as online, but a quarter of the participants might choose to complete it on a mobile device. Whilst allowing participants a wider range of modes to choose from will tend to increase the diversity amongst the participants, it may also introduce mode effects, i.e. different modes may systematically change the results, because of the device used and the context in which the survey is taken. More information on the issues of mixed-mode research is included in the chapter on Mixed-Mode Research.

Researchers should ensure that they know which devices are suitable for their study and seek to prevent (in a polite and courteous way) anybody with an inappropriate device from taking part in the study. However, unless there are good reasons why a study should be PC only, or mobile only, most studies should be suitable for PC, tablet, and smartphone.

Researchers should capture information about the sorts of devices used by participants to take part in the study, in order to check at analysis time the nature of any mode effects.

WORKING WITH PANEL COMPANIES

Working with a panel company to create a mobile or mixed-mode study is logistically much easier than almost any other method of conducting a quantitative research study. The panel company should be able to offer advice on what is likely to work and what is likely to cause a problem. The panel company will deal with the invitations, all or most of the queries, and the incentives. Some panel companies will also script and host the survey and supply the data, either as a data file or as data tables.

The main task for the researcher, when working with a panel company, is to ensure that the project has been properly specified and to check the data to ensure that only people with the right sort of devices have taken part. When first dealing with a new panel company it is a good idea to check how their panel was recruited, whom it represents (e.g. in China it might be focused on Tier 1 and Tier 2 cities), whether they 'blend' participants from other panels, and whether they abide by the relevant codes and standards. One good starting point, when finding out about a new supplier, is to ask for their answers to ESOMAR's 28 questions.

ESOMAR's 28 Questions to Help Research Buyers of Online Samples

ESOMAR (2012b) maintain a list of key questions that can be asked to the providers of research samples to help understand the nature and quality of the service they provide.

At the time of writing, the list had 28 questions, covering five key areas:

1.   Company profile

2.   Sample sources and recruitment

3.   Sampling and project management

4.   Data quality and validation

5.   Policies and compliance.

The current version of the questions can be obtained from the ESOMAR website, www.ESOMAR.org.

PANELS AND APPS

A growing number of access panels are developing apps to allow them to offer both browser-based and app-based projects. Because panels have an ongoing relationship with their members it is easier to spread the cost of apps over multiple projects. Similarly, since panel members are keen to do more surveys they are often more willing than ad hoc participants to download an app onto their phone and/or tablet.

CUSTOMER LISTS

A customer list is provided by the researcher's client and can be as simple as an Excel file, with names, email addresses, and/or telephone numbers, or it can be part of a comprehensive CRM database. Most client owned lists are based on customers registering and supplying their details, as part of buying some product or service, or through opting in to receive communications. But some client owned lists are much broader than this and will include names purchased from list vendors, ex-customers, and prospective customers.

Compared with access panels, using a customer list requires the researcher to be more aware of potential pitfalls and to take responsibility for the sample being a suitable proxy for the population being studied. For example, the researcher needs to ensure that a suitable subset of the total list has been selected.

When using a customer list for market research, the researcher should check that the appropriate permissions are in place, that is to say that the people on the list have consented to be contacted for market research. Note, consent means different things in different markets. In some locations consent will be by opting in, in others it is via not opting out.

INVITING PARTICIPANTS

Potential research participants will either be invited by the client or the research agency. There are two potential advantages of the client sending the invitations:

1.   In general, the response rate to the invitation will be higher if the client sends the invitation rather than if a third party sends it. Even when the client prefers that the researcher send the invitation, including the client's name in the invitation has been shown to increase response rates.

2.   There may be fewer data protection steps to navigate, for the researcher, if the client sends the invitations.

Potential participants are sent an invitation to the study, including a link to the survey. The invitation and the link should make it clear that if the recipient clicks on the link they are consenting to some data transfer to the research agency – as specified by the research project's terms and conditions and privacy policy.

Options for sending the invitations

In many cases the best option for inviting people to take part in a study, even a mobile study, is via email. However, if the client has telephone numbers, then SMS or some other telephone related messaging can be more appropriate. For example, if the client is a telecommunications provider (a telco) then SMS can be much better way of connecting with potential participants for a mobile study.

DRAWING A SAMPLE

When using a client's customer list, it is important to draw a sample that reflects the target population. In most cases, the sample will either be:

1.   a quota controlled sample, for example the right number (or proportion) of males, females, young, and old, etc.;

2.   a random sample from the full customer list.

Note, in traditional research, a random sample is often the best option. However, as with access panels, a client's list may contain distorting factors that have contributed to the construction of the list. For example, newer customers might be more likely to have recorded their email address, so a random sample of customers with email addresses may over-recruit new customers. Therefore, a quota controlled sample will often be the best approach.

When drawing a sample from a client list, care needs to be taken not to introduce systematic biases. For example if a sample of 10 000 contacts was created by taking the first 10 000 records from the client database, the market researcher might find that:

1.   The list might have been sorted alphabetically, producing a list of people whose family names starts with A, which could relate to a specific ethnic group or culture.

2.   The list might reflect the order that people became customers, so the first 10 000 records might be the people who have been customers longest.

3.   The list might be organized by geography, so the first 10 000 records could come from a single region or sales account.

DATA PROTECTION AND PRIVACY

The first step in using a client list is to ensure that the client has the appropriate permissions in place in order to allow the research to take place, in the way intended. For example, if the researcher will be sending the invitations, permissions need to be in place for the data to be transferred.

In most cases, it is not possible, under market research rules and guidelines, to transfer individual results back to the client after the research takes place. For example, market research rules do not normally allow usage information from a customer's survey responses to be added to the customer database. If there is a need to transfer individual information back to the client, then care should be taken to (a) obtain clearly expressed consent from the participants, (b) ensure that the client agrees to protect the confidentiality of respondents, and (c) check on the research status of the project, in accordance to market research guidelines.

If invitations to take part in the study have been sent by the research agency, then there is typically personally identifiable information. Care needs to be taken to keep this secure, and to make it anonymous at the first suitable opportunity.

SCREENING FOR DEVICE USAGE

Most client lists are going to be out of date to some extent. Therefore, when inviting customers to take part in the survey, care needs to be taken to ensure that people still meet the criteria for the study, including possession of a suitable mobile device.

RESEARCH COMMUNITIES

Research communities, including insight communities, MROCs (Market Research Online Communities), and community panels, may be operated and managed by either clients or researchers. In either case, the result is a very 'hands on' experience for the researcher, both in general and in the area of mobile communications and market research. This section of the chapter provides an overview of research communities and outlines the various ways in which mobile devices are used.

One key difference between research communities and the other two sample sources mentioned so far in this chapter, panels and lists, is that communities are commonly associated with both quantitative and qualitative research. Panels and lists can be used to obtain participants for qualitative research, but they are more typically focused on quantitative research.

AN OVERVIEW OF RESEARCH COMMUNITIES

A typical research community is a private, branded, online community composed of customers who have agreed to participate in research projects. In a private community the members of the community are only available to the brand or organization that commissioned and/or runs the community, unlike the members of an access panel who are available to a variety of organizations.

Most research communities are branded. The purpose of these communities is to foster a conversation between customers and the brand. In these communities, customers are encouraged to speak to the brand, directly, rather than talking through intermediaries.

Most communities are based on customers, rather than the whole market place. Brands and customers have a community of interest with each other, and there are many topics that only customers can speak knowledgeably about.

Not all research communities fit neatly into the categories just described (private, branded, and customer-based). Some are themed (e.g. looking at a topic such as cooking or drinking) rather than branded and some are open to everyone rather than recruited to represent a specific target population. However, the majority of communities are private, branded, and focused on customers.

Short-term and long-term

Research communities come in both short-term (anything from a few days to a few weeks) and long-term (typically ongoing and commissioned in multiples of 6–12 months). Mobile research can be used with both long and short-term communities.

Most of the notes in this section relate to ongoing communities, as the continuous nature of these communities can create more issues that need to be monitored and addressed.

MOBILE DEVICES AND COMMUNITIES

Mobile devices can be used by community members to complete research tasks and also for the management of the community itself. The types of research tasks that community members may take part in using a mobile device include:

- *Surveys*

- *Passive data collection approaches*

- *Qualitative research*

- *Multi-stage projects (for example a survey followed by a discussion)*

- *Community/member communications, for example facilitating people signing up to the community and as a medium for communication with the team managing the community.*

MANAGING MOBILE COMMUNICATIONS

Contact with mobile participants starts with the sign-up process. For most communities, the main issue is to ensure that members have the choice of using a mobile device or PC to register. However, if the community members are expected to use their mobile devices to interact with the community, then the community administrator may require them to use their device to complete the initial stages, typically registering and taking part in any initial profiling surveys.

Two key issues that community administrators face with mobile devices and communities are:

1.   Keeping the contact and device details of members up to date. One good tip is to have an alternative way of contacting members, for example a second email address or their mobile phone number.

2.   Avoiding alienating or annoying members. It is important for researchers to respect people's private time and not interrupt or disturb them at the wrong time of day or too often. Most people keep their mobile devices close at hand during the night (especially their phone), so messages should not be sent when the member might be asleep. This means knowing the time zone the members are in and ideally giving the member an easy option to change their time zone or to request no contact for a specific period of time (e.g. during a holiday or work trip). The number and frequency of reminders should be managed to avoid antagonizing members.

Members should be offered a variety of ways that they want to be contacted by the community and of interacting with the community, such as SMS, email, instant messaging, and social media. Communications should be a combination of push (where a message is sent to the community member) and pull (where members check to see if there are any messages).

THE CONTINUOUS NATURE OF COMMUNITIES

The key difference between a research community and an access panel or a customer list is that a community is part of an ongoing relationship between the researcher and the member. Access panels and client lists typically are a single interaction between the researcher and the participant, but a research community is more like an ongoing discussion. Therefore, it is important that the researcher secures the long-term cooperation of participants from the beginning of the relationship, even though this can mean increased complexity by having multiple ways of communicating with members.

USES OF MOBILE MARKET RESEARCH WITH A RESEARCH COMMUNITY

This section of the chapter briefly outlines the main uses of mobile market research in the context of research communities.

Mobile quantitative research

Mobile devices can be used for both active and passive quantitative market research. Because community members tend to have a good relationship with their community, it is often easier (compared with ad hoc samples) to find people willing to download apps or to take part in more invasive types of research, such as tracking their mobile device usage.

In terms of surveys, the ongoing relationship between the brand, the researcher, and members makes it easier to break a study into several parts and easier to draw on previously stored information, which helps produce shorter surveys.

Mobile qualitative research

A wide range of qualitative exercises are conducted with community members, including:

- *Online discussions*
- *Online focus groups*

- *Collection of ethnographic information*
- *Capturing images and photos.*

When designing a research project, the researcher should determine whether a project is mobile only, or whether the participants in mobile qualitative research projects should have a choice of device on which to complete the exercises, including phones, phablets, tablets, and also PCs.

Because researchers have an ongoing link to community members and links to past responses, qualitative research projects can be targeted at specific people or groups of people. These could be people who have particular behaviours or needs, who have expressed specific views, or whose previous responses require clarification. The analysis of the qualitative information can draw on information collected during previous research projects.

Mixed-mode studies

A large proportion of mobile research projects, particularly surveys, are mixed-mode projects. This includes intentional and unintentional mixed-mode research. In online mixed-mode research the researcher makes surveys available to community members using a platform that supports a range of devices, typically PCs, tablets, and smartphones. More information about mixed-mode studies, and the potential impact on data, can be found in the chapter focusing on mixed-mode research.

Engagement activities

The management of research communities tends to include a range of engagement activities. Sometimes these engagement activities may address a real research need, but part or all of their rationale is to provide tasks to the members that are fun, challenging, interesting, or simply different. There is a widespread view that engaging community members results in higher levels of cooperation and lower levels of churn or turnover. Mobile devices are particularly suitable for these engagement exercises. Examples include the collection of audio-visual diaries, images of meals, or tracking members' geo-location.

However, the most important element of engagement is to make sure the members know they are having an impact on products and services. This means listening to a member, acting on the insight gathered, and closing the feedback loop.

Communications

Communications include updates, queries, support, and reminders. A mobile strategy should include a variety of methods of communication, often including voice as well as email, IM, and SMS.

PANELS VERSUS LISTS VERSUS COMMUNITIES

This chapter has covered three methods for contacting and communicating with market research participants. Each method has its comparative strengths and weaknesses and these are summarized in Table 13.1.

Table 13.1   Strengths and weaknesses of methods for contacting and communicating with market research participants

	Strengths for mobile research	Weaknesses for mobile research
Access panel	A large part of the work is done by the panel company, who should be experienced, skilled, and efficient in the area. Online access panels are globally the leading method of conducting market research, so their use for mobile research adds credibility. Samples can be selected on a wide range of background variables, such as age, gender, location, and potentially: income, topics of interest, types of phone etc.	The research is based on people who have joined a panel and who are used to being paid. This means the sample is potentially a skewed sample and drawn from a potentially skewed group. If the panel is an online access panel, and if mobile usage is more widespread than internet usage, then the sample will be skewed. The cost can be too high for surveys with very large numbers (tens of thousands or more) of participants, even if the survey length is very short.
Client list	If the client's list is comprehensive, then it can be a good source of customers for research. The researcher can leverage the client's positive relationship with customers to increase cooperation rates. Can be the lowest cost of all the options.	The list, typically, only includes customers and does not cover the whole market. If the client's list only covers some types of customer, then results may be skewed. Care needs to be taken to draw an appropriate sample. Client lists are sometimes out of date and may need to be verified/ updated first.
Research community	Deep profiles of users are usually available. A high level of cooperation is typical, which facilitates a wide range of active and passive quantitative research and synchronous and asynchronous qualitative research. The use of mobile devices supports the communication strategy of the community and can enable the researcher to get closer to the member's day-to-day life.	Only represents the market to the extent the community represents the market. Adding mobile communications and research to a community typically increases the costs of running the community due to more queries, more data, and greater diversity of data.

The two key dimensions of difference amongst these are ownership and specificity to research. In terms of the ownership dimension: a client list is owned by the client company; a research community is typically owned by the client, but often managed by a third party; and an access panel is owned by a third party.

Online access panels and research communities are specific to market research, i.e. they are not used for other purposes, such as marketing. Client lists often have more uses, beyond market research. The primary uses of client lists tend to be focused on commercial activities, such as service delivery and marketing activities such as: promotions, sales, loyalty and rewards programmes, and so on.

ALTERNATIVE SOURCES OF RESEARCH PARTICIPANTS

This chapter has described the use of access panels, client lists, and research communities for mobile market research. The common element among these three sample sources is that they are all based on existing collections of people, although each has a number of distinct differences.

There are a range of alternative methods to find and recruit participants for mobile market research, including:

- *QR codes and/or short URLs (for example, in conjunction with print and outdoor advertising, in-store and point of sale initiatives, and requests on sales receipts)*
- *Social media activities*
- *Online advertising*
- *Mobile advertising*
- *Marketing lists*
- *Face-to-face recruitment*
- *Telephone recruitment.*

These and similar alternatives differ quite markedly from the three methods reviewed in this chapter. In most of these alternatives there are not ongoing relationships, and in most cases participants' identities are hard to validate.

SUMMARY

The key innovation that facilitated the growth of online research, from the mid-1990s, was the emergence and growth of online access panels. It is likely that the continued growth and development of mobile research will depend on the growth of access panels offering mobile services. Beyond panels, the two major sources of participants for mobile market research are client lists and research communities.

Key points to consider are:

- *Access panels have numerous advantages for market researchers, including not having to handle sample management, incentives, reminders, and so on.*

- *Access panels have traditionally focused on online surveys via PCs, but a growing number of specifically mobile solutions are being provided.*

- *However, online access panels have had their detractors, in terms of representing 'ordinary' customers, and this will be true of mobile panels too.*

- *Client lists can provide the lowest cost option, in terms of connecting with a mobile sample, but it can require the greatest amount of work to ensure that an appropriate sample is used. Additionally, researchers need to verify that appropriate permissions are in place to use the list for research.*

- *Research communities tend to combine both quantitative and qualitative uses, and mobile devices can have a vital role in the management of the community as well as being a mode for conducting market research.*

- *Panels and communities are making it easier to conduct app-based research, because of their ongoing relationships with members.*

- *Whilst panels, lists, and communities are likely to provide the majority of mobile quantitative samples, it is likely that traditional recruitment channels will continue to be important for mobile qualitative market research projects.*

- *Beyond panels, lists, and communities there are a wide range of alternatives, none of which are major resources, but can be the right solution to a specific research need.*

14 International Mobile Research

INTRODUCTION

International market research is a category of research that many consider to be a discipline in its own right. Countries differ in many ways including language, culture, affluence, and technology, and these differences create issues, problems, and opportunities for market researchers. International research requires special skills and knowledge, in addition to those required to conduct research within a researcher's home market. In a field like mobile market research, which is still developing and evolving, the challenges of conducting international projects can be even greater.

The term 'international research' used in this book includes: research conducted in a country other than the researcher's home country, research conducted in two or more countries, and research that is conducted in multiple countries.

This chapter focuses on the use of mobile market research in conducting global or multi-country mobile market research. The reason for this focus is that these are the harder cases, i.e. the cases where differences are more likely to create issues. A mobile market research project in, say, the USA and Canada is international, it will throw up some interesting issues (such as the need to support English and French in Canada), but the project is less complex than a study with, say, ten very different countries, in regions as different as Asia, Africa, and Europe.

AN OVERVIEW OF MULTI-COUNTRY RESEARCH STUDIES

Before looking at the complexities of international mobile market research, it is useful to consider the issues that make international research special.

GLOBALIZATION

International research has developed in the context of changes in the way businesses operate, in particular the growth in multi-national businesses and globalization.

Globalization has been one of the major trends in markets for the last 20 to 30 years, driving the growth and prominence of international brands and services, and of multinational corporations. In order to market products and services around the globe international companies need to understand multiple markets, cultures, and people.

With the international marketing of brands and services comes the need for international and standardized market research programmes to find insights in different locations. However, brands often need to balance international standardization with local preferences, laws, customers, and competitive situations.

International market research seeks to resolve a tension between the standardization of products and services with the diversity of the people who constitute local markets. For example, although products may be physically the same in each market, the packaging, communication, and the relationship they share with consumers is often country specific. In one country a product may be seen as the height of luxury, in another it might be seen as just one option amongst many.

MANAGING INTERNATIONAL PROJECTS

Whilst there is no single model that describes all international research projects there are some patterns that are more common than others. The key patterns are shown in Table 14.1.

Because international projects are often designed and managed by a lead team, often based in a single country, the design and management of the study can become quite separate from some of the markets being researched. Separate in terms of distance, time zones, and often in terms of language and culture.

Table 14.1   Some approaches for managing international research projects

Issue	Options
Client management	Normally managed and commissioned by a single team, often through a regional or global insights team.
Supplier	The most common option is to place the contract with a single agency. However, sometimes a client will place the contract with multiple agencies, e.g. one per country.
Fieldwork	Supplied by an agency with operations in each country or by sub-contractors or by an international fieldwork provider.
Project design	Typically designed by the lead team, often a combination of the client and agency lead teams.

Table 14.2   Implementing a multi-country market research study

Steps	Overview	Description
1	Objective	• Client defines the insights required, i.e. the business and research objectives.
2	Brief	• Research brief is prepared, outlining the key project specifications, often including: countries, languages, sample sizes, methods, and deliverables. • The brief usually specifies key parameters, such as the time available for the project. • The brief may also detail benchmarks or action standards that the research will be compared with.
3	Design	• A research agency is appointed to design, manage, and implement the research, often in conjunction with the client. • Define items such as the countries, target respondents, data collection methods, sample sources, and the questionnaire. • For each country, the design is expanded to include languages, translations, and any special/local considerations.
4	Data Collection	• The data collection is conducted by the research agency, often in conjunction with teams from each country, or via third parties such as access panels or fieldwork companies.
5	Insight and Analysis	• Agency conducts the analysis, seeking to identify the big picture across the countries, and the important differences between them. • If the research is quantitative, then the analysis is typically conducted centrally. • If the research is qualitative then there is often a need for the analysis to involve the central and local teams.

PROJECT IMPLEMENTATION

The key steps in implementing a multi-country market research study, in terms of a single client working with a single lead agency, are described in Table 14.2.

DIFFERENT COUNTRIES, DIFFERENT MODES

In multi-country projects the methods used for data collection may vary from one country to another. For example, the data collection mode might be mobile in one group of countries, CATI in another group, and face-to-face in others. This is because, often, no single mode is available in every country, and even where it is available, it is not always cost-efficient. For example, in-home face-to-face interviews are rare in the US, online is rarely appropriate in Mexico, and CATI is usually not suitable in Bangladesh.

However, if a relatively inexpensive and fast mode of data collection is available in each market for a specific research project, then it will tend to be the preferred option. For example, a research project in the USA, UK, Australia, and Germany is likely to be conducted via online panels. Which, as has been mentioned before, is likely to mean that large numbers of the participants will use mobile devices to take part.

A multi-country mobile market research project may need to utilize different mobile devices in different markets. For example, smartphones and tablets might be used for the project in the more advanced markets, such as Singapore. However, feature phones might be used in less developed markets, where smartphones are less common, internet connections less widely available, and data contracts are expensive.

KEY ISSUES IN INTERNATIONAL RESEARCH

Amongst the issues that need to be identified and clarified in international research are:

- *What local factors will shape the research being conducted? These factors will include the technology available, the sample options, and expectations in terms of things like incentives.*

- *What local regulations/laws could impact the research design and implementation? For example, data privacy laws can limit what can be collected and dialling rules can limit how mobile phones are called.*

- *Is the project going to be managed and debriefed centrally or will the client's local teams be involved in the management or debriefs?*

- *What translations are needed and how are they going to be handled? When using new technologies, such as smartphones and tablets, it is important that translations use contemporary language, which usually requires translations being conducted by people who are in the country and familiar with the technology.*

SPECIAL CONSIDERATIONS FOR INTERNATIONAL QUALITATIVE RESEARCH

If multiple languages are going to be used to implement the project, then there are a number of issues that relate specifically to qualitative projects. This is because the translations often need to be conducted whilst the project is happening, making it more demanding, more time consuming, and more expensive. For example:

- *In a mobile-enabled online focus group, the client and the lead researcher may want to see translations of the participants' replies as they are being collected, to help them suggest further questions and prompts.*

- *In a mobile discussion the participants will be posting replies and expecting prompt replies from the moderator.*

- *In a mobile ethnography project the researcher will need to monitor what people are collecting and ask for further information as needed.*

In a quantitative project, the most common approach is to manage the project centrally, especially if international access panels are being used. The most common pattern is for all the questionnaires to be translated at the start of the project, and all the open-ends dealt with at the end of the project, creating just two points where translations are relevant (other than handling any logistical and technical problems that occur during the project).

In international qualitative projects, the translations take place at the start (e.g. to create the discussion guide), and at the end (to aid the analysis), but translations are also needed throughout the project. In qualitative projects, the balance between central management and devolved management is less clear and there is less agreement. Some projects seek to control everything centrally, employing translators or multi-lingual researchers, whilst other recruit local researchers to localize a research plan and often to conduct the first stage of the analysis.

More information about qualitative research is available in Chapters 4, 5, and 6 that look specifically at qualitative research.

DESIGNING MULTI-COUNTRY MOBILE PROJECTS

Whilst one of the most exciting parts of being involved in multi-country market research projects is analysing the diversity of opinions and insights, the implementation of a project can be challenging and often throws up unexpected problems. Multi-country mobile market research projects go through the same processes as most other types of multi-country studies, but with the additional complexities created by using a mode that is neither mature nor internationally consistent in its form and application. Key issues include:

- *Differences in the sorts of mobile devices available*
- *Differences in the availability of reliable and affordable internet connections*

- *Differences in the ability of research software platforms to handle variations in languages and scripts*

- *Differences in the market research infrastructure to handle mobile data collection.*

The next section offers a step-by-step discussion of how the international issues facing a mobile market research project can be addressed.

WHY IS THE PROJECT USING MOBILE MARKET RESEARCH?

There are several reasons why a project might be using mobile market research, including such things as conducting research-on-research, or to pilot a new method, but there are two core reasons for choosing mobile:

1.   The nature of the research requires mobile approach, for example to conduct an 'in the moment' study as people are going about their lives.

2.   Mobile is felt to deliver the best combination of quality, price, and speed.

The reasons why a project has been deemed to require a mobile approach are important as they will help determine the answer to some of the other key questions. For example, if mobile research is not an option in one country, should the country be dropped from the project or should the method be changed?

WHAT COUNTRIES ARE GOING TO BE RESEARCHED?

Although identifying the countries that the research should cover is one of the first steps, researchers should be aware this is often a decision that is changed. Countries are sometimes removed from the research project if they are too expensive, too difficult, or if conducting research in a country is likely to take too long. Countries are also added if stakeholders within the client company press for them.

For each country the mobile ecosystem should be assessed along with normal factors to consider, including:

- *The types of mobile devices that research participants are likely to use. Including phones versus tablets, feature phones versus smartphones, and operating systems.*

- *If the internet is going to be used, what is the coverage of the internet like, for example is mobile internet common, or should the research assume that participants will need to be in a Wi-Fi zone to be able to connect?*

- *If the research is not going to be based on internet-enabled phones, what specification of phone is needed and what is the incidence of those phones?*

As well as published data, local offices and fieldwork partners can help answer these questions. Characteristics such as rural versus urban, economic status, and age are often good indicators of the type of mobile devices one might expect to find within the target population. In a few markets literacy is an issue that should be checked, especially before deciding to use a self-completion mobile mode. Some researchers have found that mobile familiarity helps them conduct research with participants who have limited formal literacy (Williams 2014a).

IS MOBILE A VIABLE OPTION?

It is important to identify as quickly as possible whether mobile is a viable option for the research. If the answer is 'yes', then the question shifts to which mobile channels are the best for the study, for example SMS, downloadable app, or browser-based. It should be noted that even if mobile is viable, it might not be the best option.

In a perfect solution the same mobile approach will be used in each country, but this is not always possible. So, the second part of this question is to identify what sort of mobile options are available in each country. Even within a single region, for example South-East Asia, different methods might be needed in advanced markets like Korea and Singapore, than in less developed markets like Cambodia and Myanmar.

UNDERSTANDING THE MOBILE RESEARCH LANDSCAPE

In designing a mobile market research study, the following information should be assessed for each country:

- *The penetration of mobile devices within the target groups.*

- *The types of mobile devices being used and their capabilities.*

- *The relevant functions (e.g. text messaging, email, game playing, banking, etc.) used by the target population on their mobile devices.*

- *The cost and quality of mobile data networks. For example, is the network fast enough to support the streaming of videos, is the network reliable, and is the network affordable?*

- *The type of mobile networks on offer. For example, some countries have proprietary networks that require some solutions to be tailored in order to work.*

- *The speed of internet connections if the internet is part of the mobile solution. This issue is broader than just network coverage and reliability, it can also relate to where the servers for a project are hosted. For example, servers based outside China can behave very sluggishly, whereas local servers can be very fast.*

- *Localization and translation issues. The mobile market research approach being used should be delivered in the local language, or languages. This does not just mean translating the survey, it means support, training, and error handling should all be localized too.*

IMPLEMENTING INTERNATIONAL MOBILE MARKET RESEARCH PROJECTS

Implementing an international market research project, including mobile ones, involves more elements than a project limited to a single country. This section looks at some of the key issues that a researcher managing an international mobile market project should keep in mind.

LOCALIZING THE RESEARCH

In most cases, an international market research project will be developed in one language, often for a single market, and then localized for the other countries. In this case localizing includes translating the questionnaire, adding in local brands and contexts, and testing locally.

In the context of a mobile market research project, this localizing might also include catering for different mobile devices, different operating systems, and different internet and mobile networks.

FIELDWORK

A researcher might prefer to complete the fieldwork one country at a time, to enable local conditions and variations to receive the maximum level of attention. However, in most projects the fieldwork for all the countries will take place at approximately the same time. The researcher needs to use all the tools provided by the data collection system to monitor the fieldwork in each country.

One key issue to determine is how problems with the technology will be dealt with. Mobile technologies are as likely as any other technology to suffer from occasional problems, and dealing with them needs to be factored into the procedures. Questions to consider include:

- *If participants have a problem, they will want to be able to ask for help in their language and expect replies in their language. Will this be provided by the fieldwork partners, by a third party, or by the lead agency?*

- *If some aspect of the technology fails, for example if there are problems uploading images from a specific brand of mobile device, who has the local technical knowledge to solve the problem?*

Key issues to watch out for in a mobile study are differences between the countries in terms of dropout rates, differences in the average survey completion time, and the integrity of paradata items such as location of the surveys and time of day.

CREATING A SINGLE DATASET

Unless the mobile data has been collected via an online research platform linked to an international server, the data from the project needs to be gathered together and transferred to the researcher. This should be the responsibility of the local partner and the process will depend upon local circumstances.

Some of the options that are used, in different parts of the world, and with different projects include:

- *Asking participants (or interviewers) to go to a location with Wi-Fi to upload the results.*

- *Participants returning the mobile devices to the local partner who uploads the data from the phone or tablet.*

- *The local partner visiting the research participants and collecting the information, using data transfer methods such as cables or Bluetooth.*

The process for gathering and transmitting the data should be agreed before the project starts. Clear specifications should be provided to all local partners before the start of the project that only clean, acceptable data is delivered. It is important that the data is fully secured; it should be password protected and access limited to authorized personnel only. All local and international laws and rules about data transfer must be adhered to.

DATA ANALYSIS

Multi-country studies usually produce separate datasets, each with their own idiosyncrasies that need to be considered when conducting the analysis. Many researchers have their own approaches to analysing data, including international data, however, a common process is:

1.   Check the integrity of the data. For example, does anything look wrong? Do some interviews need removing, replacing, standardizing, and so on?

2.   Analyse the data to find the big picture, the messages that are consistent, or at least dominant, in the data across the countries.

3.   Identify the material differences in the data, including those relating to countries.

4.   Take the information gathered and create business insights, typically by answering the business and research questions that were specified at the start of the project.

The items listed here apply to all data collection modes. In terms of a mobile market research project the researcher should be looking for any effects caused by the data collection method, especially if the mode varied from country to country. If smartphones were used by some participants and feature phones were used by others, the researcher should investigate and understand any differences.

In an international project, any differences caused by modes can be strongly correlated with country differences. For example, if smartphones are mostly used in rich countries, and feature phones are mostly used in poorer countries, there may be differences in the data, but they are more likely to be due to inter-country differences than differences between the ways the phones have been used to collect data.

THE DEBRIEF, REPORT, OR PRESENTATION

When mobile market research has been used, it is often useful to describe how the use of mobile may have influenced (hopefully positively) the findings produced.

Because mobile market research is still relatively rare, researcher should be prepared to explain and (and sometimes defend) the method and the mode more than might be the case with a more established data collection modality. For example, by preparing and having available a summary of why mobile research was selected and what it has helped contribute to the findings.

BUILDING AN INTERNATIONAL MOBILE MARKET RESEARCH SOLUTION

The majority of international mobile market research projects use a commercially available software platform and often conduct their fieldwork via access panels, especially for quantitative research. However, some projects require customized or ad hoc solutions.

In this context, 'customized or ad hoc' can mean one or more of the following:

- *Using a software platform that has not been used in that country before.*

- *Recruiting mobile respondents who have not taken part in mobile research before.*

- *Modifying a software solution to achieve a specific aim.*

One of the most common examples of this situation is when conducting a qualitative ethnographic or mobile diary project. The software platform might be from one of the leading providers, but the sample may be recruited and supported by an agency that has not used that platform before, and the research participants may not have taken part in mobile research before.

SELECTING A MOBILE TECHNOLOGY AND TECHNOLOGY PARTNER

If a research project is more complex than working with an international provider of services (e.g. the international access panels) and a standard research platform, then the researcher will need to select the mobile technology and a technology partner.

For example, if the project requires the local recruitment of participants and the use of apps downloaded onto participants' phones, the choice of technology and technology partner is likely to determine the success of the project. Not all research suppliers have the technical expertise required to run a complex mobile market research project. Similarly, technology companies that build mobile market research tools may lack the experience and know-how to design and deliver a market research project in the target countries.

It is important that the researcher delivering the service to the end-client is comfortable with the capabilities of the technology and any technology partners to deliver the research. The mobile technology partner in turn needs to be able to clearly communicate to the researcher and research teams the risks as well as the benefits that come with using a specific mobile market research solution. A checklist for evaluating technologies and technology partners is shown in Table 14.3.

SELECTING LOCAL PARTNERS

If the fieldwork is not being sub-contracted to an international panel or fieldwork organization, then local partners are likely to be required, especially if the mobile solution requires local recruitment, briefings, and/or support.

Table 14.3   A checklist for evaluating technologies and technology partners

Topic	Issues
Experience of market research	A supplier with great mobile technology, but little experience of market research can be a problem, no matter how good they are in areas like sales leads or gaming.
Experience of the specific proposed mobile channel	For example SMS, apps, WAP, or HTML5.
Mobile experience in the target countries	Somebody on the project needs to know about each market; if that is not the researcher, it needs to be the technology partner.
Familiarity with the different languages being used	This is especially important if the languages include double-byte languages (e.g. Japanese), and/or right-to-left scripts (e.g. Arabic).
Understanding of the project parameters	Does the partner understand and sign up to the project's timelines, costs, and deliverables?
Respondent briefings	If the research participants will need to be briefed and supported, does the partner have the experience and capacity?
Laws and market research codes of conducts	Does the proposed partner understand what can and can't be done with market research data?
Monitoring services	Do the technology and the technology partner provide monitoring services to the researcher? For example does it have a dashboard showing fieldwork progress?

Some of the key responsibilities of a local partner are shown in Table 14.4.

GLOBAL DIVERSITY IN THE MOBILE LANDSCAPE

This section provides a brief snapshot of the mobile landscape that researchers conducting international mobile market research projects will encounter.

THE UBIQUITY OF MOBILE PHONES

At the time this book was written there were about seven billion mobile devices in use globally. Which means there are approximately as many mobile devices around the world as people. However, this does not mean that everyone had a mobile phone by the end of 2014. This is simply because some people have two or more devices whilst others have none.

Table 14.4   Key responsibilities of a local partner

Responsibility	Description
Recruitment	Unless participants for a project are recruited by the client (e.g. from client lists) or from an international panel organization, then a local partner can ensure a higher standard of recruitment. This is particularly true if in-person recruiting is being used. Partners with knowledge of the local options, customs, and rules can make a major difference to the project.
Fieldwork monitoring and quality control	The need for a local team is particularly important in projects such as a mobile diary project, where participants might be supplied with a product, asked to download an app, and record their experiences on a daily basis for two weeks.
Motivating participants	Researchers need to ensure that the demands being made on participants are reasonable, whilst at the same time motivating participants to complete assigned tasks. A local partner can be helpful in establishing boundaries between what is reasonable and what is not, and in employing locally accepted methods of ensuring project completion.
Replacement and dropout management	Local partners can use motivation to reduce dropouts and handle participant replacement.
Data integrity	Standards of what is considered acceptable in terms of data integrity and quality can vary from country to country. A good local partner will understand local perceptions and your requirements.
Local input to the analysis and debriefing	A local partner can provide useful feedback on how local conditions might have impacted data collection, which can help interpret the findings. A local partner is usually a good sounding board for creating a useful debrief that is likely to deliver insights as well as information.

What is becoming clear is that soon every economically active adult who wants a mobile phone will have one (plus plenty of other people too). The trend is towards smartphones, and the growth of tablets and phablets is strong.

The high incidence of mobile phones can make data collection via mobile devices a better option than either data collection using online via PCs or CATI to landlines.

MOBILE DIVERSITY

Even though most people have a mobile device, the challenges of diversity and mobile network fragmentation remain an issue. People use mobile devices differently, across different geographies, and within individual markets.

Some of these differences relate to owning different devices, for example feature phones, smartphones, phablets, and tablets. However, other differences relate to what people do with their phones. Some users download hundreds of apps, others use just those that came with the phone; some use their phone as a camera, others don't; some just use their tablet to read eBooks while others use it as their main IT device.

It should be noted that changes do not always flow from the most developed markets to the less developed. For example, mobile payments and banking are widely used in large parts of Africa, but are much less developed in Europe and North America.

TECHNOLOGY, SERVICE, AND USAGE DIFFERENCES

Some of differences between countries, in terms of technology, services, and usage, are highlighted in the sections that follow.

SMS

SMS, or text messaging, is a widely utilized service in all markets. In developing markets, the SMS share of all phone usage tends to be higher than in the more developed markets, because fewer alternatives are available and/or affordable. One of the key reasons for the strength of SMS is that it is an alternative to more expensive mobile uses, such as voice calls or emails.

SMS is particularly strong amongst younger people, in both developed and less developed markets, but its dominance may be challenged by the growth in messaging apps, such as WeChat and WhatsApp.

The main advantage of SMS, for market research, is that it is available to almost all phone users, everywhere in the world. The main downside to SMS is that it is a very limited mode, in terms of the numbers and types of questions that can be asked. Another text-based protocol that is used in some countries is USSD.

Mobile banking and payments

The absence of comprehensive banking services in many developing countries and the need to handle very small sums of money have given rise to innovative alternatives, in particular, using mobile devices to execute financial transactions. For example, in East Africa, mobile operators run a service, started in Kenya, called M-Pesa to deliver money to anyone with a mobile phone via SMS. In Kenya M-Pesa transferred the equivalent of 31% of Kenya's GDP, according to a report in the *Financial Times* in 2013 (Manson 2013).

M-Pesa gives access to financial transfer services to people who don't have access to banks and to those who don't have sufficient funds to maintain or to pay service charges.

M-Pesa is also credited with the continued and phenomenal growth of mobile access across Africa.

Social messaging applications

Declining data package costs across mobile networks and across the globe are resulting in a steady rise in the use of mobile applications like WeChat and WhatsApp that allow SMS-like connectivity to others who have the application on their phones. Additionally, they allow for exchange of multimedia, such as photos and videos, adding another dimension to social messaging.

Growth of services like WeChat has been rapid, with *The Economist* (2014) reporting in January 2014 that WeChat had over 270 million active members in China alone, with others reporting 400 million as the global figure. It is possible that messaging apps will shift the balance of usage away from services like SMS and from social networks like Twitter and Facebook.

Social media channels

Many of the successful online social channels, like Facebook, Twitter, Ren Ren, and Weibo, allow users to access these social networking services from either PCs or mobile devices. Different demographic groups and people from different countries appear to have different habits and preferences. These differences include the way that mobile devices are used with social media channels.

Differences in network infrastructures

Differences in networks arise from two key reasons: either because a network is at a different level of development (e.g. Korea and Singapore are ahead of most countries, whilst Myanmar and Ethiopia are less advanced), or because of specific local decisions (e.g. internet censorship in Cuba and Kuwait).

The most significant difference, because of the size of the market, is China. Restrictions on social networks such as Facebook and Twitter have helped develop local alternatives such as Ren Ren and Weibo. One key factor for market researchers is the so-called 'great firewall of China'. One consequence of the firewall is that servers based outside China tend to perform very slowly for participants based in China.

SUMMARY

International market research is a major component of global market research spend and it is not surprising that the mobile mode is of growing interest. However, there are several challenges in conducting multi-country mobile market research, with the key ones being:

- *The differing levels of development in the mobile ecosystem in different countries. For example, smartphones might be common in one country, but relatively rare in another.*

- *The existing structure of research modes differs by country, for example the more developed markets have online as the most frequently used mode, in the less developed markets CATI or face-to-face are more common. When mobile is added to the mix, the existing research structure has an effect.*

- *In developing markets one of the key roles for mobile market research is in improving the quality and timeliness of face-to-face research, something that online had already largely done in the developed markets.*

- *Conducting international mobile market research (other than via unintentional mobile as part of using international online panels) requires the research team to be competent with both mobile research and international research.*

- *If the research uses custom or non-standard elements the researcher will need to select an appropriate technology partner and in most cases a local fieldwork partner too.*

- *The global direction of travel appears to be towards every customer owning a phone, and increasingly a smartphone. This suggests that mobile international research could, within a few years, be the mode that is the most consistent, from one country to another.*

PART IV

Researching the Mobile Ecosystem, Ethics, and the Future

This final part of the book is intended as a reference section and a guide. Researching the Mobile Ecosystem is a resource for anybody wanting to conduct research into areas like mobile advertising and gives an additional perspective on the technology of mobile devices and mobile market research. The Ethics and Evolving Picture chapters provide a guide on how mobile market research should be conducted and glimpse into what might be coming next, whilst the Research-on-Research chapter summarizes the research that has been accessed in creating this book

Part IV covers:

15 Researching the Mobile Ecosystem

INTRODUCTION

Throughout the rest of this book the term 'mobile market research' has focused on using mobile devices to conduct or aid existing market research, for example using mobile market research in concept testing. However, the term 'mobile market research' can also be applied to market research into the mobile ecosystem.

The term 'mobile ecosystem' encompasses every aspect of the mobile world, including:

- *Devices, such as phones, phablets, and tablets*

- *Telephony and internet services*

- *Operating systems and apps*

- *Mobile shopping and commerce*

- *Mobile marketing and advertising.*

The scale of the mobile ecosystem is immense. The world is moving to a point where every economically active adult who wants a phone has one, and there are already about 7 billion mobile phones in use. The growth of mobile phones is being followed by several other adoption waves, including mobile internet, smartphones, tablets, and mobile social networks.

As well as being immense in terms of the number of people who are using mobile devices, the mobile ecosystem is immense in terms of service provision, manufacturing, R&D, finance, shopping, entertainment, and advertising. In December 2013, Forbes' list of the World's Most Valuable Brands had five companies with significant roles in the mobile ecosystem in its top nine: Apple, Microsoft, Google, Intel, and Samsung – the other four being Coca-Cola, IBM, McDonald's, and General Electric.

This chapter starts by reviewing the non-market research approaches to insight generation that are common in the mobile ecosystem. The chapter then looks at several aspects of the mobile ecosystem and considers the extent to which conventional research, mobile market research, and other techniques can be combined to support business decisions.

NON-MARKET RESEARCH OPTIONS

Organizations in the mobile ecosystem employ a wide range of non-market research techniques to gather data and insights and market researchers need to be aware of these approaches.

The list that follows includes techniques frequently used in the mobile ecosystem that are either not typically offered by market researchers or are offered by a range of other providers as well as market researchers.

- *Usage data.* For example, web logs from online services, telephone usage from the telcos, and usage information from third-party suppliers.

- *A/B testing.* Testing variants of a product or service in live situations to determine winners.

- *Agile development.* Launching products into the market quickly and adapting them in the marketplace, to optimize their appearance or performance.

- *Crowdsourcing.* Using the wider world to help solve problems, including the use of open-source development and crowdfunding.

- *Usability testing.* Ensuring products and services work properly for their intended users.

USAGE DATA

The mobile and online worlds create an extensive electronic record of the activity of users. Accessing a website tells the website owner a large amount about the user, in terms of: hardware, location, operating system, language the device is using (e.g. English, French etc.), and it might make an estimate of things like age and gender based on the sites you visit and the answers you pick. Use a mobile phone and you tell the telco who you contacted, where you were geographically, how long the contact lasted, what sort of contact it was (e.g. voice or SMS). Use email, such as Gmail, and you tell the service provider who you contacted, which of your devices you used, and the content of your email.

In many fields, market research is used to estimate usage and behaviour, but in the mobile ecosystem there is often at least one company that can provide this information without using market research, and provide it in much better detail. For example, a telco does not need to conduct a survey with a sample of its subscribers to find out how often they make calls or to work out how many texts they send, and how many of those texts are to international numbers. Telcos have this information, for each of their users.

Usage data tends to be better, cheaper, and often quicker than market research for recording what people did. However, this data is less powerful in working out why patterns are happening, and it is thought (by some people) to be weak in predicting what will happen if circumstances change. However, it should be noted that the advocates of big data and in particular 'predictive analytics' believe that it is possible to work out the answer to 'what if' questions, just from usage/behaviour data.

Unique access to usage data

One limitation of usage data is that in most cases only one organization has primary access to a specific section of usage data. In most cases, no single organization has a complete usage picture. For example, in a country with two mobile telephone operators, each will only have access to the usage data for their subscribers, plus some cross-network traffic information.

The segmented access model appears in many areas of usage data, for example the owner of a website is the only company that can track the people who visit that site. A bank has access to the online and mobile banking data and other data from its customers, but not data about the users of other banks. This segmented access feature of usage data is one of the reasons why organizations buy data from other sources and conduct market research to get a whole market picture.

Third-party estimates of usage

A number of organizations have created services and models that allow usage data to be acquired or estimated. For example, if users can be persuaded to download a tracking device, such as a useful toolbar, then that service can build a large, but partial picture of users of other services. For example, Alexa.com offer a toolbar that enables it to collect website usage data.

Another route to usage information is where the provider of a service buys or uses a utility from a third party to improve its services, but in turn provides usage data to the third party. Two examples of this route are Google Analytics and Flurry.

Flurry provide tracking software to app developers to embed in their applications. Each time the applications are run data is sent to Flurry, who share it with the app developer and utilize it for their services. Google offer web analytics to websites, which allows Google to gain a large but partial picture of online and mobile behaviour. In Google's case this can be added to any other services, such as search and ad serving, to build a much larger picture of internet usage patterns.

Legal implications of usage data

Usage data, whether it is browsing, emailing, mobile, or financial, is controlled by law in most countries, although the laws tend to vary from one jurisdiction to another. Because the scale and depth of usage data is a new phenomenon and because the tools to analyse it and the markets for selling/using it are still developing, the laws are tending to lag behind the practice.

Most services that track usage data have terms and conditions that tell the user what is happening and require them to agree to these terms if they want to use the service. The issue that the courts have with some companies is whether the terms and conditions are sufficiently prominent and clear.

A/B TESTING

The definition of A/B testing is a developing and evolving one; and it is likely to evolve and expand further over the next few years. At its heart, A/B testing is based on a very old principle: create a test where two offers only differ in one detail, present these two choices to matched but separate groups of people to evaluate, and whichever is the more popular is the winner.

What makes modern A/B testing different from traditional research is the tendency to evaluate the options in the real market, rather than with research participants. One high profile user of A/B testing is Google, who use it to optimize their online services. Google systematically, and in many cases automatically, select a variable, offer two options, and count the performance with real users. The winning option becomes part of the system.

Google's A/B testing is now available to users of some of its systems, such as Google Analytics. There is also a growing range of companies offering A/B testing systems. Any service that can be readily tweaked and offered is potentially suitable for A/B testing – in particular virtual or online services.

The concept of A/B testing has moved well beyond simply testing two options and assessing the winner, for example:

- *Many online advertising tools allow the advertiser to submit several variations and the platform uses an algorithm to adjust which execution is shown most often and to whom it is shown, to maximize a dependent variable, for example to maximize click through.*

- *Companies like Phillips have updated their direct mailing research/practice by developing multiple offers, for example 32 versions of a mailer, employing research design principles to allow the differences to be assessed. The mailers are used in the marketplace, with a proportion of the full database, to assess their performance. The results are used in two ways. Firstly, the winning mailer is used for the rest of the database. Secondly, the performances of the different elements are assessed to create predictive analytics for future mailings.*

- *Dynamic pricing models are becoming increasingly common in the virtual and online world. Prices in real markets, such as stock exchanges, have been based for many years on dynamic pricing, but now services such as eBay, Betfair, and Amazon apply differing types of automated price modelling.*

- *Algorithmic bundling and offer development. With virtual products and services, the components can be varied to iteratively seek combinations that work better than others.*

The great strength of A/B testing is in the area of small, iterative changes, allowing organizations to optimize their products, services, and campaigns.

AGILE DEVELOPMENT

Agile development refers to operating in ways where it is easy, quick, and cheap for the organization to change direction and to modify products and services. One consequence of agile development is that organizations can try their product or service in the marketplace, rather than assessing it in advance.

Market research is of particular relevance when the costs of making a product are large, or where the consequences of launching an unsatisfactory product or service are serious. But, if products and services can be created easily and the consequences of failure are low, then 'try it and see' can be a better option than classic forms of market research.

Whilst the most obvious place for agile development is in the area of virtual products and services, it is also used in more tangible markets. The move to print on demand books has reduced the barriers to entry in the book market and facilitated agile approaches. Don Tapscott and Anthony Williams (2008) in their book *Wikinomics: How Mass Collaboration Changes Everything* talk about the motorcycle market in China, which adopted an open-source approach to its design and manufacture of motorcycles, something which combined agile development and crowdsourcing.

CROWDSOURCING

Crowdsourcing is being used in a wide variety of ways by organizations, and several of these ways can be seen as an alternative to market research. Key examples of crowdsourcing include:

- **Open source.** *Systems like Linux and Apache are developed collaboratively and then made freely available. The priorities for development are determined by the interaction of individuals and the community, and the success of changes is determined by a combination of peer review and market adoption.*

- *Crowdfunding. One way of assessing whether an idea has a good chance of succeeding is to try and fund it through a crowdfunding platform, such as Kickstarter. The crowdfunding route can provide feedback, advocates, and money.*

- *Crowdsourced product development. A great example of crowdsourcing is the T-shirt company Threadless.com. People who want to be T-shirt designers upload their designs to the website. Threadless displays these designs to the people who buy T-shirts and asks which ones people want to buy. The most popular designs are then manufactured and sold via the website. In this sort of crowdsourced model there is little need for market research as the audience get what they want, and the company is not paying for the designs, unless the designs prove to be successful.*

USABILITY TESTING

Some market research companies offer usability testing, but there are a great many providers of this service who are not market researchers and who do not see themselves as market researchers. The field of usability testing brings together design, HCI (human computer interaction), and ergonomics professionals, as well market researchers.

Usability testing for a mobile phone, or a mobile app, or mobile site can include:

- *Scoring it against legal criteria to make sure it conforms to statutory requirements.*

- *Scoring it against design criteria, including criteria such as disability access guidelines.*

- *User lab testing, where potential users are given access to the product or service and are closely observed as they use it.*

- *User testing, where potential users are given the product or access to the service and use it for a period of time, for example two weeks. The usage may be monitored, there is often a debrief at the end of the usage period (which can be qualitative, quantitative, or both), and usage data may have been collected and analysed.*

MOBILE DEVICES, SUCH AS PHONES, PHABLETS, AND TABLETS

The history of mobile devices shows that the same organization can make great decisions on some occasions and really bad decisions on others. The rise and fall of Psion,

Nokia, and BlackBerry show the strengths and weaknesses of how product development is often conducted in the mobile ecosystem.

In terms of issues such as branding, advertising, and customer satisfaction, the market research needs for manufacturers and sellers of mobile devices are similar to the needs of organizations in other sectors.

Two key category specific challenges for mobile device designers and manufacturers are:

1.   What is the right way to offer features, in terms of usability and appeal?

2.   What features will the next generation of devices need?

Both of these areas are ones where market research can help, but given the failure of brands to master either of them, that help will probably only provide part of the answer.

1. THE BEST WAY TO OFFER FEATURES

There is a wide range of ways of assessing this issue, and the right tool will depend on the situation. Options include:

- *Assessing usage data, to see how the device is used at the moment. This usage data can include passive data from the device, diary information, and options such as eye-tracking.*

- *User labs, where participants are shown prototypes and where they can discuss and explore how they would use them.*

- *Testing, where participants are given a device to test over a period of time.*

- *Using approaches like insight communities to develop ongoing conversations about how products are used and how they could be tweaked to make them better.*

2. WHAT FEATURES WILL BE NEEDED IN THE FUTURE?

People are often unable to say how they will react in the future. This is a major problem for mobile device manufacturers. Major issues over the last few years have included:

- *The rise of cameras on phones: some brands missed this at the time.*

- *Touchscreens: the early touchscreens were not successful; BlackBerry and Nokia were too slow to see that the iPhone had changed the game.*

- *The iPhone/Android smartphone growth story: companies like Nokia and BlackBerry did not see that a very large part of the phone buying world would settle, for the time being, on the paradigm of the current smartphone, rejecting (to a large extent) physical keyboards, other operating systems, styluses, and so on.*

- *Voice command, which has not yet happened to the degree that was expected.*

One of the interesting things about both Nokia and BlackBerry is that before some recent problems they had got many of the previous big decisions right, both in terms of things they did pursue, for example, cameras and business email, and things they did not, such as flip-phones.

The successful cases in mobile devices seem to be based on a combination (a) understanding what technology is capable of and where technology is going, (b) the wider context of people's needs and lives, not just their articulated demands, and (c) then making an intuitive jump based on these two inputs. Market research can be used to help determine which features can be discontinued (although usage data from logs can often help answer that question too) but its role in assessing the next big thing is much less proven and reliable.

MOBILE TELEPHONY AND INTERNET SERVICES

Market research for mobile telephone services needs to be constructed in the context of the information clients already have, in particular the usage data for their subscribers. Many of the research needs of telephone service providers are the same as for other service providers, such as brand and advertising tracking, ad testing, pricing research, and to an extent customer satisfaction.

One of the notable trends in the area of telephone service providers has been the adoption of insight communities as a method of having ongoing dialogues with customers and of conducting rapid, low cost, often tactical market research.

Because the research is with mobile phone users it is important that market research is at least platform agnostic (i.e. capable of being answered via PC or an internet-enabled mobile device), and in many cases, especially outside the most developed markets, mobile specific.

MOBILE OPERATING SYSTEMS AND APPS

Market research for operating systems and apps has to be conducted in the context of the following:

- *The non-market research information available, for example usage and registration information.*

- *The scope for action for the organization, for example a phone manufacturer can choose exactly which generation Android to use and which features to highlight, but is not going to re-write a key feature of Android.*

- *Whether the new product or service can be envisaged by potential users. If users would struggle to understand how or why they would use it, adopting agile development might be more helpful than trying to research a hard to envisage future.*

- *The scale of risk (in terms of investment or in terms of user backlash if the new service is not right when launched).*

The range of companies looking to commission market research into the performance and opportunities of mobile operating systems is relatively few, but the number looking to understand and research apps is enormous and varied. Banks, retailers, service providers, sports, media, and many more are offering apps – and the market research for each needs to combine knowledge of the sector with knowledge of app testing.

MOBILE SHOPPING AND COMMERCE

Mobile shopping and commerce borrow heavily from online shopping and commerce, and are widely offered in two formats, i.e. via browser and online site and via an app.

The key things that market researchers are typically called on to investigate, in the area of mobile shopping and commerce, are:

- *Why some customers shop in-store, via catalogues, online, or via mobile.*

- *The attribution of different parts of the marketing mix to mobile sales.*

- *Why some customers use the online version versus the app, and how to persuade people to move from one to another.*

- *Why shopping exercises are not being completed, often referred to as abandoned shopping carts.*

- *Assessing the usability and technical characteristics of the shopping experience.*

- *Suggesting enhancements to the process.*

In assessing these elements, market researchers need to work within the context of the non-market research inputs that are available, such as usage data, purchase patterns, and A/B testing. The market research tools that can be used in these situations include the traditional tools of qualitative research, quantitative research, mystery shopping, along with the newer mobile approaches, such as utilizing passive data and participant ethnography.

MOBILE MARKETING AND ADVERTISING

Mobile marketing and advertising covers all forms of marketing that utilize mobile devices and mobile channels. These can broadly be broken into two groups: (a) traditional marketing delivered via mobile and (b) new forms of marketing that are pure-play mobile.

An example of extending a traditional campaign to mobile could be to add a QR code to an existing (traditional) marketing communication. The QR code could link to a game or engagement exercise, linking to marketing activities or promotions. Or, at a simpler level, the QR code could direct users to a website or campaign banner, optimized for viewing on mobile phones.

Pure play mobile campaigns are ones that only exist in mobile. The early versions of these were simple forms such as SMS messages. More contemporary campaigns include branded mobile games, where a game is sponsored to promote the brand, or campaigns delivered via devices like iBeacon.

In countries where more people access the internet via mobiles than via PCs (e.g. Korea and China) mobile advertising is expected to continue to increase sharply and some people, like Mary Meeker and Liang Wu, think it may eventually be the medium of choice (Meeker and Wu 2013).

Mobile advertising tends to be managed through mobile ad networks such as AdMob (owned by Google), InMobi, and others. Mobile ad networks buy and barter media inventory from publishers and content providers, including: game manufacturers, mobile sites, and other mobile content providers. The agencies then resell to those advertisers looking for mobile media opportunities.

As mobile media users become more sophisticated, mobile media planning and targeting of consumers is expected to become more accurate and focused. In the online space, the traditional media model has already been greatly influenced by the features of that environment. For example, services like Facebook now are considered media platforms, allowing advertisers to target consumers based on preferences and habits rather than by demographics. This targeting is different from other traditional media, like TV, where targeting by demographics has been the norm, and where the focus has been more on reach and frequency of exposure.

METRICS

Global consumers are increasing in their number, in the time they spend connected to the mobile ecosystem, and the amount they spend through mobile channels. As a consequence, mobile marketing and mobile advertising budgets are increasing across mobile device channels. Given the large scale of mobile marketing and advertising, marketers need to measure the ROI and effectiveness of these mobile marketing and advertising investments.

Some measurement tools, such as cookie-based tracking and IP tracking, which are commonly used to measure the effectiveness of online campaigns, have been replicated to measure mobile marketing activity. However, given the diversity of mobile approaches and the existence of some unique elements, mobile market research is evolving to address the specific information and insight needs that arise from mobile-based campaigns.

RESEARCHING MOBILE MARKETING AND ADVERTISING

As with other sections in this chapter, discussion of market research in this field starts by recognizing what is available without market research, in particular:

- *Exposure. How many people saw the marketing and how many times? This data will normally include lots of information about dates, times of day, locations, types of device, operating systems, and so on.*

- *Actions. How many people clicked on links, sent an SMS in reply, checked in, or whatever other action the campaign was designed to elicit?*

- *Fulfilment. How many people bought, joined, contributed, or did whatever the end point of the campaign was intended to deliver?*

- *Measures of ROI that simply link the cost of the marketing or advertising to those elements of the fulfilment process that can be tracked.*

Areas where market research (e.g. quantitative, qualitative, and social media research) is especially applicable for mobile marketing and mobile advertising include:

- *Profiling of mobile consumers, to help design and target campaigns.*

- *Measuring usage patterns and trends, to help design and target campaigns.*

- *Pre-testing campaigns, to help optimize and target them.*

- *Measuring and evaluating mobile campaigns and activities in terms of brand values.*

- *Measuring virality components and the potential for engagement.*

- *Measuring the impact of gamification on a brand, including engagement with the brand.*

- *Monitoring and reporting on trends and shifts in intentions.*

- *Assessing the impact of changes in devices and device usage on consumer wants and needs.*

- *Measuring the ROI of marketing and advertising in wider terms than just clicks and buys.*

One challenge for market research when working with mobile marketing and advertising is that many mobile campaigns are very inexpensive. The cost of an ad and its deployment can be less than the normal cost for a market research test. This is one of the reasons why some organizations prefer to try new campaigns, rather than pre-test them. Market research needs to tackle this challenge in two ways: (a) find cheaper/faster ways to test mobile campaigns, (b) focus on the bigger picture, to help design multiple executions of a broader theme, where it is the broader theme that is more fully researched.

Another challenge for market research, in this area, is to combine market research insights with the outputs from other providers, for example people producing the data logs, the predictive analytics, and performance statistics. Whilst some market research providers may have all of these skills in-house, it is likely that partnerships and collaboration will be the norm in the future.

SUMMARY

The mobile ecosystem is already enormous, indeed it touches more people on the planet that any other modern form of communication and its commercial and social importance are set to grow rapidly for many years. The growth of the mobile ecosystem is creating new challenges and opportunities for market researchers.

Key elements to highlight are:

- *The range of non-market research solutions available in the mobile ecosystem and the need for market researchers to understand them, not to underestimate them, and to seek to provide offers that complement them.*

- *In the mobile ecosystem a large amount of data exists that explains what people are actually doing; the opportunity for market research lies in understanding why and what-if.*

- *The complexity created by the diversity of mobile devices needs to be accounted for in research designs.*

- *The challenges created by the relatively low cost of many forms of mobile marketing and advertising mean that market researchers need to find research solutions that are appropriate.*

- *The need to show that there is more to advertising and marketing than clicks, by showing the value of brand building.*

16 Ethics, Laws, and Guidelines

INTRODUCTION

Ethics are a central tenet of market research, and most chapters in this book have touched on ethics, along with rules, laws, and guidelines, and the need to gain informed consent. The core issues relating to mobile market research ethics are similar to the issues for other forms of market research. However, there are specific considerations that are either unique to mobile market research or have different characteristics in a mobile context, and these are the issues reviewed in this chapter.

Specific topics covered include key stakeholders in terms of privacy and ethics, the interplay of laws, guidelines, and ethics, and how to conduct ethical mobile market research. The chapter finishes with a checklist of the key questions that should be addressed.

KEY STAKEHOLDERS IN TERMS OF PRIVACY AND ETHICS

The key stakeholders in most forms of market research are:

- *Research participants*
- *Research agencies and their employees*
- *Research clients and users*
- *The market research profession, including the bodies that represent it*
- *Legislators and regulators.*

When conducting mobile market research there are additional groups of people who may need to be considered, for example:

- **People who might be recorded by the participants in mobile research studies.** For example, people who might be photographed or videoed during a mobile ethnography project.

- **People whose digital details may be accidently or unintentionally collected by the researcher.** *For example Bluetooth or Wi-Fi information might be gathered, by participants or interviewers, about people not participating in the research.*

- **Mobile service providers.** *Mobile service providers may have restrictions relating to how their services can be used.*

- **Owners of locations visited by participants.** *For example, retailers seek to control what happens in their stores, schools are often covered by regulations, and airlines often ban the use of electronic devices during take-off and landing.*

THE INTERPLAY OF LAWS, GUIDELINES, AND ETHICS

As with any other form of market research, there is interplay between laws, guidelines, ethics, and best practice. No single resource can list all the relevant rules and how they interconnect and any such list would soon be out of date. Researchers need to make themselves familiar with the ethical and regulatory framework surrounding mobile market research in the countries in which they are conducting research. The best starting place is often the local market research organization.

Anyone planning to conduct international mobile market research needs to take advice about each market where research is proposed. Good sources of advice for international projects include colleagues, local agencies, and in particular the national market research associations, and ESOMAR.

LAWS

Laws are the most important element within the framework of laws, regulations, and guidelines and usually cover data protections and privacy. In addition, laws often cover the following:

1.   The different ways that a phone can be contacted. For example, some countries do not allow auto-diallers to be used when contacting mobile phones.

2.   Where a phone/camera can or cannot be used. For example, laws may restrict the use of mobile devices on government property or near airports.

3.   The times of day that somebody can be contacted. Many countries have laws that limit unsolicited calls to specific times of day.

4.   The need to respect 'do not call/contact/email/SMS' lists. 'Do not contact' laws vary considerably from country to country. Some have exemptions for market

research, and some do not. All contact lists should be checked to see if the appropriate permissions to call/text/email exist.

5.   The sorts of services that can be used, for example, some countries have banned specific services such as Twitter and Facebook.

6.   The collection of passive data. In some countries the collection of traffic and location data is controlled by legislation.

Whilst laws in some countries are relatively clear and uniformly enforced, in others they may be unclear or unevenly enforced. In situations where specific mobile laws do not exist, courts often need to try to retrofit disputes to laws dating back to older technologies, sometimes even as far back as telegraphy. In locations where the laws are less defined or effective, guidelines and ethics become even more important.

GUIDELINES

Guidelines are typically rules and advice that market researchers have agreed to as a condition of membership of a trade body or professional association, or which they have agreed to without necessarily joining the relevant body. Sometimes guidelines have the force of law behind them, other guidelines are linked to the potential to be sanctioned by a relevant body, and other guidelines are simply recommendations. The ESOMAR/ICC market research guidelines are widely adopted around the world and are a useful starting point for any market researcher seeking to understand market research guidelines. ESOMAR (2012a) produces a specific Guideline for Conducting Mobile Market Research, which is available from www.esomar.org.

When conducting mobile market research, researchers should respect the general guidelines for market research as well as any specific guidelines for mobile market research. Researchers should note that the absence of a specific clause in mobile specific guidelines does not mean it is not covered. For example, if the general guidelines specify protecting respondent anonymity, it might not be explicitly repeated in the text of mobile guidelines, because the clause about anonymity in the general guidelines automatically applies.

ETHICS

Laws and guidelines tend to come from external bodies, such as governments and trade bodies and associations. By contrast, ethics tend to relate to the organization the researcher is employed by and the individual researcher's own value structure.

In a fast moving field like mobile market research, ethics become even more important than in a more stable field. Laws and guidelines, governing the mobile ecosystem, tend to lag behind what is technically possible. Until laws and codes catch up with what is possible, consideration of the ethical issues is the best way for market researchers to do the right thing, and the best way to stay on the right side of the law and public opinion.

Some organizations, especially academic institutions, have a formal ethical review process, but for most market researchers the process is more informal. Researchers should ask themselves whether their actions would attract criticism or scorn from the general public, their family, and their peers, if they were to become aware of what the researcher was doing. If in doubt, don't — or at least make sure you gain consent.

Often the difference between an ethical project and an unethical one is the quality of the disclosure and the quality of the informed consent obtained. The key consideration for market researchers to remember is that just because something is possible, it does not mean it should be done.

CONDUCTING ETHICAL RESEARCH

The key to conducting ethical research is to be aware of the guidelines and laws, to consider the issues raised by a specific research project, and to discuss the implications and best practices with peers. This section covers the key issues that researchers should consider.

SAFETY CONCERNS

One of the core assumptions of market research is that the participants will not be put at risk by taking part in the research. One of the eight 'fundamentals' of the ESOMAR/ICC Codes says that respondents shall not be harmed or adversely affected as the direct result of cooperating in a market research project.

Some of the safety concerns about mobile market research are the same as they would be for other modes of data collection. For example, not exposing participants to the risk of fraud or identity theft, or making it more likely they will lose their job. But there are also concerns that are quite specific to mobile market research, including:

1. Ensuring that the participant is not doing something hazardous, such as driving, at the same time as taking part in a market research study.

2. Checking that the participant is not likely to be observed while entering sensitive data into a mobile device. For example, if a respondent is using a tablet on a train, their responses may be viewable by people sitting near them.

3. Not asking the participant to do things that may be seen as illegal or threatening. For example, researchers should avoid asking participants to take videos/pictures of the sensitive parts of airports or of other people's children.

COSTS AND ANNOYANCE

Not harming the participants means more than just safety issues, it also includes not inconveniencing them, not costing them money, and not annoying them. Market researchers should ensure that participants do not incur expenses as a result of taking part in mobile studies (e.g. data charges). Or, if costs are incurred, the participants should be compensated or reimbursed.

Researchers need to avoid annoying or distressing people, for example they should avoid sending SMS messages to a participant's phone at a time when they may be sleeping. In a global study, or in a country with multiple time zones, extra steps are required to ensure that mobile market research does not become a source of annoyance. Similarly, researchers should seek to provide participants with methods of avoiding being contacted when travelling into other time zones or when on vacation.

PERSONALLY IDENTIFIABLE INFORMATION

The term 'personally identifiable data or information' (often shortened to PID or PII) includes anything that can identify individuals. Obvious examples of personally identifiable data include names, email addresses, and phone numbers. However, less obvious forms of data, such as photographs of people's faces or location data showing where somebody lives, are also personally identifiable data. In many countries the use of personally identifiable data is governed by data privacy and data protection laws.

When collecting personally identifiable data, researchers need to secure informed consent and follow data protection and privacy rules. Researchers should only collect personally identifiable data that is needed by the project and for which the participant has given permission.

PRIVACY CONCERNS

Mobile privacy concerns tend to involve: anonymity, security of participants' personal information, and consent.

Market researchers should already be familiar with the need to protect the anonymity of research participants. However, when using mobile devices, there are a number of extra ways that anonymity can be compromised. Mobile web browsing records can identify the participant. Images and recordings on the mobile device may include personally identifiable data. Various codes and information on the phone (including its phone number) can identify an individual. Even location data can identify people. All of these routes to compromising participant anonymity need to be addressed by the research design.

DATA ABOUT THIRD PARTIES

Mobile phones typically hold personal information about people other than the participant. For example, personally identifiable information about third parties can be found in: contact lists, telephone numbers called, email histories, text messages, calendars, and in some apps. As a general rule, researchers should not collect information about third parties without the permission of those whose personal information is accessed. The core issue is that the research participant may not have the right to give consent to this third-party information being passed on to the researcher. This is a complicated area and researchers should seek legal advice before accessing information about third parties.

INFORMED CONSENT

Informed consent is the bedrock of most research and all market research. Researchers should ensure that each participant understands what data is being collected, what it will reveal about them, and who it will be shared with. If their device is being recorded, for example storing GPS, Bluetooth, and web-browsing information, they may not immediately realize how much of their privacy they are sharing.

Informed consent requires that people are fully informed about:

- *The purpose of the research.*

- *The information to be collected, including passively collected information.*

- *The use to which it will be put. For example, is it market research or does it include other uses?*

- *Who it will be shared with. For example, will it be shared with other organizations?*

- *The form in which it will be shared. For example, will only aggregated information be shared or will personally identifiable information such as images be shared?*

Informed consent can be especially difficult when collecting data that includes third parties. If videos and images of people other than the research participant are collected, then the researcher should have their permission as well, or put procedures in place to protect their identity (e.g. by pixelating images for their faces).

In order to avoid difficult decisions, a number of researchers have adopted a policy of not collecting information that is potentially embarrassing. For example, some tracking software can be set to not record visits to adult entertainment sites; other software can be set to automatically delete potentially embarrassing information at the early stages of cleaning/consolidation.

DATA SECURITY ISSUES

The two key elements of data security are keeping data secure from unauthorized access and safe from becoming corrupt or lost. Personal and sensitive data should be encrypted; access should be regulated and monitored.

As a general rule, personally identifiable information should not be shared with clients unless the participant has given explicit permission for it to be shared. Where personally identifiable information is transferred (with the participants' permission) to clients, the client needs to be aware that they are accepting responsibility for protecting the data with appropriate procedures.

The three key mobile elements of data security are ensuring the device is not lost, not hacked, and not damaged. In most cases this means ensuring that data is moved from the mobile device to central servers as promptly as possible and removing data from the mobile devices as quickly as possible.

IS IT MARKET RESEARCH?

Market researchers are increasingly being called on to use their skills on projects that are not market research – in terms of what market researchers define as market research. For example, if a client wants to improve the mobile sign-up process to collect richer information for their CRM system, a market researcher can use their skills to design a better set of questions, but this is not market research.

If a project is not market research, the researcher should ensure that it is not called, or made to appear as, market research and should abide by the relevant laws and guidelines. ESOMAR (2009) has a 'Guide on Distinguishing Market Research from Other Data Collection Activities' and the UK's MRS (2010) has a set of guidelines called 'Using Research Techniques for Non-Research Purposes', which discuss this topic.

RESEARCH QUALITY ISSUES

Providers of research need to ensure that the buyers and users of market research are aware of the confidence they can have in the data collected and conclusions and insights generated from the data. Methodologies and approaches with a long history, such as face-to-face surveys or in-person focus groups, tend to have well-understood properties in terms of the confidence that users can place in the findings. However, in a new and fast changing field, such as mobile market research, the picture is less settled and clear.

The way market research is conducted has an impact on what is collected. Any new research method needs to be assessed to identify:

1.   How it affects the research process, in comparison with other methods.

2.   Whether the differences between the new and established methods can be removed.

3.   Whether any differences are the result of better data, worse data, different data, or some combination of better, worse, and different.

4.   What 'new' types of data are provided by the method, and how this new data can be utilized.

ETHICS CHECKLIST

No list can be complete or fully up to date, but the checklist in Table 16.1 should be useful when scoping a mobile market research project, in terms of laws, ethics, and guidelines:

Table 16.1   Ethics checklist

Question	Comments
Is it legal?	Researchers should verify that their mobile research project complies with the relevant laws in the countries where they plan to conduct it.
Are you putting participants at risk?	Never ask a participant to do something that may be illegal or potentially put themselves or others at risk. For example, researchers should check that participants are not driving a car and should advise participants not to take pictures or videos of unsuitable subjects, such as other people's children or in areas where photography is prohibited.
Is it market research?	If it is not market research, the researcher needs to ensure that it does not appear to be market research.
Are you collecting personally identifiable data?	Researchers need to identify what information is being collected, how permission will be obtained, and how the data will be protected.
Do you have informed consent from each participant?	Informed consent depends on sharing enough information with participants to ensure they can give informed consent.
Is information being gathered abut third parties?	If third-party information is being collected, how will permission be gathered? Or, will the information be rendered anonymous?
How will you avoid annoying people?	Review issues such as time zones to avoid causing annoyance or distress.
What confidence can the user of the research have in the findings?	The researcher needs to evaluate the impact of the mobile method on the research findings and ensure the client is made aware of the potential impact.

SUMMARY

This chapter has highlighted the key issues that market researchers should be aware of, both in terms of the ethical issues that relate to market research in general and those that relate specifically to mobile market research. Researchers should stay up to date with changes in the field and develop their own moral compass (so they instinctively know right from wrong). They may find a checklist approach to be helpful.

17 Research-on-Research

INTRODUCTION

Research-on-research, often referred to as RoR, refers to research about the research process, conducted by research vendors and/or research users. RoR can be similar to, or overlap with, academic research.

This chapter highlights a number of RoR studies that help illustrate aspects of mobile market research. The studies in this chapter are referred to in other sections of the book and inform recommendations made in the book. The authors extend their thanks to the organizations that have made these studies available.

The notes about each study in this chapter are in a very short format. A fuller commentary on each of these studies, plus a number of additional studies, is available via the accompanying online site www.handbookofmobilemarketresearch.com. The studies below are grouped by fieldwork date.

2010

Does Adding One More Question Impact Survey Completion Rate? (Chudoba 2010)

Meta-analysis of 100 000 online surveys conducted on the SurveyMonkey platform 2009 and 2010, looking at 2000 single question surveys, 2000 two question surveys, 2000 three question surveys, and so on up to 2000 50 question surveys.

This study confirmed that longer surveys lead to more dropouts. The paper highlights that from 1 to 15 questions the growth in dropouts is relatively steep. From 16 to 35 questions the increase in the dropout rate slows, and above 30 questions there is relatively little additional increase in dropouts.

2011

Differences Between Mobile and PC Responses
(Vision Critical 2014)

This study was conducted in 2011 with a sample of 2025 participants, spread across the USA, UK, and Canada. The three key findings were that most survey question types give similar answers on PCs and smartphones, that multi-select grids tend to give different answers on PC and smartphone, and that smartphone versions of PC surveys can take 50% longer.

How Much Time Are Respondents Willing to Spend
on Your Survey? (Chudoba 2011)

A meta-analysis of 100 000 online surveys conducted on the SurveyMonkey platform in 2011. The key finding was that respondents spend longer per question when answering shorter surveys, and less time per question with longer surveys. This finding supports the suggestion that research participants can sometimes engage in satisficing, i.e. just doing enough to be able to complete the survey (Krosnick 2000).

Impact of Survey Length on Responses (Vision Critical 2014)

This study was conducted in 2011 with a sample of 2000 participants spread across the USA, UK, and Canada. Participants were allocated to a PC or a smartphone cell and three survey lengths were tested. The longest survey length tested had a mean completion time of 9.5 minutes.

The two key findings were: (a) forcing participants to respond via mobile reduced the response rate, and (b) the completion rate for a 9.5 minute survey was the same as for shorter mobile surveys.

2012

Australian Mobile Test 2012 (Ipsos ASI 2014)

The study was conducted in 2012 to evaluate mobile ad testing in conjunction with MobileMeasure, using three TV ads with a sample size of approximately 120 participants seeing each ad. The test used a subset of the normal Ipsos ASI test. For those items included in the mobile test the results were comparable.

Harnessing Mobile Technology to Draw Insights from Health Care Professionals (Kantar Health 2014)

The study looked at using a mobile survey with 600 US doctors, comparing the results with a reference study conducted as a conventional online study. The survey was re-designed for mobile and reduced in length from 45 minutes to 15 minutes.

The three key findings included: (a) the results from the mobile study were comparable with the online study, (b) some doctors expressed reluctance at being allocated to the mobile cell, and (c) the surveys on smartphones took longer than the same surveys on iPads.

I Would ... But the Data Would be Different (Courtright 2013)

The presentation was based on 30 000 interviews conducted by Research Now in 2012. The analysis covered multiple countries and compared results from participants using PC and mobile. The study showed very comparable responses in mean responses in attitudes towards sports and in the proportions of participants choosing to follow the Olympics via different media.

Research Goes Mobile: Findings from Initial Smartphone Application Research (Dubreuil and Joubert 2012)

This paper reported two separate advertising comparison tests. The first was in 2011 and used a sample of 400 people to evaluate a print ad, the second test was in 2012 and evaluated two TV ads. Both waves of testing were based on Luma's ad+impact test.

The two key findings were: (a) the results for the TV ad were comparable between PC and mobile, and (b) the print ad results were generally comparable, but the 'stand out' score for the print ad was lower for the mobile cell.

The Who, When, Where, and How of Smartphone Research (Fine and Menictas 2012)

The study comprised 1514 participants in 2011 and a further 640 in 2012, in Australia. The three key findings were: (a) the mobile responses had a different demographic profile, (b) after controlling for demographic differences the survey responses were similar, and (c) the response rates and results for 5, 10, and 15 minute long surveys were similar.

Touchscreen Devices Versus Non-Touchscreen Devices
(Vision Critical 2014)

The study investigated 902 participants with touchscreen phones and 1115 non-touchscreen (BlackBerry) users. The three key findings were: (a) the response rate amongst non-touchscreen users was lower, (b) the non-touchscreen participants were less happy with the process, and (c) the non-touchscreen users took about 40% longer than the touchscreen users.

Using Dual-Frame Telephone Surveys to Include the 'Mobile Phone-Only' Population (Pennay et al. 2013)

This study was conducted as a CATI (telephone) study in Australia in 2012, with a sample of 2000 people. The key finding, for mobile market research, was that the profile and responses of people with both a mobile phone and landline differed depending on whether the interviews were completed on a landline or a mobile phone.

2013

Can Mobile Web Surveys Be Taken on Computers?
A Discussion on a Multi-Device Survey Design
(de Bruijne and Wijnant 2013)

This study was a two cell study with a sample size of 2722 and was conducted in The Netherlands. Both cells answered via mix of devices (about 15% using a mobile device). One cell saw a PC style survey, the other saw the survey configured for mobile devices.

The key findings were that the results were similar, but the mobile version took slightly longer and was slightly less popular.

GRIT Consumer Participation in Research Report (GreenBook 2013a)

This study reported the findings from using the RIWI method globally in 2013, utilizing data from about 1.6 million devices. About 19% of the survey invitations were served to mobile devices, with iOS as the most commonly used operating system.

Participation of Mobile Users in Online Surveys (Jue and Luck 2014)

This report was based on the surveys delivered by the Decipher platform in 2013, with the numbers of survey starts varying from 1.5 to 5 million per month. The key findings included:

1.   The number of people using mobile devices to take online surveys has grown from less than 10% in Q1 2012 to about 20% in Q4 2013.

2.   Panel members are less likely to be using mobile devices (7%) and participants from client lists are more likely to be using mobile devices (27%).

3.   Completion rates are lower for mobile devices (59%) than for PCs (76%), but Decipher report that well-designed mobile studies do better than this.

4.   60% of mobile devices used in Q4 2013 were iOS, 38% Android, with all other operating systems coming to just 2%.

SUMMARY OF THE RESEARCH-ON-RESEARCH REVIEWED

The papers reported in this chapter represent an interesting cross-section of research-on-research in the area of mobile market research. Not all of the findings are in the same direction, but several key strands suggest themselves as findings that appear to be consistent:

- *Adding mobile to online can widen the reach of the research in terms of who takes part. This means that the data from a mixed-mode study can be more representative than a study offering fewer choices, but that it can also result in differences in the results because the sample has changed.*

- *In general the differences in answers resulting from the question being viewed on a different device are small, although some differences do exist. Questions that appear to produce similar results include single response questions, multi response questions, sliders, numeric questions, and simple grids.*

- *Multi-select grids, where the participant can select multiple items per row or per column in a grid, tend to produce different answers on PCs and smartphones, with the mobile participants tending to make more selections.*

- *When a mobile survey is created by taking an online survey and simply rendering it for mobile, the average length of interview appears to increase. However, this increase does not appear to result in lower satisfaction with the survey, or higher dropout rates, or changes in the data.*

- *Mobile surveys of up to 15 minutes do not appear to be too long, compared with online surveys of a similar length.*

- *Forcing participants to use mobile devices, as opposed to offering them a choice, can result in lower completion rates.*

- *Participants completing a survey on their mobile tend to respond to the survey invitations faster than those completing it on a PC.*

- *Most participants completing mobile surveys do so from home or the office.*

- *When given the choice to complete a survey on a PC or mobile, more participants choose PC than mobile, but this may be changing.*

- *Longer surveys result in more dropouts and may encourage satisficing (participants answering quickly in order to finish the survey with the minimum effort).*

- *Ad tests, particularly TV ads, seem capable of producing similar results between mobile and PC-based tests. However, print ads may appear to have less impact on a mobile screen than a PC screen.*

A much fuller version of these studies is available online, along with additional studies. The online material, which includes a longer version of the glossary, can be found at www.handbookofmobilemarketresearch.com.

18 The Evolving Picture

INTRODUCTION

The world is moving towards a situation where the vast majority of the world's population are likely to own a powerful, internet connected mobile device. Already most people have a mobile phone and in the developed economies a majority have a smartphone. Other mobile devices are growing rapidly, from tablets through to navigation devices to fitness monitors. This is a change in society on a par with the invention of the printing press, and unlike the printing press its impact is on a truly global scale.

The world of mobile market research is changing, firstly to catch up with what has already happened, secondly to embrace current changes, and finally to try to work with what will come next.

This chapter reviews the evolving picture facing mobile market research by examining four perspectives:

- *Technology*
- *Society*
- *Methodology*
- *Practical issues in using emergent mobile technologies.*

TECHNOLOGY

As mobile technologies, both hardware and software, continue to evolve, phone calls have become a smaller and smaller part of what people do with their mobile phone. Mobile phones have evolved into something like a Swiss Army knife, with manufacturers and third-party providers adding multiple, often unrelated, tools and apps to products. Most of these additions remain unused for most people, but a few become runaway successes.

The scale of the challenge of picking winners was shown by a forecast in 2014 by Gartner that predicted just 1-in-10 000 apps would be considered a financial success by 2018 (Gartner 2014).

This section reviews some of the mobile technologies that are already of interest to market researchers and some that may be of interest soon

LOCATION-BASED SERVICES

Location-based services (or LBS) have been around for some time and features such as GPS receivers and apps to utilize GPS information are now common on phones. As mentioned in The Technology of Mobile Market Research and Utilizing Passive Data chapters, a variety of location techniques are available and are being developed, including cell tower tracking, Wi-Fi related systems, NFC, and audio-based tracking.

The potential benefits of using location-based services to monitor consumers' location and movements are easy to understand. For example:

1.   Knowing the routes that consumers take, either as part of their normal day or prior to purchasing an item, opens up a wide range of marketing and research opportunities.

2.   Geofencing allows researchers to trigger 'in the moment' research activities, for example a survey, when somebody enters or leaves a specific location, such as a restaurant or station.

Location-based research is in its infancy, but is widely expected to grow. In terms of the evolving picture, key issues include:

-    *Strategies for using location based services without draining batteries.*

-    *Improving the accuracy of GPS estimates of location.*

-    *More innovations in the technologies providing location-based services, for example short distance Wi-Fi and Apple's iBeacon to help locate people in relation to shelves, advertising, point-of-sale promotions.*

-    *Improvements in the analysis of routes, particularly in the analysis of large samples of location/movement data.*

-    *Creating larger panels of participants willing to engage in location-based research projects.*

Location-based services raise a number of privacy issues and a number of governments and regulatory bodies around the world are discussing limitations and restrictions. At the very least location data is likely to be classed as sensitive personal information. Market researchers will need to ensure that the concept of informed consent is a major part of their procedures if they are to minimize potential restrictions.

VOICE SERVICES

Interest in voice-enabled services and speech recognition goes back at least three decades, but recently has gained the attention of consumers after Apple utilized it in the form of Siri, the voice-enabled personal assistant. Introduced in 2011, Siri was described at that time, by some pundits, as being the most important new feature of the iPhone4. However, once the hype wore off, the limited utility of the feature, at least in its current form, became apparent.

Given time, voice recognition/activation will become more accurate and may become a major element in utilizing mobile devices. For example, the default way of operating Google Glass is via voice commands.

For market researchers, a major aspect of interest in voice services is that they imply voice recognition, not just audio capture. Responses captured via voice recognition are stored as digital information, which can be searched and processed in ways that are very difficult with traditional recordings.

QR (QUICK RESPONSE) CODES

QR codes are usually thought of as two-dimensional barcodes. They were initially used by the Japanese auto industry, and can encode a wide variety of machine readable information. Mobile phones can use an app, such as Google Goggles, to process, scan and interpret QR codes. The user scans the QR code using the device's camera and the app determines what action to take.

Figure 18.1 is a QR code. If you have a QR reader on your phone you should find it takes you to NewMR.org. If you don't have a QR code reader, then you can try downloading Google Goggles, which is one of many apps capable of reading QR codes.

In terms of market research, QR codes can be used to trigger a survey, share information, or download mobile apps and content to a consumer's phone. When QR codes first appeared, a few years ago, they were hailed as the 'next big thing', with their supporters claiming they would make it much easier to reach consumers. The outcome has been much less useful from a market research point of view, at least in the West. MarketingCharts.com compiled a selection of reports, which indicated that in the US about 10% of smartphone users regularly scanned a code, and about 20–25% had done so in the last few months (Marketing Charts Staff 2013).

Figure 18.1   Example of a QR Code

However, QR codes have been successful in places like China, where WeChat makes use of QR codes to simplify entering contact information, and there have been successful campaigns in the West when the campaign was well designed.

QR codes are an interesting technology for market researchers to keep an eye on. The technology works, is very low cost, and the only thing holding it back in the West is that consumers have not found a good enough reason to use it. All of that could change if one of the leading online services were to give people a reason to use it.

MOBILE 3D ANIMATION

Mobile 3D animation is a widely utilized technology in the mobile gaming industry and is a readily available service.

Currently, 3D animation is not widely used in market research. However, it is a service with considerable potential. For example, mobile 3D animation could be used to allow users to get a better representation of products, both for existing products and products at the design stage.

The key difference between gaming and mobile market research is that in gaming a 3D animation can be created once and used many times, but in mobile market research, most projects are ad hoc, so the costs for a specific 3D animation often have to be recovered from a single project. For this approach to have major market research applications the cost of creating animations needs to fall, or reusable applications need to be found.

USING SOUND IN RESEARCH

There are a number of approaches being explored that utilize sound for research purposes, for example audio signature and sound location.

Audio signature for advertising reach measurement

Audio signature is highly experimental and still in its infancy, but it has been explored by a number of researchers in the past few years. All audio and audio-visual ads have a distinct digital audio signature. A mobile device embedded with an audio signature reader and the appropriate software is capable of identifying the advertisements a research participant is exposed to during their day. The use of mobile devices in this way holds the prospect of better measures of reach, broader samples, and adding location and behaviour tracking.

Sound location

With a suitable app, non-audible sound signals can be used to record the phone's location, a technology sometimes referred to as sound beacons. For example ShopKick and Sonic Notify use high frequency signals to tell the phone that they have walked into a participating store, or that they are in a specific part of the store. This information can be used by the app to gain shopping coupons or to receive a message from the store.

Sound beacons can be placed around a store (in the way iBeacons can be placed) to trigger messages and location detection. The sound location can be as simple as recording that somebody has visited a specific branch of a specific retailer, or with more beacons it can track the participant around the store or request feedback.

The key challenges in this approach include:

- *Fitting the locations with the technology*
- *Persuading sufficient participants to download the app and take part in the research*
- *Ensuring that the techniques used do not run batteries down too fast.*

MOTION SENSOR TECHNOLOGY

Gaming was an early adopter of motion sensor technologies, for example in the consoles of games such as Nintendo Wii and Xbox Kinect. While the Nintendo Wii requires a user to carry an external device to interact with the sensor, the Xbox Kinect does not require a device to be held by the user. The sensors placed on the gaming console detect the gamer's physical movements and allow them to interact with the game.

Motion sensors are highly sensitive, very accurate, and capable of recording not just movement but also the intensity of movement. From a market research perspective, if sensors are placed near a store shelf stocking soft drinks, then the sensor would be able to record the number of people who touched products on the shelf and identify which products were touched. Researchers would also be able to identify which products were 'chosen', 'chosen and returned', 'lingered on', and so on. Using data like this, researchers might infer which promotions are working, how they are working, and their impact on sales. Technologies such as Apple's iBeacon could be used in conjunction with this approach, or as an alternative. An iBeacon signal can push a message to a compatible phone, recording what the research participant was doing at that moment in time.

WEARABLE TECHNOLOGIES

Wearable technologies appear to have three core uses at the moment:

1.   The quantified self

2.   Passive recording

3.   Wearable computing.

1. Quantified self

Currently, the most popular aspects of the 'quantified self' focus on exercise and weight loss, with products like Garmin Vivofit, FitBit, and Jawbone. These devices follow a much longer tradition of walkers, runners, and cyclists using devices such as pedometers, heart monitors, and GPS watches to track their exercise. However, the breadth of the quantified self is much wider, with people measuring things as variable as mood, blood sugar, heart rate, location, and sleep. This area also connects with a growing interest in biometrics and research.

The quantified self presents an enormous opportunity for market researchers along with considerable challenges. At the individual level, the data collected by a 'quantified self' project is relatively easy to analyse, for example looking at one month of data for ten people. However, the market research tools for combining data from 1000 people into a form that will generate insight are not generally available, although they do exist in other areas.

2. Passive recording

Passive recording can be achieved in a variety of ways, including using mobile phones, wearable video cameras like GoPro, life-logging cameras like Memoto, eye tracking devices like Tobii Glasses, or devices like Google Glass. The two big pluses of these approaches are:

1.   The participant does not have to decide what to take a picture or video of, which removes the subjective bias.

2.   The systems provide a complete record, either as a video or as a series of still images.

These approaches have two main challenges (in addition to getting the technology working the way it needs to work):

1.   Cameras recording everything the participant sees create enormous data privacy issues that the industry needs to work its way through.

2.   Beyond qualitative analysis there are very few tools for processing images and videos. This is a pressing need for market research.

3. Wearable computing

The epitome of wearable computing is, currently, Google Glass, although there are a variety of other approaches, such as Samsung's Galaxy Gear worn as a wrist watch. Wearable computing creates an almost endless list of possible market research opportunities. At one end of the spectrum devices like Google Glass could be used to test products, stores, and shelf layouts, at the other end of the spectrum these technologies could allow researchers to sit on the participant's shoulder, see what the participant sees, and send questions in response to what is happening in the participant's world.

Like passive recording, these technologies are going to raise a considerable number of legal, ethical, and privacy related questions and like the quantified self- and location-based services they will generate a need for new tools capable of processing large amounts of observational data.

NEW WEB AND MOBILE MESSAGING SERVICES

One of the recent growth areas has been in messaging applications, such as WeChat, SnapChat, and WhatsApp. These services are growing at enormous rates, with hundreds of millions of people using these sorts of services.

At present there is no clear model of how they might be used in market research, other than as a method of communication, but given the scale of these messaging applications there is no shortage of people looking for ways to utilize them. However, researchers should remember the lessons of Facebook, Twitter, and LinkedIn, which, despite their enormous size and usage levels, have not had a major impact on market research, beyond social media mining/monitoring.

SOCIETY

As well as technologies evolving, what people do with their mobile devices also changes, and in some cases the devices change how people live their lives. This section looks at some of the key issues relating to what people do with their mobile devices in ways that might impact market research.

THE UBIQUITY OF THE MOBILE PHONE

As mentioned at the start of the chapter, mobile phones are becoming omnipresent. The ITU's ICT 2013 Facts and Figures report estimated that 'Mobile-cellular penetration rates stand at 96% globally; 128% in developed countries; and 89% in developing countries'. However, the ITU figures do not account for multiple phone ownership, and other estimates based on allowing for multiple device ownership put the global penetration figure at about two-thirds, rather than almost 100% (Poynter 2013).

The second key aspect of the ubiquity of mobile phones is that people tend to have their phone with them all the time. Phones are near people when they sleep, when they go shopping, when they go to work, and many people even use them in the bathroom.

Market research today has to deal with a world where not everybody of interest has a mobile phone, and not everybody has a smartphone, but this is changing. The numbers will never reach 100%, but they will approach 100% of economically active adults who want to have a phone, and in many cases already represent 100% of the target group of interest. By contrast, the number of people who can be reached via a landline is falling.

At the moment people offering mobile market research often have to defend the mode, but it may well soon be the mode with the most respectable claim to breadth of reach.

MULTIPLE MOBILE SUBSCRIPTIONS

In many countries there are more mobile phone subscriptions than people, because some people have more than one mobile subscription. In broad terms the number of mobile subscriptions is the number of SIMs in use in a country. Somebody who has a personal phone, a work phone, a SIM in their tablet, and a SIM in their car dashboard has four subscriptions, and can look like four people to, say, a random digit dialling CATI system.

The number of people with multiple mobile subscriptions is likely to grow and so is the number of subscriptions that the average person has. This is partly a consequence of the growth in the use of phones and the projected trend to put mobile connectivity into more devices.

As people have more subscriptions, there are potential gains and losses for market research. The potential loss is that it makes it harder to say a phone is the same thing as a person. This can increase the complexity of sampling and the complexity of ensuring that participants are not interviewed (or annoyed) twice. The positive side of multiple subscriptions per person is that there will be more aspects of people's lives that are capable of being observed.

MOBILE DEVICES AND THE INTERNET

The number of mobile phones in a country is not the same thing as the number that are reliably and regularly connected to the internet. In wealthier, more developed, countries, not being reliably connected to the internet tends to be as a result of somebody making either a personal choice or because they have a relatively low income. In many of the developing countries the patchy nature of internet coverage and the high cost of data connections exacerbate this situation. For example, the ITU's 2013 ICT Facts and Figures (ITU 2013) briefing suggests that connecting a mobile phone to the internet costs ten times as much (as a proportion of annual income) in the developing world as in the developed world.

Costs are coming down, and mobile coverage is increasing, in both the developed and developing worlds, but it will be some time before market researchers can assume everybody of interest is connected to the internet via their mobile device(s). However, the growth of CATI in the 1990s and the growth of online in the mid-1990s showed that it is not necessary for 100% of people to be connected in order to conduct a wide range of market research projects.

SoLoMo

'SoLoMo' is a term that has been created by combining social, local, and mobile, and refers to the way that people are using different technologies and systems in an integrated way. People are using their phones to announce where they are, to find who else is where they are, to upload or post images and observations about their surroundings, to seek out opportunities (e.g. sales, meals, people), and to leave a digital impression on the social and geographical landscape.

SoLoMo creates interesting opportunities for market research, in the collection of ethnographic data, in using citizens as researchers, and in terms of collecting holistic, tracked, passive data about what people do during their everyday lives.

PRIVATE VERSUS PUBLIC LIVES

There are two current societal trends that seemed destined to clash. The first is the growing willingness of billions of people to share details about their lives online, for example, snapping a picture on their phone and uploading it to Facebook, along with automatically appending date, time, and location. The second strand is concerned with privacy, data theft, and over-intrusive marketing.

The growing sharing/public nature of social media and mobile usage is mostly driven by what people do. The concerns about privacy are mostly driven by what people say and the concerns of legislators. However, it could take only a few more scandals for people to radically change their behaviour, towards a more secure and private way of operating.

Market researchers are currently benefiting from the fact that so many people are willing to share so much information about their lives and actions. However, if the public climate changes, or if legislators extend the barriers to sharing and using information, this could have a major impact on market research.

MOBILE DEVICES AS A RESOURCE FOR SHOPPING

Mobiles are changing the way people shop, both online and in physical locations.

Browsers and apps

For some people shopping online means logging into a retail website via a browser and shopping and this can be done from a PC or from phones and tablets.

However, mobiles have ushered in a new form of online shopping, via apps. Apps can streamline the shopping process, can more easily be personalized to the shopper, can create a feeling of security (particularly in terms of using things like credit cards), and, from the retailer's point of view, lock a shopper into one destination to a greater extent than the browser option does.

Shopping assistants

Mobile devices, especially phones, are having a major impact on the way that some people conduct their 'real world' shopping. People are using their phone to gain extra information whilst on a shopping trip, including browsing the web for information, comparing prices, scanning QR codes, and taking pictures for later review and discussion. One of the challenges for researchers is to help brands gain a complete view of the pathways to purchase, and the interaction of different advertising and promotional material along the way; understanding more about the complete role of mobile devices in shopping will be part of this process.

SOCIAL GAMING AND SHARING

The success of the Facebook game Farmville a few years ago highlighted that there are many people who want to take part in activities that combine a pastime or game with a social aspect. This form of social living is particularly relevant to mobile devices and underpins the use of services such as Foursquare and Facebook Places.

Social sharing is also a key part of many people's fitness regime, using service such as MyFitnessPal, where mobile devices are used to record activities, and the service is used to share the results via the web and social networks. Sharing raises a number of possibilities for market researchers, including reviewing existing shared information or creating projects that utilize people's willingness to share aspects of their lives.

MOBILE WALLETS, MOBILE BANKING, AND MICRO-CREDIT

One change that has happened much faster in the developing world than in the developed world is growth in various forms of mobile payment and banking. In large parts of sub-Saharan Africa payment by SMS-enabled phones is fast becoming the norm for a large range of services.

For researchers this raises the opportunity for micro-payments as incentives for people taking part in research projects. This approach has been made popular by organizations such as Jana.com (formerly txteagle).

METHODOLOGY

Technology is changing, society is changing, and consequently market research methods are evolving. This section looks at some of the ways that market research methods are changing.

SHORTER SURVEYS

There is a widespread view that surveys on mobile phones cannot last 20, 30, and 40 minutes. There is a perception that too many potential participants will refuse to do long surveys, either because they are disinclined to do them, or that the units of time they have available on a mobile device are too short.

This drive towards shorter surveys focuses attention on issues like micro-surveys and chunking or modularizing. Using micro-surveys tends to mean running more studies, but asking fewer questions, whilst chunking tends to be used to ask longer surveys, but to spread them over several sessions.

COLLABORATION AND CO-CREATION

The use of mobile devices, especially phones, is encouraging researchers to enlist consumers to play an active, collaborative, and co-creational role in research projects.

Current examples of collaborative mobile research include:

- *Participants collecting ethnographic or mobile diary data about their everyday lives.*
- *Participants actively researching the lives of people around them.*
- *Participants collecting data about their experiences with advertising, products, or customer service.*

As the use of mobile devices evolves, these approaches are likely to make greater use of life-logging approaches to combine observational data with research data.

PROFESSIONAL RESPONDENTS

'Professional respondents' is a term that can have negative connotations, but it is a useful reminder that the use of access panels represents a major change in the way market research is conducted, and it should not be confused with fraudulent or rogue respondents. Before the advent of online access panels, most research participants were deemed to have been new to the research process; in particular they were assumed not to have taken part in similar research recently. Active members of online access panels take part in very large numbers of surveys, often more than 100 a year. Studies of high frequency respondents tend to show that they are people who like doing surveys and who value the financial incentives they receive. Fraudulent or rogue respondents are people who change their behaviour and answers to obtain the maximum reward, usually for the minimum effort (Walker et al. 2009).

A large number of mobile surveys are completed by members of online access panels who have chosen to use their mobile devices. So mobile research is already intertwined with the world of professional respondents, that is high frequency participants who are, to a greater or lesser extent, motivated by the incentives they receive for taking part.

Apps may produce another form of professional respondents: people who download apps with the intention of taking part in research projects.

OBSERVATIONAL TECHNIQUES

The recent reporting of neuroscience and behavioural economics has increased the interest of clients and market researchers in observational research, as opposed to the mediated and potentially over-rationalized responses to surveys or depth interviews.

Mobile devices support this interest in observational research in a variety of ways, including the collection of passive data by mobile phones, the use of geofencing to trigger surveys or research exercises, and by collaborating with participants to log and record some aspect of their everyday lives.

Observational research has been very successful at the qualitative level, dealing with data at the level of the individual. There are fewer examples, so far, of mobile-based observational data being widely used in quantitative projects, partly due the shortage of good analysis options.

PRACTICAL ISSUES IN USING EMERGENT MOBILE TECHNOLOGIES FOR MARKET RESEARCH

This section looks at some of the practical issues surrounding the use of emerging mobile technologies in market research.

ADOPTION AND PENETRATION?

One of the key issues when considering a new technology is the degree of adoption and penetration that is required before it can be used. When considering a new approach, the degree of adoption or penetration will be a key factor in determining whether potential participants already have the relevant device, or whether the device needs to be supplied to them.

Are consumers expected to own the technology?

Most consumers, in most markets, own a phone; in developed countries most have access to the internet, so these are suitable channels for broad sample market research. Most consumers do not scan QR codes and most consumers do not possess devices like Garmin Vivofit, so these are not suitable for mass market research, but they can be used for niche research.

Researchers are generally looking for a technology to be adopted by more than 50% of the population before using it for mass research, and typically they are looking for penetration rates to be growing quickly in addition to being well above 50%.

Is the technology going to be supplied to people, for example to interviewers?

If the research company (or field company) is going to buy the technology, mass adoption by consumers is not relevant. The key issues tend to be whether the technology is cheap enough and stable enough to be used for research. In this context 'stable' means two things: does the technology work and is there some stability in the supply chain? The use of tablets for mCAPI has been an example of using a technology that has become affordable and stable for interviewers, even before the devices are ready to be used for general consumer samples.

MARKET RESEARCH INHIBITORS

There tend to be two main inhibitors for market research adoption of new technology, infrastructure, and commitments to existing methods.

In order for most market research companies to make use of new technology it needs to be capable of being integrated into market research projects. This typically means being able to input standard questionnaires, use discussion guides, conforming to market research ethical standards, and producing outputs in the form that market researchers are used to. Without this sort of infrastructure, new technologies are often too time consuming and too expensive to be widely adopted.

Market research adoption of new technologies can be delayed because of companies being heavily invested in existing methods and approaches. Existing methods and techniques often have a large number of norms and benchmarks, based on years or even decades of use. Moving away from these norms and setting up new norms requires a significant investment in time, money, and a willingness to create new norms and benchmarks. In many cases, adopting a new technology requires training in new protocols and for people to 'unlearn' things they had previously been trained to do.

SKIPPING TECHNOLOGIES

Sometimes a technology can allow countries or organizations to skip a technology level. For example, in some of the developing and unorganized markets, jumping from pen and paper methods to data capture based on mobile devices (skipping approaches such as CATI and online) is leading to cost savings in paper, elimination of transmission time (e.g. couriers), improved accuracy of data, and shortened delivery times.

RESEARCH AGENCY ISSUES

For research agencies two major issues around new technology are:

1.   Avoiding being left behind by a major change.

2.   Only having the resources to look at a limited range of options at any one time.

The second of these two issues is crucial to understanding why the adoption of new technologies is much slower than proponents think it should be. If an agency is focusing on adopting, say, facial coding, it usually can't, at the same time, be adopting passive tracking and mobile ethnography.

The need to focus is true for most sizes of agency. The smaller agencies only have limited resources (especially people and money), but the larger agencies have much bigger and more complex systems into which they have to fit any new approach.

Agencies can loosely be divided into two categories: those who follow the market adopting new approaches once they become widely accepted, and the innovators. The innovators typically focus on applying a small number of new approaches and tend to simply follow the pack in terms of other emergent approaches.

ACCESS PANELS AND COMMUNITIES

Access panels and online communities have the advantage of dealing with the same research participants over an extended period of time. This relationship makes it easier to generate ROI, because new tools are used repeatedly, rather than as one-off solutions.

Panel companies and providers of research communities have been rapid adopters of mobile approaches. To date their progress can be seen as comprising three phases:

1.   Identifying the devices their members used, and warning them when a survey was unsuitable, whilst at the same time increasing the range of phones and devices their surveys supported.

2.   Moving to a platform agnostic approach, where most of their surveys and discussions will run seamlessly on PCs, tablets, phablets, smartphones, and some feature phones.

3.   Creating research options that use apps, either by providing a research app, or by facilitating third-party apps.

In terms of members, access panels and communities started by adding mobile functionality to members who had initially been recruited to do online activities via PCs. In the new phase of development the panels and communities are recruiting people whose only engagement is via mobile, especially in markets where internet access via PCs represents less than 50% of the population, i.e. where mobile is needed in order to be representative.

RESEARCH BUYERS AND USERS

Although some research users are very interested in how research is conducted and how data is collected, most are more concerned with the results, as opposed to the process. Three criteria for a research buyer or user are better, faster, and cheaper.

In most cases mobile market research has not been cheaper than online research in the developed markets and rarely cheaper than paper-based face-to-face in the least developed markets. This has resulted in the key driver being 'better' and to an extent faster.

In developing markets the use of mobile devices is speeding up the process and improving the quality control processes, which are tangible benefits that help fuel change.

In the more developed research markets 'better' has tended to mean moving away from surveys that ask people to recall events and instead capture views, experiences, and reactions 'in the moment'. Mobiles can also be 'better' in the sense of reaching a wider range of participants, in a wider range of situations, and in ways that suit the participants.

Cheaper?

The drive for cheaper research is likely to help create a move to new solutions rather than trying to offer a like-for-like solution. Shorter questionnaires, utilizing 'in the moment' targeting, and adaptive approaches could deliver something that is better, faster, and cheaper – and offer something different from what has gone before.

FEARS OF NEW SOURCES OF BIAS

New techniques often reduce some sources of bias, for example self-completion mobile surveys reduce the interviewer effect found in CATI and face-to-face research, but they typically introduce new sources of bias, such as higher refusal rates. Adoption of new research can be delayed if the industry focuses on just the new sources of bias, rather than the overall impact. This is because the industry is often reconciled to existing problems, even when they are worse than those the new technology offers.

The true nature of the changes associated with mobile market research will only become fully apparent as the method becomes more widely established. However, early indications suggest that the key issues are:

- *Mobile research can broaden the range of people reached by the research, which can in turn impact the results.*

- *When comparing online via PCs and mobile devices, the results are in most cases similar, with some important differences.*

- *Collecting 'in the moment' data results in more information about the topic being investigated, but there are concerns that this is partly the result of participants being too primed/sensitive to the topic.*

PRIVACY

The privacy of respondents is essential to existing market research methods and the success and acceptance of a new method often rests on its ability to comply with market research expectations and guidelines. In fields where technological possibilities outstrip the pace of regulation there tends to be a tension between market researchers, who have signed up to codes of conduct, and non-researchers, who are not aware of these codes of conduct and do not feel constrained by them. This pattern is true of social media research, big data, and it is certainly true of many of the opportunities created by mobile market research.

TECHNOLOGY FRAGMENTATION AND TECHNOLOGY CHANGE

Because mobile technology is evolving quickly and in a fragmented way, mobile market research solutions must be designed to take advantage of the features used today as well as those that are likely to evolve in the near future. For example, until recently Nokia and BlackBerry phones were seen as being potentially central to mobile market research. Following the launch of the iPhone, the direction of developments has changed. The widespread adoption of Android has moved the centre of gravity for mobile market research again. Researchers need to move with these changes, as and when they occur.

KEEPING IN TOUCH WITH THE LEADING EDGE

A book can only capture the mobile picture at a moment in time. The following resources are all likely to be of benefit to anybody who wants to keep in touch with the changes happening in the mobile world:

- *The companion website for this book, www.handbookofmobilemarket research.com, contains a fuller glossary, more details on the case studies included in the book, and more case studies. It will also contain updates on developments in mobile market research.*

- *Workshops and conferences organized by research bodies such as ESOMAR and MRS, and other local associations.*

- *The MRMW series of conferences (Market Research in the Mobile World) organized by the Merlien organization.*

- *The MMRA (Mobile Marketing Research Association) is a global trade body that develops and promotes professional and ethical standards for mobile market research.*

- *The Global Market Research report (annual) and the Global Prices Study (every two years) from ESOMAR.*

- *The yearly GRIT report from GreenBook.*

- *The Confirmit Annual Market Research Software report.*

- *The Mobile Course provided by the University of Georgia's Principles of Marketing Research course.*

- *Online events and recordings at NewMR.org, and its Mobile reference page NewMR.org/mobile.*

- *Useful sources of data and information include ITU (www.itu.int), press releases and reports from IDC and Gartner, and reports available from the Pew Research Center (www.pewresearch.org/).*

- *Useful news sites/blogs include: Mashable.com, Techcrunch.com, ZDNet.com, and cnet.com.*

- *Academic and practitioner journals will be a good source of information about the latest research-on-research findings.*

SUMMARY

2500 years ago the Greek philosopher Heraclitus said 'the only constant is change'. This is certainly true of market research and especially relevant to the evolving picture of mobile market research. The key themes of this evolving picture are:

- *The world is moving to a situation where nearly everybody of interest to market research has a mobile phone, and in many markets that will tend to be a smartphone.*

- *Beyond smartphones there are many other changes, for example tablets, web messaging, improved location-based services, and mobile payments.*

- *However, most innovations will not have a major impact on the world, or market research. Winners are rare.*

- *The key driver of mobile research in the developed markets has been 'better', in particular, in collecting 'in the moment' information.*

- *In the developing markets another key driver has been 'faster', in addition to 'better'.*

- *One of the key requirements for a new technology is its ability to fit into the market research ecosystem, for example can it handle market research questions, can it produce market research outputs, in ways that market researchers consider practical and ethical?*

- *A specific weakness of many new approaches is that they produce large amounts of detailed information that is hard to analyse quantitatively, for example GPS coordinates of movements or large amounts of video.*

- *Even innovative agencies can only explore and implement a small number of new approaches at any moment in time.*

Glossary

3G Third generation mobile technology, supports mobile broadband facilitating use of the internet from mobile devices. The roll-out of 3G dates from about 2001.

4G Fourth generation mobile technology, faster mobile broadband than 3G. The roll-out of 4G dates from about 2009.

Accelerometer A sensor in a mobile device that detects and measures movement.

Android An operating system for touchscreen mobile devices, developed by Google and currently the most common operating system on new phones sold.

App A piece of software that runs on a mobile device, such as a game, a browser, or a survey app.

App store An app store is a service where apps can be downloaded, including free and purchased apps. Apps downloaded from an approved app store such as iTunes or Google Play are more likely to be trusted than those downloaded from other locations.

Asynchronous online qualitative research Qualitative approaches, such as online discussions, that do not require the participants and the moderator to be online at the same time. (See also 'Synchronous online qualitative research'.)

Avatar The way somebody is identified online: it can be a name, or it can include an image, or it can be more complex.

BlackBerry Messenger (BBM) A low cost, relatively secure messaging system that connected (and still connects) BlackBerry devices together. BBM is now available for other devices.

Bluetooth A technology protocol used for short distance transmissions between mobile devices.

Bluetooth LE A low energy (LE) version of Bluetooth.

CAPI Computer Assisted Personal Interviewing, usually a form of face-to-face interviewing where the questionnaire is administered via a computer.

CATI Computer Assisted Telephone Interviewing, where interviews are conducted via telephone with an interviewer in conjunction with a PC.

CCTV Closed circuit TV, often referred to as security cameras.

Cell tower tracking A method the telcos can use to track where people are located by checking which towers they are connected to.

Chunking Chunking is a process for reducing the length of a survey. The survey is divided into sections so that the participant can complete it one or more sections at a time. This is also referred to as modularizing.

Crowd (as in 'the wisdom of the crowd' or crowdsourcing) The crowd refers to ordinary people, as opposed to experts or professionals. *The Wisdom of Crowds* was the title of a book by James Surowiecki (2005) which suggested the average estimate of ordinary people can be as good as experts.

Device agnostic Device agnostic, or platform agnostic, in the context of mobile research, means allowing participants to choose whether to use a PC or a mobile device, and the type of mobile device they prefer.

Environmental sensors Sensors on a mobile device that can measure some aspect of the environment, such as air pressure, temperature, or light.

Ethnographic data Data about people's everyday lives, for example images and videos from people's day-to-day experiences.

Ethnography The study of the lived experience, usually consisting of collecting ethnographic data, analysis, and the creation of an explanatory narrative.

Feature phone There is no phone that is a 'feature phone'. The term has been retrofitted to describe phones that are not smartphones.

Flash Flash was a widely used tool to provide graphics and animation on websites. It has fallen into decline in recent years as it is not supported by iOS or Android, the leading smartphone and tablet operating systems. The owner of Flash, Adobe, has largely discontinued the production, development, and support of Flash.

Forums An online discussion. Either a single conversation or a collection of discussions.

Gamification The utilization of game-like elements into a survey or process to make it more engaging.

Geofencing Geofencing is where a boundary is established for a location (for example a specific restaurant) and technologies are used to identify when somebody enters or leaves that particular location. The information about people entering or leaving an area can be used to trigger location-based activities, such as a survey.

Geolocation Working out where somebody is, for example by using GPS.

Geotagging Adding location information to other data, for example adding location to a survey or image.

Google Glass A piece of wearable technology from Google, including a camera, voice recognition, and a screen.

GPS Global Positioning Satellite. GPS uses satellites to locate a device.

Gyroscope Sensor that measures the turning and rotation of a device.

HTML HyperText Markup Language. HTML is the main method of creating web pages for the internet, using text commands.

HTML5 HTML5 is the latest version of HTML. HTML5 is, amongst other things, very suitable for mobile devices.

iBeacon A new device from Apple that uses Bluetooth to recognize when a phone is nearby, for example when entering a store.

IM (Instant messaging) A method of real-time chat, usually text, usually via the internet.

Installed base The devices that are in use. The installed base is often used in contrast to the recent device sales figures, which reflects what has been bought recently.

iOS The operating system from Apple used by the iPhone and iPad.

ITU (International Telecommunication Union) The United Nations specialist telecommunications agency.

Location analytics Analytics based on location data, for example GPS information.

Location-based Services (LBS) Services based on location information, for example sending a message to a shopper's phone as they enter a store.

mCAPI or Mobile CAPI Mobile CAPI (Computer Assisted Personal Interviewing), using a mobile device to assist with face-to-face interviewing.

mCATI Mobile CATI (Computer Assisted Telephone Interviewing), conducting telephone (voice) interviews via participant's mobile phone.

Metaphor (of the device) The metaphor of a device describes the way people interact with a device, for example GUI (graphical user interface) or WIMP (windows, icons, menus, and a pointer).

Micro-payments Very small payments, typically conducted via mobile devices.

Micro-surveys Very short surveys, typically three or fewer questions.

Mixed-mode Using more than one mode for a study, for example some participants taking part in the study by completing an online questionnaire and some taking part by completing a paper questionnaire.

MMR An abbreviation of Mobile Market Research.

MMRA The MMRA is the Mobile Marketing Research Association – see more at www.mmra-global.org.

MMS Multimedia messaging service, used to send messages containing media files to or from mobile phones.

Mobile app See 'App'.

Mobile device In most cases this refers to a phone, tablet, or phablet, but can also refer to wearable technologies.

Mobile diary/diaries Using a mobile device (phone or tablet) to keep a research diary, typically as part of a qualitative research project.

Mobile discussions Accessing online forums and/or discussions from a mobile device.

Mobile forums See 'Mobile discussions'.

Mobile homework Task or assignment given to a research participant to undertake using their mobile device.

Mobile only Describes a project where all the participants are using mobile devices, as opposed to a mixed-mode or device agnostic project.

Mobile service provider The companies that provide the mobile phone networks that connect mobile phones to the wider telephone network.

Modularizing See 'Chunking'.

Motion sensor Sensor in a mobile device that detects movement.

Multi-mode See 'Mixed-mode'.

NFC (Near Field Communication) A telecommunication protocol that allows two devices to talk to each other when they are close together or in contact. It can be used to send and/or receive information when it is embedded in a mobile phone.

Operating system (OS) The operating system manages the hardware and allows programs and apps to provide services. Two leading mobile operating systems are Google's Android and Apple's iOS.

Paradata Data about the research process, for example how long participants took to answer each question.

Passive data Data that does not require the active participation of a user to be collected. For example, the route taken by a participant on their way to work, collected via their mobile phone and GPS.

Passive data collection See 'Passive data'.

PDA (Personal Digital Assistant) A mobile digital device. These have been largely superseded by tablets and modern mobile phones, but some are still in use for specialist purposes.

Phablet A phablet is a mobile device that is larger than a typical phone, smaller than a typical tablet, with the features of a phone. The word phablet is a combination of PHone and tABLET.

Pinging To send a signal from one device to another to either check a connection exists or to check the speed of a connection.

Platform agnostic See 'Device agnostic'.

Professional respondents Research participants who are either (a) mostly or (b) entirely motivated by incentives and who take part in a large number of research projects.

Pure play A company that just uses a single channel, for example a retailer that only sells online.

QR (Quick Response) codes A two-dimensional bar code that can contain a variety of information, for example instructions or a URL. QR codes can be used to launch a survey. QR codes can be read by phones, if they have a suitable app.

QR reader A mobile phone app that uses the phone's camera to read and interpret a QR code.

Quantified self The trend in people keeping an ongoing record of some aspect (or multiple aspects) of their life – for example using Garmin Vivofit to track their activities and food intake.

Research-on-research Often referred to as RoR. Research about the research process, to help explore or explain research processes.

Return on investment Return on investment (often expressed as ROI) is the result of an investment. A positive ROI is where the return on the spending is at least more than the amount spent, and typically better than other uses the money could have been put to. The ROI can also be expressed as a percentage (ROI = net profit/investment × 100).

RFID Radio Frequency Identification. A low-power wireless communication protocol. RFIDs are often used in badges, cards, and devices to permit entry, record activity, or to track location.

ROI See 'Return on investment'.

RoR See 'Research-on-research'.

Screen resolution The resolution of a screen describes the number of pixels, i.e. the number of separate items that can be turned on or off. The resolution is normally expressed as the number of rows and columns, for example 1024 x 768, which means 768 rows of 1024 pixels.

Screen size Physical size of a screen. It is normally the diagonal length of a mobile screen measured in inches.

Scripting In market research scripting refers to creating a computer administered questionnaire. In particular it often means being able to use a language to enter commands, either a survey language or a computer language such as JavaScript.

SIM (card) Subscriber Identity Module. A small card containing an integrated circuit that establishes the identity of a mobile device to a telephone service provider. For example, a SIM is used in a mobile phone to allow it to subscribe to a network.

Siri An Apple app that uses voice recognition to allow the user to issue commands and queries to a mobile device, such as an iPhone.

Smartphone The definition of a smartphone evolves over time. At the time of this book being researched it tends to refer to devices with a touchscreen, internet access, multimedia features, and capable of running a wide range of apps.

SMS Short Messaging Service. A method of sending text messages to and/or from mobile phones.

Software as a Service (SaaS) In a SaaS solution the software is accessed, typically, via the internet, and the user pays to use it, rather than paying to buy a copy of the software.

SoLoMo A combination of social, local, and mobile, used to refer to the convergence of these three elements.

Synchronous online qualitative research Synchronous refers to the moderator and the participants being online at the same time, as in an online focus group. The alternative is an asynchronous technique, such as an online forum.

Tablet A touchscreen computer, such as an iPad.

Telco Short for telecommunications company. The telcos provide the telephone services, including fixed lines, mobile, and internet.

Thread In an online discussion each separate discussion is known as a thread.

Unintentional mobile Unintentional mobile, also known as accidental mobile, refers to surveys where the research is designed or intended for participants using PCs, but where some participants choose to use a mobile device.

URL Uniform Resource Locator. The URL is also known as a web address. It is a text string that usually defines a specific web page.

USSD Unstructured Supplementary Service Data allows a participant's phone to be connected to the researcher's computer via a gateway, allowing for messages of up to 182 characters to be sent backwards and forwards. Some agencies have had success using this method for research surveys, particularly in countries where smartphones and/or internet access are relatively rare, such as many countries in Africa.

Voice recognition Voice recognition is software that interprets the spoken word. Voice recognition is used in voice commands (such as those used by Siri and Google Glass).

VOIP Voice Over Internet Protocol, a method of using an internet connection to have voice or video conversations, for example Skype.

WAP Wireless Application Protocol was an early method of providing internet to mobile devices and is still used when faster methods are not available.

Wearable technologies Devices that are worn, such as smart glasses or watches, which connect to mobile devices or the mobile network.

WE-research Enlisting people to collaborate in market research processes.

References

AAPOR Cell Phone Task Force (2010) *New Considerations for Survey Researchers When Planning and Conducting RDD Telephone Surveys in the U.S.* With Respondents Reached via Cell Phone Numbers.

Bain, R (2011) *The power of text in the developing world*, 20 January, viewed 15 February 2014, <www.research-live.com/features/the-power-of-text-in-the-developing-world/4004395.article>.

Ballve, M (2013) 'How Much Time Do We Really Spend On Our Smartphones Every Day?' *Business Insider*, viewed 18 February, <www.businessinsider.com.au/how-much-time-do-we-spend-on-smartphones-2013-6>.

Blumberg, P and Luke, J, (2012) *Wireless Substitution: Early Release of Estimates From the National Health Interview Survey, July–December*, CDC Centers for Disease Control and Prevention, <www.cdc.gov/nchs/data/nhis/earlyrelease/wireless201212.PDF‎>. ESOMAR Global Market Research 2012.

Cattell, J (2001) *The mobile internet revolution and it implications for research*, ESOMAR Net Effects 4, Barcelona, February 2001, pp. 191–213.

Chudoba, B (2010) 'Does Adding One More Question Impact Survey Completion Rate?', web log post, 8 December 2010, viewed 24 February 2014, <www.surveymonkey.com/blog/en/blog/2010/12/08/survey_questions_and_completion_rates/>.

Chudoba, B (2011) 'How Much Time are Respondents Willing to Spend on Your Survey?' web log post, 14 February 2011, viewed 24 February 2014, <www.surveymonkey.com/blog/en/blog/2011/02/14/survey_completion_times/>.

de Bruijne, M and Wijnant, A (2013) 'Can Mobile Web Surveys Be Taken on Computers? A Discussion on a Multi-Device Survey Design', *Survey Practice*, Vol. 6, no. 4, viewed 5 July 2014, <http://surveypractice.org/index.php/SurveyPractice/article/download/238/pdf>.

Deloitte (2013) viewed 15 February 2014, <www.deloitte.com/assets/Dcom-United States/Local%20Assets/Documents/us_Retail_2013HolidaySurveyResults_102113.pdf>.

eMarketer (2013) viewed 15 February 2014, <www.emarketer.com/newsroom/index.php/emarketer-tablets-smartphones-drive-mobile-commerce-record-heights/>.

ESOMAR (2009) *ESOMAR Guide on Distinguishing Market Research from Other Data Collection Activities*, viewed 16 February 2014, <www.esomar.org/uploads/pdf/ESOMAR_Codes&Guidelines_MaintainingDistinctionsMRDM.pdf>.

ESOMAR (2012a) *ESOMAR Guideline for Conducting Mobile Market Research*, viewed 16 February 2014, <www.esomar.org/uploads/public/knowledge-and-standards/codes-and-guidelines/ESOMAR_Guideline-for-conducting-Mobile-Market-Research.pdf>.

ESOMAR (2012b) *28 Questions to Help Research Buyers of Online Samples*, viewed 16 February 2014, <www.esomar.org/uploads/public/knowledge-and-standards/documents/ESOMAR-28-Questions-to-Help-Buyers-of-Online-Samples-September-2012.pdf>.

ESOMAR (2013) *Global Market Research 2013*, prepared by ESOMAR in conjunction with BDO Accountants and Advisors, ESOMAR, The Netherlands.

Gartner (2014) 'Gartner Says Less Than 0.01 Percent of Consumer Mobile Apps Will Be Considered a Financial Success by Their Developers Through 2018' 13 January 2014, viewed 24 February 2014, <www.gartner.com/newsroom/id/2648515>.

GreenBook (2013a) *GRIT Consumer Participation in Research Report: A Study of Survey-Takers in 200+ Countries and Regions around the World*, GreenBook, viewed 22 January 2014, <www.Greenbook.org/GRITCPR>.

Greenbook (2013b) GRIT (Greenbook Research Industry Trends) Report, Winter 2013, viewed 1 July 2014, <www.greenbookblog.org/grit-winter-2013/>

Greenbook (2014) GRIT (Greenbook Research Industry Trends) Report, Winter 2014, viewed 1 July 2014, <www.greenbook.org/grit>

Hofmeyr, J (2013) *From the handset to the client: Marketing research without researchers*, Market Research in the Mobile World, 8–11 October 2013, London, viewed 16 February 2014, <mrmw.net/eu-2013-london-day-1>.

Hu, Sean S, Ballus, L, Battaglia, MP, and Frankel, Martin R (2011) 'Improving Public Health Surveillance Using a Dual-Frame Survey of Landline and Cell Phone Numbers' *American Journal of Epidemiology*, Vol. 173, No. 6, 703–711, viewed 12 May 2014, <http://aje.oxfordjournals.org/content/173/6/703.full.pdf+html>.

ITU (2013) *Measuring the Information Society*, International Telecommunication Union, Geneva Switzerland, viewed 4 January 2014, <www.itu.int/en/ITU-D/Statistics/Documents/publications/mis2013/MIS2013_without_Annex_4.pdf>.

ITU (2013) *The World in 2013: ICT Facts and Figures*, viewed 24 February 2014, <www.itu.int/en/ITU-D/Statistics/Documents/facts/ICTFactsFigures2013-e.pdf>.

Jue, A and Luck, K (2014) *Update: Participation of mobile users in online surveys*, Decipher White Paper, viewed 4 July 2014, <www.decipherinc.com/n/uploads/images/pages/Decipher_Mobile_Research_White_Paper_Update.pdf>.

Kearon, J and Earls, M (2009) *Me-to-we research – From asking unreliable witnesses about themselves to asking people what they notice, believe & predict about others*, ESOMAR, Congress, Montreux, September 2009.

Kravets, D (2013) 'Cops and Feds Routinely "Dump" Cell Towers to Track Everyone Nearby', *Wired.com*, viewed 18 February 2014, <www.wired.com/threatlevel/2013/12/massive-domestic-monitorning/>.

Krosnick, J (2000) 'The Threat of Satisficing in Surveys: The Shortcuts Respondents Take in Answering Questions', *Survey Methods Newsletter*, Vol. 20, No. 1, <https://pprg.stanford.edu/wp-content/uploads/2000-The-threat-of-satisficing-in-surveys-The-shortcuts-responde.pdf>.

Leadbeater, C (2009) *We Think: Mass Innovation Not Mass Production*, Profile Books Ltd, London, UK.

MacKerron, G and Mourato, S (2013) 'Happiness is greater in natural environments', viewed 15 February 2014, <http://personal.lse.ac.uk/mackerro/happy_natural_envs.pdf>.

McCormick, R (2014) 'Grocery stores push coupons to iPhones with iBeacons', *The Verge*, viewed 15 February 2014, <www.theverge.com/2014/1/7/5282872/ibeacons-in-grocery-stores-for-inmarket-app-users>.

Manson, K (2013) 'From oil painter to the C-suite', *Financial Times*, viewed 16 February 2013, <www.ft.com/intl/cms/s/0/c62cf5aa-7b8a-11e2-95b9-00144feabdc0.html#axzz2rMS8u28g>.

Marketing Charts Staff (2013) 'Data Dive: QR Codes', *Marketing Charts*, 8 July 2013, viewed 24 February 20014, <www.marketingcharts.com/wp/direct/data-dive-qr-codes-29525/>.

Meeker M and Wu L (2013) *Internet Trends*, KPCB Kleiner Perkins Caufield Byers, viewed 21 February 2014, <www.kpcb.com/insights/2013-internet-trends>.

MRS (2010) MRS Regulations for Using Research Techniques for Non-Research Purposes, MRS, November 2010, viewed 16 February 2014, <www.mrs.org.uk/pdf/2012-02-23%20Regulations%20for%20Non%20Research%20Purposes.pdf>.

Ofcom (2013) 'Communications Market Report 2013', 1 August 2013, viewed 24 February 2014, <http://stakeholders.ofcom.org.uk/binaries/research/cmr/cmr13/2013_UK_CMR.pdf>.

OnDevice Research, viewed 24 February 2014, <http://ondeviceresearch.com/media/content/20130923055108_mobile-survey-chunking-whitepaper.pdf>.

Pennay, D, Misson, S, and Vickers, N (2013) *Using Dual-Frame Telephone Surveys to include the 'Mobile Phone-Only' population*, AMSRS Conference, Sydney, Australia, 5–6 September.

Pew Research Center's Internet & American Life Project (2012) *The Best (and Worst) of Mobile Connectivity*, Pew Research Center, Washington, viewed 15 February 2014 <www.pewinternet.org/files/old-media//Files/Reports/2012/PIP_Best_Worst_Mobile_113012.pdf>.

Pew Research Internet Project (2013) *Mobile Technology Fact Sheet*, 27 December, 2013, viewed 22 February 2014, <www.pewinternet.org/fact-sheets/mobile-technology-fact-sheet/>.

Poynter, R (2010) *The Handbook of Online and Social Media Research: Tools and Techniques for Market Researchers*, John Wiley & Sons, Ltd, Chichester UK.

Poynter, R (2013) 'The ITU is 100% Wrong on Mobile Phone Penetration, IMHO', web log post, 29 June 2013, viewed 24 February 2014, <http://newmr.org/the-itu-is-100-wrong-on-mobile-phone-penetration-imho/>.

Poynter, R (2014a) 'Stop Asking When Mobile will be the Next Big Thing, it Happened a Year or Two Ago!', web log post, 27 January 2014, viewed 16 February 2014, htttp://newmr.org/stop-asking-when-mobile-will-be-the-next-big-thing-it-happened-a-year-or-two-ago/>.

Poynter, R (2014b) 'The Shape Of Mobile Market Research Over The Next Three Years', web log post, 3 February 2014, viewed 24 February 2014, <www.greenbookblog.org/2014/02/03/the-shape-of-mobile-market-research-over-the-next-three-years/.

Rosling, H (2013) <http://edition.cnn.com/2013/12/10/opinion/gapminder-hans-rosling/>.

Surowiecki, J (2005) *The Wisdom of Crowds*, Anchor Books, New York.

Tapscott, D and Williams, A (2008) *Wikinomics: How Mass Collaboration Changes Everything*, Atlantic Books, London, UK.

The Economist (2014) 'From Weibo to WeChat', *The Economist*, viewed 16 February 2014, <www.economist.com/news/china/21594296-after-crackdown-microblogs-sensitive-online-discussion-has-shifted-weibo-wechat>.

Walker, R, Pettit, R, and Rubinson, J (2009) 'A Special Report from the Advertising Research Foundation – The Foundations of Quality Initiative: A Five-Part Immersion into the Quality of Online Research', *Journal of Advertising Research*, Vol. 49, No. 4, December, 464–485.

Weisberg, J (2003) 'The MCAPI primer', *Quirks Marketing Research Media*, February 2003, viewed 21 February 2014, <www.quirks.com/articles/a2003/20030209.aspx?searchID=906234243&pg=1>.

Williams, N (2014a) 'The Mobile Advantage In Illiterate Or Limited Literacy Populations', Greenbook Blog, web log post, 20 January 2014, viewed 16 February 2014, <www.greenbookblog.org/2014/01/20/the-mobile-advantage-in-illiterate-or-limited-literacy-populations/>.

Williams, N (2014b) 'The Mobile Players in 2014 & Mobile MR' web log post, 14 January 2014, viewed 24 February 2014, <http://newmr.org/the-mobile-players-in-2014-mobile-mr-navin-williams/>.

Witt, K (2000) *Moving Studies to the Web: A Case Study*, Proceedings of the Sawtooth Software Conference, March 2000, Hilton Head Island, viewed 24 February 2014, <sawtoothsoftware.com/download/techpap/2000Proceedings.pdf>.

About the Authors

RAY POYNTER

Ray has spent the last 35 years at the interface of technology, innovation, and market research, and sees his mission as 'To have fun, help people, advocate change, and ideally make some money along the way'.

Ray is the author of *The Handbook of Online and Social Media Research*, joint editor of ESOMAR's *Answers to Contemporary Market Research Questions* book, a contributor of courses to the University of Georgia's Principles of Marketing Research distance learning course, and the founder of NewMR.org. Ray is in regular demand as a workshop leader, conference speaker, contributor to magazines, blogger, and consultant.

Ray is the Managing Director of The Future Place, a director with Vision Critical (heading up their knowledge gathering and sharing operation), and has been the independent research consultant on the last four ESOMAR Global Pricing Studies. Previous roles include director-level appointments with Virtual Surveys, Millward Brown, IntelliQuest, The Research Business, and Sandpiper International.

You can follow Ray on Twitter using @RayPoynter.

NAVIN WILLIAMS

Navin Williams is the founder and CEO at MobileMeasure Consultancy Limited. Navin has extensive experience in the Market Research, Technology, and Media & Telecom sectors. Navin has worked for some of the world's market research leaders across the disciplines of media, consumer (IMRB, RI & Nielsen), and retail (Nielsen). He has held senior roles in four countries, spanning two continents. His last assignment with Nielsen was as Head of Consumer Research (FMCG) in China.

He has spent a large part of his career introducing pioneering digital and mobile data collection methods in Asia, Africa, and other parts of the world. His quest to drive mobile and digital adoption in market research led him to found MobileMeasure.

A digital pioneer, Navin is widely regarded as a thought-leader in the evolution of mobile technology in research. Navin is the co-author of University of Georgia's MRII curriculum Mobile Marketing Research and is part of ESOMAR's Mobile Monitoring Group. A frequent speaker at conferences, he also lends his time to universities and schools introducing mobile market research to students and professionals.

Navin holds an MBA from the University of Pune, India. He is based in Shanghai, China with his wife and their two children.

SUE YORK

Sue is a market and social researcher working at the Institute for Social Science Research at The University of Queensland in Australia. She has more than 15 years' experience in market research across a wide variety of sectors and research approaches, and of utilizing advances in technology in data collection.

Sue enjoys working at the intersection of research methodology, technology, and innovation. She has a love of new methods and techniques, and is a strong advocate of methodological rigour, and the need for research-on-research to continually improve research approaches.

Sue has a high profile within the global market research community, and has run workshops for bodies such as ESOMAR, AMSRS (Australian Market and Social Research Society), and the MRSS (Singapore).

She is joint editor and curator of the ESOMAR book and ongoing project *Answers to Contemporary Market Research Questions*.

Sue is an active member of the market research online community and was a founder of NewMR.

Sue tweets as @1sue3, mostly about research methods and related innovations.

A Note of Thanks

There is a saying that it takes a village to raise a child, and our experience is that it takes a research community to produce a better book. We have been astounded and pleased by the amount of help and advice that we have received over the last year whilst writing this book and we'd like to put our thanks on record to as many of those people and organizations as possible.

In this section there are lists of the people and organizations who have contributed to the book, via online discussions, reviewing content, or by contributing material.

However, special thanks are extended to The University of Georgia and to Reg Baker. This book draws on material developed by Navin Williams and Ray Poynter, under the editorial leadership of Reg Baker, for the University of Georgia's Principles of Marketing Research course 'Mobile Marketing Research', launched in 2014.

ORGANIZATIONS

The following organizations have kindly supplied access to materials, case studies, advice, support, and the results of research-on-research:

Australia Online

Confirmit

CrowdLab

Curious Analytics

Decipher

Dub

ESOMAR

Google Consumer Surveys

Greenbook

IPSOS

Join the Dots

Kantar

Locately

Lumi Mobile

Marketing Sciences

Merlien

MESH

MFour Mobile

MMR Research Worldwide

MMRA (Mobile Marketing Research Association)

MobileMeasure

NewMR

OnDevice

Research Now

Revelation

SKIM

SSI

Tesco

TNS South Africa

The University of Queensland

University of Georgia's Principles
of Marketing Research Course

Vision Critical

Wallis Group

Wiley

PEOPLE

The following people have all helped with the book, in a variety of ways. For example, some have reviewed chapters, some have contributed to our online crowdsourcing of ideas, and some have highlighted alternative sources.

Ansie Lombaard

Bernie Baffour

Betsy Leichliter

Brian Fine

Cao Shuai

Carolyn Hall

Dan Foreman

Darren Pennay

Don Marek

Emma Earl

Fiona Blades

Frankie Johnson

Gerard Loosschilder

Gerry Nicolaas

Guy Rolfe

Heidi Swanepoel

Helen Bartlett

Inge Nel

Jan Wegelin

Jasper Lim

Jayne Van Souwe

Jenny Ng

John Davidson

Jon Beaumont

Karine Del Moro

Lara Hoppe

Lenny Murphy

Mark Michelson

Matthew Lintern

Melanie Courtright

Michele Haynes

Michèle Poynter

Miguel Ramos

Monica Gessner

Niall Smith

Noah Marconi

Pam Bracken

Paul McDonald

Pete Cape

Priya Williams

Ranjit Singh

Ravi Shankar Bose

Richard Owen

Rick Wilson

Siim Teller

Siobhan Churchill

Soudamini Bose

Stephen Cribbett

Steve August

Thaddeus Fulford-Jones

William Poynter

Yoshida Tomoko

Index